AF554009

Reader's Guide
to
WILLIAM SHAKESPEARE

Reader's Guide
to
WILLIAM SHAKESPEARE

John T. Nichol

CENTRUM PRESS
NEW DELHI-110002 (INDIA)

CENTRUM PRESS
H.O.: 4360/4, Ansari Road, Daryaganj,
New Delhi-110 002 (India)
Ph.: 23278000, 23261597

B.O.: No. 1015, Ist Main Road, BSK IIIrd Stage
IIIrd Phase, IIIrd Block,
Bangalore - 560 085 (India)
Tel.: 080-41723429
Visit us at: www.centrumpress.com

Reader's Guide to William Shakespeare

First Edition, 2009
ISBN 978-93-80106-57-1

PRINTED IN INDIA

Printed at Salasar Imaging Systems, Delhi-110035 (India)

Contents

Contents

Preface

William Shakespeare was an English poet and playwright, widely regarded as the greatest writer in the English language and the world's preeminent dramatist. He is often called England's national poet and the "Bard of Avon". His surviving works consist of 38 plays, 154 sonnets, two long narrative poems, and several other poems. It is all the more wondrous when one can study the works and see Shakespeare developing as a playwright right there upon the pages.

Love's Laboures Lost and the early comedies are the work of a gifted and clever author. Perhaps such plays alone would have earned him literary fame in later days. The grandeur of a *Hamlet of King Lear*, however, its the work of a master who learned from his own writing and long practice. In his time, Shakespeare was the most popular playwright of London. As centuries have passed, his genius eclipses all others of his age; *Jonson, Marlowe, Kyd, Greene, Dekker, Heywood*—none approach the craft or the humanity of character that marks the Bard's work.

He took the art of dramatic verse and honed it to perfection. He created the most vivid characters of the Elizabethan or any other stage. His usage of language, both lofty and low, shows a remarkable wit and subtlety. Most importantly, his themes are so universal that they transcend generations to stir the imaginations of audiences even to this day." His plays have been translated into every major living language, and are performed more often than those of any other playwright.

Author

Politics and Society in Renaissance England

An excursion into Renaissance society and politics would provide for a better understanding of Elizabethan literature. Shakespeare's plays can be fully understood only if the socio-political and intellectual tradition that inspired their creation is discovered, as these plays and their staging are very much a product of their socio-cultural milieu.

Politics and social life in Renaissance England was closely related to religion, particularly the establishment of the Church of England which wrought immense changes on the English society. The causes of English Reformation were both political and personal. In 1509, Henry VIII succeeded his father, the first Tudor king, Henry VII, to the throne. In fact, the Tudors had no dynastic claim to the English throne. The Lancastrian Henry Tudor had come to power by killing the Yorkist Richard III in the Battle of Bosworth in 1485, thus putting an end to the Plantagenet dynasty as well as the Middle Ages in England. England was still smarting from the Wars of the Roses, which Henry VII had effectively ended, by marrying Elizabeth of York. So the first priority for the young king Henry VIII was to marry and father sons who would secure his dynasty. In

1509 itself, Henry married the widow of his elder brother Prince Arthur, Catherine of Aragon, who was related to the ruling families of Spain, Portugal and Burgundy. However, the marriage produced only one child who survived beyond infancy—Mary. In 1525, Henry fell in love with the daughter of a Kentish knight, Anne Boleyn, and badly needed a divorce in order to marry her.

The erosion of the power of Roman Catholic Church in England started when Pope Clement VII dismissed Henry's request. Earlier, in Oct 1517, a disillusioned former monk, Martin Luther had effectively launched the Reformation, nailing 95 theses to the door of the castle Church in Wittenberg in Germany, questioning the authority of the Roman Catholic Church.

Lutheran Protestantism gave Henry the pretext to challenge Papal authority, and in 1533 he declared himself the Supreme Governor of the Church of England and married Anne Boleyn. [She was then pregnant with Elizabeth I. Soon after, she too fell from the King's favour for failing to provide a male heir and was beheaded for treason in 1536.] Partly because he feared retribution from Catherine's relatives, including the Holy Roman Emperor Charles V, Henry closed down England's numerous wealthy abbeys and monasteries, and gifted part of the gains to the knights and nobles, thus ensuring their allegiance. The money also raised a fleet of ships to ward off invasions, thus founding the British navy.

In 1547, Henry was succeeded by his 10-year-old son Edward VI (by his third wife Jane Seymour), and when Edward died in 1553, Mary Tudor (daughter of Catherine of Aragon) came to power. When Mary I (popularly known as Bloody Mary for having burnt almost 300 religious dissenters at stake, re-establishing Catholicism in England in the process) also died in 1558, Elizabeth I succeeded her. The 25-year-old

Elizabeth was unmarried and remained so till the end of her 45-year reign. Even though an anomaly in the sixteenth century, the virgin queen could easily fill the psychological and cultural vacuum of the intercessory role of Virgin Mary and the saints in the Protestant society. A cult quickly grew around her when she was celebrated like a goddess.

Meanwhile, Elizabeth's cousin Mary, Queen of Scots, a Catholic brought up in the French tradition, facing serious problems in Scotland, escaped to England. Elizabeth could not offend her friendly Protestant neighbours, the Scots, and imprisoned Mary for 19 years, in England. This badly strained relationships with France and Spain (the latter ruled by Philip II, who was Mary I's husband), and an atmosphere of extreme paranoia about domestic security overcast England. Finally, Mary was executed in 1587 and the Spanish Armada that set sail to invade England was defeated in 1588. Towards the end of Elizabeth's reign, a series of economic and military setbacks did weaken her popularity. However, Elizabeth's reign provided valuable stability for the kingdom and helped forge a strong sense of national identity.

Elizabeth was succeeded by James VI of Scotland, the only child of Mary, Queen of Scots, who ascended the throne as James I. He wished to end all hostilities with foreign powers and unite Scotland, England, Wales and Ireland under a unified British Empire. James had a number of male favourites in court which gave rise to many scandals. So it is little wonder that corruption in court is a recurrent theme in Jacobean literature. James's son Charles I proved to be an even more unpopular king, much too dependent on his father's favourite, the Duke of Buckingham, and his equally unpopular Catholic queen Henrietta Maria. Charles's increasingly strained relationship with the Parliament led to its suspension for over 11 years. This was the time when the landed gentry and the

Puritans were gaining control of the nobility in England. War broke out in 1642 between the King and the Parliament, immediately resulting in the closing down of theatres and the end of the Renaissance period.

The Renaissance period in England was marked by socio-cultural upheavals, like in the rest of Europe. Gutenberg's invention of printing had brought an unprecedented number of literary works into European society, and literatures in the vernacular languages began to develop, primarily through translations, imitations and adaptations. For the first time in the modern world, ordinary people began to hanker after literacy and education, and there was a race for cultural development.

Humanism—the belief in the centrality and dignity of man—took central stage in all discourses, endorsing the concerns and experiences of the individual, the spirit of freedom and the authority of the subject. New developments in art and literature, sociology, polity and other branches of social inquiry, as well as science and technology opened the floodgates of a new era where fear and superstition were replaced by rational thinking and knowledge.

However, early Renaissance society was still primitive in science and technology, by today's standards. Printing was a luxury; even local travel was arduous and limited; and scientists and witches were often mistaken as in the same trade. A number of women were executed for witchcraft in England during the Renaissance, and many literary works of the period bear testimony to the public interest in the subject.

Renaissance scientists held that each individual is a microcosm that reflects and is in tune with the macrocosm of the universe. Everybody possessed a soul, for which the body was only an imperfect and temporary container. In a society where the basic tenets of hygiene were unheard of, when plagues swept through the cities occasionally, killing multitudes, the death of the body was an everyday reality. Like everything else, the human body was believed to be composed of the varying proportions of the four elements—earth, water, air and fire—that manifested as the four humours—blood, phlegm, choler and melancholy.

A disproportionate composition of these resulted in a characteristic personality trait. The Renaissance people held that all human beings—man and woman—ultimately had the same bodies, arranged differently. This also involved the idea of gender as not biologically stable, which gives fresh insight into the practice of cross-dressing and gender transgression in Renaissance plays.

The Renaissance notion of the four humours, which in turn is a manifestation of the four elements and related to astronomical processes, is indicative of the sixteenth century conception of society as part of the "great chain of being"—that everything in the universe is interconnected, with God at the pinnacle. This ordered and hierarchical society is headed by the monarch, who enjoys the Divine Right to govern the country and its people.

The monarch exerted his power through the institution of the court, a privileged group of the richest and most powerful aristocrats in the country. Below the aristocrats came the gentry and the citizens. The gentry, usually denoted by the title 'Sir', held their wealth as landed property outside London, inherited by birth or acquired by marriage.

The gentry exercised feudal authority over those who worked in their country estates; served the king at his court and raised an army for him as well, in times of need. Unlike the gentry, the citizens generally lived in London and derived their wealth from trade. They never attended the court, but sponsored entertainments and ran the "apprentice system", by which young men learned a trade as an employee of a master. From the citizens' perspective, the courtier was an immoral, extravagant spendthrift, while the citizens themselves were associated with the virtues of hard work, thrift and honesty. The courtiers in turn derided the citizens as unfashionable and vulgar.

In the Renaissance mindset, a "family" included not only the husband, wife and children, but even the servants, for they were actively involved in all affairs of the family. The Renaissance nobility married early, while the common folks married in their mid-twenties. The average life expectancy was 40 and many women died in childbirth. It has been argued that due to the high rate of child mortality, adults were more attached their siblings than to their own children. The husband was held as superior to the wife, physically, morally, intellectually and spiritually. Children were regarded as miniature adults with unquestioning obedience expected of them. Renaissance culture, as evident from the literature of the time, was marked by the prevalent male anxiety about female infidelity. The greatest insult for a man was to sprout horns and turn into a cuckold. The female counterpart of this phenomenon—cuckquean—was rarely used. However in England, more than in the rest of Europe, there was more insistence on mutual affection and companionship in marriage.

Dr. Kalyani Vallath
Director, VallathsTES

Chapter 1

Introduction

William Shakespeare (baptised 26 April 1564–23 April 1616) was an English poet and playwright, widely regarded as the greatest writer in the English language and the world's preeminent dramatist. He is often called England's national poet and the "Bard of Avon" (or simply "The Bard"). His surviving works consist of 38 plays, 154 sonnets, two long narrative poems, and several other poems. His plays have been translated into every major living language, and are performed more often than those of any other playwright.

Shakespeare was born and raised in Stratford-upon-Avon. At the age of 18, he married Anne Hathaway, who bore him three children: Susanna, and twins Hamnet and Judith. Between 1585 and 1592, he began a successful career in London as an actor, writer, and part owner of a playing company called the Lord Chamberlain's Men, later known as the King's Men. He appears to have retired to Stratford around 1613, where he died three years later. Few records of Shakespeare's private life survive, and there has been considerable speculation about such matters as his sexuality, religious beliefs, and whether the works attributed to him were written by others.

Shakespeare produced most of his known work between 1590 and 1613. His early plays were mainly comedies and histories, genres he raised to the peak of sophistication and artistry by the end of the sixteenth century. He then wrote mainly tragedies until about 1608, including Hamlet, King Lear, and Macbeth, considered some of the finest examples in the English language. In his last phase, he wrote tragicomedies, also known as romances, and collaborated with other playwrights. Many of his plays were published in editions of varying quality and accuracy during his lifetime. In 1623, two of his former theatrical colleagues published the First Folio, a collected edition of his dramatic works that included all but two of the plays now recognised as Shakespeare's. Shakespeare was a respected poet and playwright in his own day, but his reputation did not rise to its present heights until the nineteenth century.

The Romantics, in particular, acclaimed Shakespeare's genius, and the Victorians hero-worshipped Shakespeare with a reverence that George Bernard Shaw called "bardolatry". In the twentieth century, his work was repeatedly adopted and rediscovered by new movements in scholarship and performance. His plays remain highly popular today and are constantly performed and reinterpreted in diverse cultural and political contexts throughout the world.

EARLY LIFE

William Shakespeare was the son of John Shakespeare, a successful glover and alderman originally from Snitterfield, and Mary Arden, the daughter of an affluent landowning farmer. He was born in Stratford-upon-Avon and baptised on 26 April 1564. His unknown birthday is traditionally observed on 23 April, St George's Day. This date, which can be traced back to an eighteenth-century scholar's mistake, has proved appealing because Shakespeare died on 23 April 1616. He was the third child of eight and the eldest surviving son.

Although no attendance records for the period survive, most biographers agree that Shakespeare was educated at the King's New School in Stratford, a free school chartered in 1553, about a quarter of a mile from his home. Grammar schools varied in quality during the Elizabethan era, but the curriculum was dictated by law throughout England, and the school would have provided an intensive education in Latin grammar and the classics. At the age of 18, Shakespeare married the 26-year-old Anne Hathaway.

The consistory court of the Diocese of Worcester issued a marriage licence on 27 November 1582. Two of Hathaway's neighbours posted bonds the next day as surety that there were no impediments to the marriage. The couple may have arranged the ceremony in some haste, since the Worcester chancellor allowed the marriage banns to be read once instead of the usual three times.

Anne's pregnancy could have been the reason for this. Six months after the marriage, she gave birth to a daughter, Susanna, who was baptised on 26 May 1583. Twins, son Hamnet and daughter Judith, followed almost two years later and were baptised on 2 February 1585. Hamnet died of unknown causes at the age of 11 and was buried on 11 August 1596.

After the birth of the twins, there are few historical traces of Shakespeare until he is mentioned as part of the London theatre scene in 1592. Because of this gap, scholars refer to the years between 1585 and 1592 as Shakespeare's "lost years". Biographers attempting to account for this period have reported many apocryphal stories. Nicholas Rowe, Shakespeare's first biographer, recounted a Stratford legend that Shakespeare fled the town for London to escape prosecution for deer poaching.

Another eighteenth-century story has Shakespeare starting his theatrical career minding the horses of theatre patrons in London. John Aubrey reported that Shakespeare had been a country schoolmaster. Some twentieth-century scholars have suggested that Shakespeare may have been employed as a schoolmaster by Alexander Hoghton of Lancashire, a Catholic landowner who named a certain "William Shakeshafte" in his will. No evidence substantiates such stories other than hearsay collected after his death.

LONDON AND THEATRICAL CAREER

It is not known exactly when Shakespeare began writing, but contemporary allusions and records of performances show that several of his plays were on the London stage by 1592. He was well enough known in London by then to be attacked in print by the playwright Robert Greene:

...there is an upstart Crow, beautified with our feathers, that with his Tiger's heart wrapped in a Player's hide, supposes he is as well able to bombast out a blank verse as the best of you: and being an absolute Johannes factotum, is in his own conceit the only Shake-scene in a country.

Scholars differ on the exact meaning of these words, but most agree that Greene is accusing Shakespeare of reaching above his rank in trying to match university-educated writers, such as Christopher Marlowe, Thomas Nashe and Greene himself. The italicised phrase parodying the line "Oh, tiger's heart wrapped in a woman's hide" from Shakespeare's Henry VI, part 3, along with the pun "Shake-scene", identifies Shakespeare as Greene's target.

"All the world's a stage,
and all the men and women merely players:
they have their exits and their entrances;
and one man in his time plays many parts..."
As You Like It, Act II, Scene 7, 139–42.

Greene's attack is the first recorded mention of Shakespeare's career in the theatre. Biographers suggest that his career may have begun any time from the mid-1580s to just before Greene's remarks. From 1594, Shakespeare's plays were performed only by the Lord Chamberlain's Men, a company owned by a group of players, including Shakespeare, that soon became the leading playing company in London.

After the death of Queen Elizabeth in 1603, the company was awarded a royal patent by the new king, James I, and changed its name to the King's Men. In 1599, a partnership of company members built their own theatre on the south bank of the Thames, which they called the Globe. In 1608, the partnership also took over the Blackfriars indoor theatre. Records of Shakespeare's property purchases and investments indicate that the company made him a wealthy man. In 1597, he bought the second-largest house in Stratford, New Place, and in 1605, he invested in a share of the parish tithes in Stratford.

Some of Shakespeare's plays were published in quarto editions from 1594. By 1598, his name had become a selling point and began to appear on the title pages. Shakespeare continued to act in his own and other plays after his success as a playwright. The 1616 edition of Ben Jonson's Works names him on the cast lists for Every Man in His Humour (1598) and Sejanus, His Fall (1603). The absence of his name from the 1605 cast list for Jonson's Volpone is taken by some scholars as a sign that his acting career was nearing its end.

The First Folio of 1623, however, lists Shakespeare as one of "the Principal Actors in all these Plays", some of which were first staged after Volpone, although we cannot know for certain what roles he played. In 1610, John Davies of Hereford wrote that "good Will" played "kingly" roles. In 1709, Rowe passed down a tradition that Shakespeare played the ghost of Hamlet's father. Later traditions maintain that he also played Adam in As You Like It and the Chorus in Henry V, though scholars doubt the sources of the information.

Shakespeare divided his time between London and Stratford during his career. In 1596, the year before he bought New Place as his family home in Stratford, Shakespeare was living in the parish of St. Helen's, Bishopsgate, north of the River Thames. He moved across the river to Southwark by 1599, the year his company constructed the Globe Theatre there. By 1604, he had moved north of the river again, to an area north of St Paul's Cathedral with many fine houses. There he rented rooms from a French Huguenot called Christopher Mountjoy, a maker of ladies' wigs and other headgear.

LATER YEARS AND DEATH

After 1606–1607, Shakespeare wrote fewer plays, and none are attributed to him after 1613. His last three plays were collaborations, probably with John Fletcher, who succeeded him as the house playwright for the King's Men. Rowe was the first biographer to pass down the tradition that Shakespeare retired to Stratford some years before his death; but retirement from all work was uncommon at that time, and Shakespeare continued to visit London.

In 1612, he was called as a witness in a court case concerning the marriage settlement of Mountjoy's daughter, Mary. In March 1613, he bought a gatehouse in the Blackfriars priory; and from November 1614, he was in London for several weeks with his son-in-law, John Hall.

Shakespeare died on 23 April 1616, and was survived by his wife and two daughters. Susanna had married a physician, John Hall, in 1607, and Judith had married Thomas Quiney, a vintner, two months before Shakespeare's death.

In his will, Shakespeare left the bulk of his large estate to his elder daughter Susanna. The terms instructed that she pass it down intact to "the first son of her body". The Quineys had three children, all of whom died without marrying.

The Halls had one child, Elizabeth, who married twice but died without children in 1670, ending Shakespeare's direct line. Shakespeare's will scarcely mentions his wife, Anne, who was probably entitled to one third of his estate automatically. He did make a point, however, of leaving her "my second best bed", a bequest that has led to much speculation.

Some scholars see the bequest as an insult to Anne, whereas others believe that the second-best bed would have been the matrimonial bed and therefore rich in significance. Shakespeare was buried in the chancel of the Holy Trinity Church two days after his death.

Sometime before 1623, a monument was erected in his memory on the north wall, with a half-effigy of him in the act of writing. Its plaque compares him to Nestor, Socrates, and Virgil. A stone slab covering his grave is inscribed with a curse against moving his bones. Shakespeare has been commemorated in a number of statues and memorials around the world.

PLAYS

Scholars have often noted four periods in Shakespeare's writing career. Until the mid-1590s, he wrote mainly comedies influenced by Roman and Italian models and history plays in the popular chronicle tradition. His second period began in about 1595 with the tragedy Romeo and Juliet and ended with the tragedy of Julius Caesar in 1599. During this time, he wrote what are considered his greatest comedies and histories. From about 1600 to about 1608, his "tragic period", Shakespeare wrote mostly tragedies, and from about 1608 to 1613, mainly tragicomedies, also called romances.

The first recorded works of Shakespeare are Richard III and the three parts of Henry VI, written in the early 1590s during a vogue for historical drama. Shakespeare's plays are difficult to date, however, and studies of the texts suggest that Titus Andronicus, The Comedy of Errors, The Taming of the Shrew and Two Gentlemen of Verona may also belong to Shakespeare's earliest period.

His first histories, which draw heavily on the 1587 edition of Raphael Holinshed's Chronicles of England, Scotland, and Ireland, dramatise the destructive results of weak or corrupt rule and have been interpreted as a justification for the origins of the Tudor dynasty. Their composition was influenced by the works of other Elizabethan dramatists, especially Thomas Kyd and Christopher Marlowe, by the traditions of medieval drama, and by the plays of Seneca.

The Comedy of Errors was also based on classical models, but no source for the The Taming of the Shrew has been found, though it is related to a separate play of the same name and may have derived from a folk story.

Like Two Gentlemen of Verona, in which two friends appear to approve of rape, the Shrew's story of the taming of a woman's independent spirit by a man sometimes troubles modern critics and directors. Shakespeare's early classical and Italianate comedies, containing tight double plots and precise comic sequences, give way in the mid-1590s to the romantic atmosphere of his greatest comedies. A Midsummer Night's Dream is a witty mixture of romance, fairy magic, and comic lowlife scenes.

Shakespeare's next comedy, the equally romantic The Merchant of Venice, contains a portrayal of the vengeful Jewish moneylender Shylock which reflected Elizabethan views but may appear prejudiced to modern audiences. The wit and wordplay of Much Ado About Nothing, the charming rural setting of As You Like It, and the lively merrymaking of Twelfth Night complete Shakespeare's sequence of great comedies.

After the lyrical Richard II, written almost entirely in verse, Shakespeare introduced prose comedy into the histories of the late 1590s, Henry IV, parts 1 and 2, and Henry V. His characters become more complex and tender as he switches deftly between comic and serious scenes, prose and poetry, and achieves the narrative variety of his mature work.

This period begins and ends with two tragedies: Romeo and Juliet, the famous romantic tragedy of sexually charged adolescence, love, and death; and Julius Caesar based on Sir Thomas North's 1579 translation of Plutarch's Parallel Lives which introduced a new kind of drama. According to Shakespearean scholar James Shapiro, in Julius Caesar "the various strands of politics, character, inwardness, contemporary events, even Shakespeare's own reflections on the act of writing, began to infuse each other".

Shakespeare's so-called "tragic period" lasted from about 1600 to 1608, though he also wrote the so-called "problem plays" Measure for Measure, Troilus and Cressida, and All's Well That Ends Well during this time and had written tragedies before. Many critics believe that Shakespeare's greatest tragedies represent the peak of his art. The hero of the first, Hamlet, has probably been more discussed than any other Shakespearean character, especially for his famous soliloquy "To be or not to be; that is the question."

Unlike the introverted Hamlet, whose fatal flaw is hesitation, the heroes of the tragedies that followed, Othello and King Lear, are undone by hasty errors of judgement. The plots of Shakespeare's tragedies often hinge on such fatal errors or flaws, which overturn order and destroy the hero and those he loves. In Othello, the villain Iago stokes Othello's sexual jealousy to the point where he murders the innocent wife who loves him. In King Lear, the old king commits the tragic error of giving up his powers, initiating the events which lead to the murder of his daughter and the torture and blinding of the Earl of Gloucester.

According to the critic Frank Kermode, "the play offers neither its good characters nor its audience any relief from its cruelty".

In Macbeth, the shortest and most compressed of Shakespeare's tragedies, uncontrollable ambition incites Macbeth and his wife, Lady Macbeth, to murder the rightful king and usurp the throne, until their own guilt destroys them in turn. In this play, Shakespeare adds a supernatural element to the tragic structure.

His last major tragedies, Antony and Cleopatra and Coriolanus, contain some of Shakespeare's finest poetry and were considered his most successful tragedies by the poet and critic T. S. Eliot. In his final period, Shakespeare turned to romance or tragicomedy and completed three more major plays: Cymbeline, The Winter's Tale and The Tempest, as well as the collaboration, Pericles, Prince of Tyre. Less bleak than the tragedies, these four plays are graver in tone than the comedies of the 1590s, but they end with reconciliation and the forgiveness of potentially tragic errors.

Some commentators have seen this change in mood as evidence of a more serene view of life on Shakespeare's part, but it may merely reflect the theatrical fashion of the day. Shakespeare collaborated on two further surviving plays, Henry VIII and The Two Noble Kinsmen, probably with John Fletcher.

PERFORMANCES

It is not clear for which companies Shakespeare wrote his early plays. The title page of the 1594 edition of Titus Andronicus reveals that the play had been acted by three different troupes. After the plagues of 1592–3, Shakespeare's plays were performed by his own company at The Theatre and the Curtain in Shoreditch, north of the Thames. Londoners flocked there to see the first part of Henry IV, Leonard Digges recording, "Let but Falstaff come, Hal, Poins, the rest...and you scarce shall have a room".

When the company found themselves in dispute with their landlord, they pulled The Theatre down and used the timbers to construct the Globe Theatre, the first playhouse built by actors for actors, on the south bank of the Thames at Southwark. The Globe opened in autumn 1599, with Julius

Caesar one of the first plays staged. Most of Shakespeare's greatest post-1599 plays were written for the Globe, including Hamlet, Othello and King Lear.

After the Lord Chamberlain's Men were renamed the King's Men in 1603, they entered a special relationship with the new King James. Although the performance records are patchy, the King's Men performed seven of Shakespeare's plays at court between 1 November 1604 and 31 October 1605, including two performances of The Merchant of Venice. After 1608, they performed at the indoor Blackfriars Theatre during the winter and the Globe during the summer.

The indoor setting, combined with the Jacobean fashion for lavishly staged masques, allowed Shakespeare to introduce more elaborate stage devices. In Cymbeline, for example, Jupiter descends "in thunder and lightning, sitting upon an eagle: he throws a thunderbolt. The ghosts fall on their knees."

The actors in Shakespeare's company included the famous Richard Burbage, William Kempe, Henry Condell and John Heminges. Burbage played the leading role in the first performances of many of Shakespeare's plays, including Richard III, Hamlet, Othello, and King Lear. The popular comic actor Will Kempe played the servant Peter in Romeo and Juliet and Dogberry in Much Ado About Nothing, among other characters.

He was replaced around the turn of the sixteenth century by Robert Armin, who played roles such as Touchstone in As You Like It and the fool in King Lear. In 1613, Sir Henry Wotton recorded that Henry VIII "was set forth with many extraordinary circumstances of pomp and ceremony". On 29 June, however, a cannon set fire to the thatch of the Globe and burned the theatre to the ground, an event which pinpoints the date of a Shakespeare play with rare precision.

TEXTUAL SOURCES

In 1623, John Heminges and Henry Condell, two of Shakespeare's friends from the King's Men, published the First Folio, a collected edition of Shakespeare's plays. It contained 36 texts, including 18 printed for the first time. Many of the plays had already appeared in quarto versions flimsy books made from sheets of paper folded twice to make four leaves. No evidence suggests that Shakespeare approved these editions, which the First Folio describes as "stol'n and surreptitious copies". Alfred Pollard termed some of them "bad quartos" because of their adapted, paraphrased or garbled texts, which may in places have been reconstructed from memory.

Where several versions of a play survive, each differs from the other. The differences may stem from copying or printing errors, from notes by actors or audience members, or from Shakespeare's own papers.

In some cases, for example Hamlet, Troilus and Cressida and Othello, Shakespeare could have revised texts between the quarto and folio editions. The folio version of King Lear is so different from the 1608 quarto that the Oxford Shakespeare prints them both, since they cannot be conflated without confusion.

POEMS

In 1593 and 1594, when the theatres were closed because of plague, Shakespeare published two narrative poems on erotic themes, Venus and Adonis and The Rape of Lucrece. He dedicated them to Henry Wriothesley, earl of Southampton.

In Venus and Adonis, an innocent Adonis rejects the sexual advances of Venus; while in The Rape of Lucrece, the virtuous wife Lucrece is raped by the lustful Tarquin. Influenced by Ovid's Metamorphoses, the poems show the guilt and moral confusion that result from uncontrolled lust. Both proved popular and were often reprinted during Shakespeare's lifetime.

A third narrative poem, A Lover's Complaint, in which a young woman laments her seduction by a persuasive suitor, was printed in the first edition of the Sonnets in 1609. Most scholars now accept that Shakespeare wrote A Lover's Complaint. Critics consider that its fine qualities are marred by leaden effects.

The Phoenix and the Turtle, printed in Robert Chester's 1601 Love's Martyr, mourns the deaths of the legendary phoenix and his lover, the faithful turtle dove. In 1599, two early drafts of sonnets 138 and 144 appeared in The Passionate Pilgrim, published under Shakespeare's name but without his permission.

SONNETS

"Shall I compare thee to a summer's day?
Thou art more lovely and more temperate..."
Lines from Shakespeare's Sonnet 18.

Published in 1609, the Sonnets were the last of Shakespeare's non-dramatic works to be printed. Scholars are not certain when each of the 154 sonnets was composed, but evidence suggests that Shakespeare wrote sonnets throughout his career for a private readership. Even before the two unauthorised sonnets appeared in The Passionate Pilgrim in 1599, Francis Meres had referred in 1598 to Shakespeare's "sugred Sonnets among his private friends". Few analysts believe that the published collection follows Shakespeare's intended sequence.

He seems to have planned two contrasting series: one about uncontrollable lust for a married woman of dark complexion (the "dark lady"), and one about conflicted love for a fair young man (the "fair youth"). It remains unclear if these figures represent real individuals, or if the authorial "I" who addresses them represents Shakespeare himself, though Wordsworth believed that with the sonnets "Shakespeare unlocked his heart".

The 1609 edition was dedicated to a "Mr. W.H.", credited as "the only begetter" of the poems. It is not known whether this was written by Shakespeare himself or by the publisher, Thomas Thorpe, whose initials appear at the foot of the dedication page; nor is it known who Mr. W.H. was, despite numerous theories, or whether Shakespeare even authorised the publication. Critics praise the Sonnets as a profound meditation on the nature of love, sexual passion, procreation, death, and time.

STYLE

Shakespeare's first plays were written in the conventional

style of the day. He wrote them in a stylised language that does not always spring naturally from the needs of the characters or the drama. The poetry depends on extended, sometimes elaborate metaphors and conceits, and the language is often rhetorical written for actors to declaim rather than speak. The grand speeches in Titus Andronicus, in the view of some critics, often hold up the action, for example; and the verse in Two Gentlemen of Verona has been described as stilted.

Soon, however, Shakespeare began to adapt the traditional styles to his own purposes. The opening soliloquy of Richard III has its roots in the self-declaration of Vice in medieval drama. At the same time, Richard's vivid self-awareness looks forward to the soliloquies of Shakespeare's mature plays. No single play marks a change from the traditional to the freer style.

Shakespeare combined the two throughout his career, with Romeo and Juliet perhaps the best example of the mixing of the styles. By the time of Romeo and Juliet, Richard II, and A Midsummer Night's Dream in the mid-1590s, Shakespeare had begun to write a more natural poetry. He increasingly tuned his metaphors and images to the needs of the drama itself.

Shakespeare's standard poetic form was blank verse, composed in iambic pentameter. In practice, this meant that his verse was usually unrhymed and consisted of ten syllables to a line, spoken with a stress on every second syllable. The blank verse of his early plays is quite different from that of his later ones. It is often beautiful, but its sentences tend to start, pause, and finish at the end of lines, with the risk of monotony.

Once Shakespeare mastered traditional blank verse, he began to interrupt and vary its flow. This technique releases the new power and flexibility of the poetry in plays such as Julius Caesar and Hamlet. Shakespeare uses it, for example, to convey the turmoil in Hamlet's mind:

Sir, in my heart there was a kind of fighting
That would not let me sleep. Methought I lay

Worse than the mutines in the bilboes. Rashly
And prais'd be rashness for it let us know
Our indiscretion sometimes serves us well...

After Hamlet, Shakespeare varied his poetic style further, particularly in the more emotional passages of the late tragedies. The literary critic A. C. Bradley described this style as "more concentrated, rapid, varied, and, in construction, less regular, not seldom twisted or elliptical". In the last phase of his career, Shakespeare adopted many techniques to achieve these effects. These included run-on lines, irregular pauses and stops, and extreme variations in sentence structure and length.

In Macbeth, for example, the language darts from one unrelated metaphor or simile to another: "was the hope drunk/ Wherein you dressed yourself?" (1.7.35–38); "...pity, like a naked new-born babe/ Striding the blast, or heaven's cherubim, hors'd/ Upon the sightless couriers of the air..." (1.7.21–25). The listener is challenged to complete the sense.

The late romances, with their shifts in time and surprising turns of plot, inspired a last poetic style in which long and short sentences are set against one another, clauses are piled up, subject and object are reversed, and words are omitted, creating an effect of spontaneity.

Shakespeare's poetic genius was allied with a practical sense of the theatre. Like all playwrights of the time, Shakespeare dramatised stories from sources such as Petrarch and Holinshed. He reshaped each plot to create several centres of interest and show as many sides of a narrative to the audience as possible. This strength of design ensures that a Shakespeare play can survive translation, cutting and wide interpretation without loss to its core drama.

As Shakespeare's mastery grew, he gave his characters clearer and more varied motivations and distinctive patterns of speech. He preserved aspects of his earlier style in the later plays, however. In his late romances, he deliberately returned to a more artificial style, which emphasised the illusion of theatre.

INFLUENCE

Shakespeare's work has made a lasting impression on later

theatre and literature. In particular, he expanded the dramatic potential of characterisation, plot, language, and genre. Until Romeo and Juliet, for example, romance had not been viewed as a worthy topic for tragedy. Soliloquies had been used mainly to convey information about characters or events; but Shakespeare used them to explore characters' minds. His work heavily influenced later poetry.

The Romantic poets attempted to revive Shakespearean verse drama, though with little success. Critic George Steiner described all English verse dramas from Coleridge to Tennyson as "feeble variations on Shakespearean themes."

Shakespeare influenced novelists such as Thomas Hardy, William Faulkner, and Charles Dickens. Dickens often quoted Shakespeare, drawing 25 of his titles from Shakespeare's works. The American novelist Herman Melville's soliloquies owe much to Shakespeare; his Captain Ahab in Moby-Dick is a classic tragic hero, inspired by King Lear. Scholars have identified 20,000 pieces of music linked to Shakespeare's works.

These include two operas by Giuseppe Verdi, Otello and Falstaff, whose critical standing compares with that of the source plays. Shakespeare has also inspired many painters, including the Romantics and the Pre-Raphaelites. The Swiss Romantic artist Henry Fuseli, a friend of William Blake, even translated Macbeth into German. The psychoanalyst Sigmund Freud drew on Shakespearean psychology, in particular that of Hamlet, for his theories of human nature.

In Shakespeare's day, English grammar and spelling were less standardised than they are now, and his use of language helped shape modern English. Samuel Johnson quoted him more often than any other author in his A Dictionary of the English Language, the first serious work of its type. Expressions such as "with bated breath" (Merchant of Venice) and "a foregone conclusion" (Othello) have found their way into everyday English speech.

CRITICAL REPUTATION

Shakespeare was never revered in his lifetime, but he

received his share of praise. In 1598, the cleric and author Francis Meres singled him out from a group of English writers as "the most excellent" in both comedy and tragedy. And the authors of the Parnassus plays at St John's College, Cambridge, numbered him with Chaucer, Gower and Spenser. In the First Folio, Ben Jonson called Shakespeare the "Soul of the age, the applause, delight, the wonder of our stage", though he had remarked elsewhere that "Shakespeare wanted art".

Between the Restoration of the monarchy in 1660 and the end of the seventeenth century, classical ideas were in vogue. As a result, critics of the time mostly rated Shakespeare below John Fletcher and Ben Jonson. Thomas Rymer, for example, condemned Shakespeare for mixing the comic with the tragic. Nevertheless, poet and critic John Dryden rated Shakespeare highly, saying of Jonson, "I admire him, but I love Shakespeare". For several decades, Rymer's view held sway; but during the eighteenth century, critics began to respond to Shakespeare on his own terms and acclaim what they termed his natural genius.

A series of scholarly editions of his work, notably those of Samuel Johnson in 1765 and Edmond Malone in 1790, added to his growing reputation. By 1800, he was firmly enshrined as the national poet. In the eighteenth and nineteenth centuries, his reputation also spread abroad. Among those who championed him were the writers Voltaire, Goethe, Stendhal and Victor Hugo.

During the Romantic era, Shakespeare was praised by the poet and literary philosopher Samuel Taylor Coleridge; and the critic August Wilhelm Schlegel translated his plays in the spirit of German Romanticism. In the nineteenth century, critical admiration for Shakespeare's genius often bordered on adulation. "That King Shakespeare," the essayist Thomas Carlyle wrote in 1840, "does not he shine, in crowned sovereignty, over us all, as the noblest, gentlest, yet strongest of rallying signs; indestructible".

The Victorians produced his plays as lavish spectacles on a grand scale. The playwright and critic George Bernard Shaw mocked the cult of Shakespeare worship as "bardolatry". He claimed that the new naturalism of Ibsen's plays had made Shakespeare obsolete.

The modernist revolution in the arts during the early twentieth century, far from discarding Shakespeare, eagerly enlisted his work in the service of the avant garde. The Expressionists in Germany and the Futurists in Moscow mounted productions of his plays. Marxist playwright and director Bertolt Brecht devised an epic theatre under the influence of Shakespeare.

The poet and critic T. S. Eliot argued against Shaw that Shakespeare's "primitiveness" in fact made him truly modern. Eliot, along with G. Wilson Knight and the school of New Criticism, led a movement towards a closer reading of Shakespeare's imagery. In the 1950s, a wave of new critical approaches replaced modernism and paved the way for "post-modern" studies of Shakespeare. By the eighties, Shakespeare studies were open to movements such as structuralism, feminism, African American studies, and queer studies.

SPECULATION ABOUT SHAKESPEARE

AUTHORSHIP

Around 150 years after Shakespeare's death, doubts began to emerge about the authorship of Shakespeare's works. Alternative candidates proposed include Francis Bacon, Christopher Marlowe, and Edward de Vere, the Earl of Oxford. Although all alternative candidates are almost universally rejected in academic circles, popular interest in the subject, particularly the Oxfordian theory, has continued into the 21st century.

RELIGION

Some scholars claim that members of Shakespeare's family were Catholics, at a time when Catholic practice was against the law. Shakespeare's mother, Mary Arden, certainly came from a pious Catholic family. The strongest evidence might be a Catholic statement of faith signed by John Shakespeare, found in 1757 in the rafters of his former house in Henley

Street. The document is now lost, however, and scholars differ on its authenticity.

In 1591, the authorities reported that John had missed church "for fear of process for debt", a common Catholic excuse. In 1606, William's daughter Susanna was listed among those who failed to attend Easter communion in Stratford. Scholars find evidence both for and against Shakespeare's Catholicism in his plays, but the truth may be impossible to prove either way.

SEXUALITY

Few details of Shakespeare's sexuality are known. At 18, he married the 26-year-old Anne Hathaway, who was pregnant. Susanna, the first of their three children, was born six months later on 26 May 1583. However, over the centuries readers have pointed to Shakespeare's sonnets as evidence of his love for a young man. Others read the same passages as the expression of intense friendship rather than sexual love. At the same time, the twenty-six so-called "Dark Lady" sonnets, addressed to a married woman, are taken as evidence of heterosexual liaisons.

LIST OF WORKS

Classification of the Plays

Shakespeare's works include the 36 plays printed in the First Folio of 1623, listed below according to their folio classification as comedies, histories and tragedies. Shakespeare did not write every word of the plays attributed to him; and several show signs of collaboration, a common practice at the time. Two plays not included in the First Folio, The Two Noble Kinsmen and Pericles, Prince of Tyre, are now accepted as part of the canon, with scholars agreed that Shakespeare made a major contribution to their composition. No poems were included in the First Folio.

In the late nineteenth century, Edward Dowden classified four of the late comedies as romances, and though many scholars prefer to call them tragicomedies, his term is often used. These plays and the associated Two Noble Kinsmen are marked with an asterisk below.

In 1896, Frederick S. Boas coined the term "problem plays" to describe four plays: All's Well That Ends Well, Measure for Measure, Troilus and Cressida and Hamlet. "Dramas as singular in theme and temper cannot be strictly called comedies or tragedies", he wrote. "We may therefore borrow a convenient phrase from the theatre of today and class them together as Shakespeare's problem plays." The term, much debated and sometimes applied to other plays, remains in use, though Hamlet is definitively classed as a tragedy. The other problem plays are marked below with a double dagger.

Chapter 2

Shakespeare's Sonnet Sequence

In William Shakespeare: A Textual Companion, which partners the Oxford Complete Works, Gary Taylor made use, amongst other approaches, of the relative frequency of various 'function words' to determine how far one could be confident that various works either were or were not within the Shakespeare canon.

He said that authors tend to have a typical pattern in the frequency with which they use various common words. The words he chose, because of what he said was the relative consistency of their use within the known Shakespeare canon, were: but, by, for, no, not, so, that, the, to and with. Surprisingly, Taylor did not use this approach in considering the chronology of the plays: surprising, since the frequency of the use of such words does sometimes show a marked increase or decrease over the course of Shakespeare's career.

Taylor's 10 function words had been from an original list of 38, some of which do change quite significantly. Figure 1, for example, gives the relative frequency of the word then (shown as a percentage of all 38 words). This is plotted against the year in which, according to Taylor, each of the works seems most likely to have been written. For the purposes of this exercise we shall be more interested in the data up to about 1609, so the graph is cut off at that date. Works thought to be from 1592 or earlier have also been excluded.

A line of best fit (least squares) is shown, with the coefficient of determination (R2) indicating the extent to which the variation about the mean is 'explained' by the trend, in other words the trend's validity.

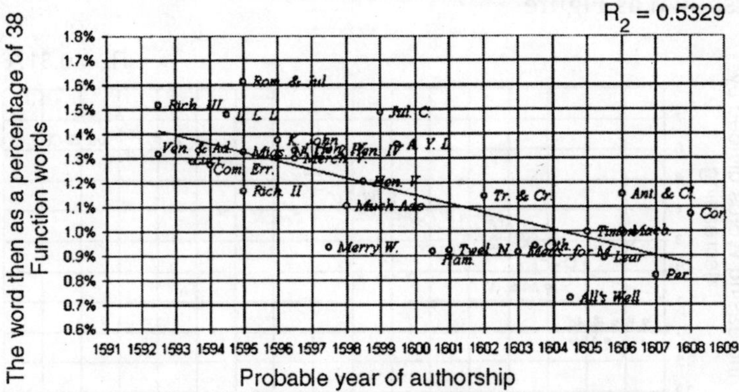

Then gives the highest R2 value of the 38 function words, as is shown below.

Decreasing	R2	N		Increasing	R2	N
then	.5329	1613		most	.3846	937
in	.3647	8810		what	.2563	3710
by	.3605	2907		than	.1913	1365
with	.1858	5961		upon	.1402	1372
so	.1794	3823		not	.1079	6521
for	.1214	5635		to	.0884	14810
these	.1013	906		which	.0829	1763
or	.0951	1753		out	.0816	1098
some	.0924	1018		all	.0812	2947
the	.0430	21068		how	.0764	1569
never	.0420	801		if	.0618	2678
from	.0329	1953		nor	.0578	696
at	.0165	1955		it	.0546	6079
when	.0064	1554		there	.0445	1758
this	.0056	4925		no	.0230	2877
that	.0020	8544		as	.0114	4311
much	.0015	789		why	.0100	1101
now	.0000	2013		but	.0094	4769
				where	.0012	1010
Taylor's words in	bold			such	.0003	1052

A graph similar to Figure, but this time dividing a group of the 'increasing' words by a group of the 'decreasing' ones, is shown as Figure .

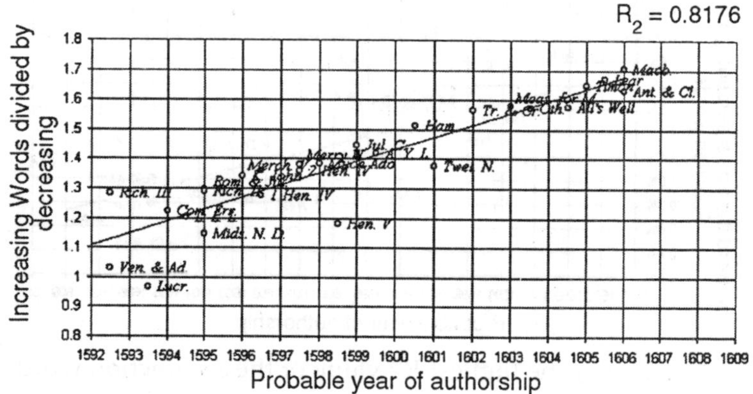

The words used were all of those with R2 values of more than .05.

Given that six of Taylor's ten words are thus included, one cannot but wonder about his definition of 'consistent'. The overall R2 value of .8176 reflects the high validity of the trend, as is clearly discernible.

The purpose of this paper is to see whether, having observed such a trend, we can use it to gain an indication of the order in which The Sonnets were written.

Was the original orders, as printed by Thomas Thorpe, more or less that in which Shakespeare wrote them, or are the many authors and editors who have attempted to find a 'better' sequence on the right track?

Clearly, the individual sonnet is far too small an entity to be dated in this way.

Dealing with groups of sonnets, however, we may be able to find patterns emerging.

We do nevertheless need to count how many of the 22 function words appears in each of the 154 sonnets. The result is fairly emphatic. Looking first of all at whether in the case of each sonnet there are more 'decreasing' words or more 'increasing', we obtain the following picture:

	More 'decreasing' words	More 'increasing' words	Totals
Sonnets 1 to 77	38	18	56
Sonnets 78 to 154	28	50	78
Totals	66	68	134

This yields a chi-squared value of 12.07, which is highly significant at the p = .001 level, and therefore lends considerable support to Thorpe's original sequence having reflected the order in which they were written. The 'missing' 20 Sonnets are those with the same number of each type of word.

Next we can consider it simply in terms of how often the two types of word appear overall in either the first half or the second half of the collection.

	'Decreasing' words	'Increasing' words	Totals
Sonnets 1 to 77	606	570	1176
Sonnets 78 to 154	517	690	1207
Totals	1123	1260	2383

This time the chi-squared value is even greater, coming out at 17.73, which is again highly significant at the p = .001 level. We can see the first of these tables illustrated quite clearly in Figure 3, which shows the difference between the number of 'decreasing' and 'increasing' words for each Sonnet.

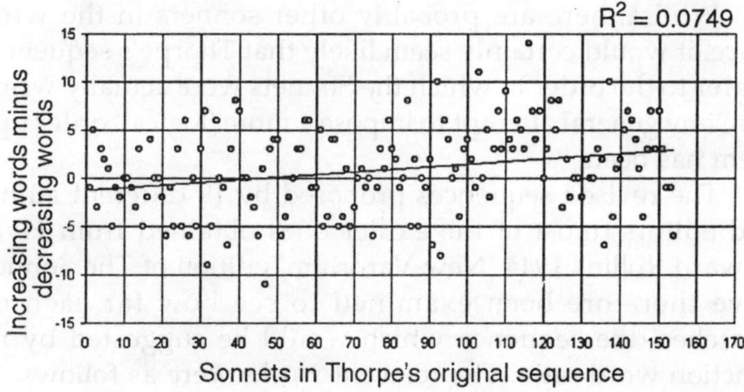

With an average of only about 114 words per sonnet there is bound to be a fairly wide variation, but the trend is clear nevertheless, even without seeing the linear trendline and its R2 value of .0749. Compare the numbers above and below the zero line in each half.

There would obviously be some disagreement as to where breaks should occur, but it is possible to identify a few points in the sequence where the overall theme seems to undergo a change. One very rough way of splitting them might be as follows, to which is added the average score of each group, found by dividing its 'decreasing' total by its 'increasing'.

Sonnet numbers	General 'theme'	Average score
1 to 17	Recommending marriage	0.9612
18 to 24	Young love	0.8281
25 to 52	Travel, absence and disgrace	0.9207
53 to 75	Relationship problems	0.9568
76 to 103	Rival poet and jealousy	1.1786
104 to 126	Reconciliation	1.7214
127 to 154	The Dark Lady	1.2570

As can be easily seen, all follow the expected sequence except the first 17, which look as though they might have been written some time nearer the middle of the sequence and the Dark Lady group, which might have been a little earlier, but not much. There can be little doubt that the use of function words does provide us with important evidence related to the overall sequence of Shakespeare's Sonnets.

Whilst there are probably other sonnets in the wrong place, it would certainly seem likely that Thorpe's sequence is nearer to the order in which the Sonnets were actually written than any general attempt to impose a more 'logical' order upon them has been.

The revised sequences proposed by 19 different authors and editors (most of the earlier ones obtained from Hyder Edward Rollins 1944 'New Varorium' edition of The Sonnets) have therefore been examined to see how far each one 'matches' the sequence which would be suggested by this function word ratio. The relevant works were as follows.

Year	Author/editor		Work
1609	Thomas Thorpe		Shake-speare's Sonnets
1841	Charles Knight		ed.
1857	F.-V. Hugo		Les Sonnets de William Shakespeare
1859	Robert Cartwright		ed.
1866	Friedrich Bodenstedt		Gesammelte Schriften
1872	Fritz Krauss		Shakespeare's Southampton-Sonette
1877	Velasco y Rojas		Shakespeare's Obras
1888	Gerald Massey		ed.
1894	Alfred von Mauntz		Gedichte von William Shakespeare
1899	Samuel Butler		ed.
1900	Parke Godwin		ed.
1904	Charlotte Stopes		ed.
1908	C.M.Walsh		ed.
1925	Rudolf Fischer		Shakespeare's Sonette
1922	Arthur Acheson		Shakespeare's Sonnet Story
1938	Sir Denis Bray		ed.
1968	Brents Stirling		The Shakespeare Sonnet Order
1978	S.C.Campbell		Only Begotten Sonnets
1981	John Padel		New Poems by Shakespeare
1995	A.D.Wraight		The Story that the Sonnets Tell

By reordering the sonnets according to the scores in Figure 3, it is possible to say what the most probable sonnet sequence is, whilst accepting that this is certainly not the actual original sequence.

I shall call this the 'stylometrically determined sequence' (the SDS). As the following table shows, using Spearman's rank order coefficient, only one of the 19 sequences is nearer to this SDS than Thorpe's is, and the further each one is from Thorpe's original sequence, the more it also tends to depart from the SDS. This is displayed as Figure.

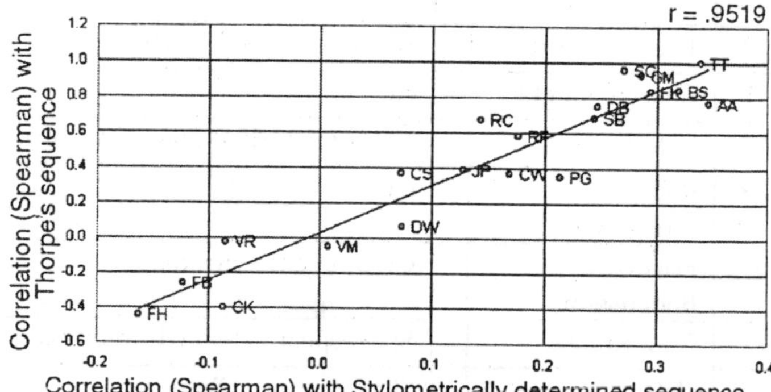

Picking numbers at random would therefore have a greater chance of being correct than those negatively correlated with the SDS.

Author/editor		Correlation with Thorpe	Correlation with SDS
Thomas Thorpe	(TT)	1.00	0.34
Charles Knight	(CK)	-0.40	-0.09
F.-V. Hugo	(FH)	-0.44	-0.16
Robert Cartwright	(RC)	0.67	0.14
Friedrich Bodenstedt	(FB)	-0.26	-0.12
Fritz Krauss	(FK)	0.84	0.29
Velasco y Rojas	(VR)	-0.02	-0.08
Gerald Massey	(GM)	0.92	0.29
Alfred von Mauntz	(VM)	-0.05	0.01
Samuel Butler	(SB)	0.69	0.24
Parke Godwin	(PG)	0.35	0.21
Charlotte Stopes	(CS)	0.37	0.07
C.M.Walsh	(CW)	0.37	0.17
Rudolf Fischer	(RF)	0.58	0.18
Arthur Acheson	(AA)	0.77	0.35
Sir Denis Bray	(DB)	0.75	0.25
Brents Stirling	(BS)	0.84	0.32
S.C.Campbell	(SC)	0.96	0.27
John Padel	(JP)	0.39	0.13
A.D.Wraight	(DW)	0.07	0.07

The correlation between the two sets of figures (r = .9519) is clearly illustrated in Figure.

We have seen that Shakespeare's use of certain function words decreased over the course of his career, while the use of some others increased. Plotting the ratio of one set of such words to the other indicated a highly significant trend over time. Using the same ratio in the case of The Sonnets, we found a similar trend occurred when plotted against the sequence in which they were originally printed. The trend was also more pronounced in this case than in that of all except one of 19 other suggested sequences.

In the case of Shakespeare's other works, the trend was chronologically based. We may therefore state with a high level of confidence that this applies in the case of The Sonnets too. In other words, that the period over which they were written probably covered several years, and that Thomas Thorpe's original sequence is to a large extent the one in which they were originally written.

Chapter 3

The Sonnet in Ruins

With this essay, I want to think about an English history whose destiny is not, after all, monarchical, anti-republican or insular. I will be reading for an England that will no longer have been England, that will have been anti-monarchical, pro-republican, cosmopolitan. The implausibility of this conjectured history is what I will be working towards and, particularly, the knowledge of this impossible history as it could have been contained within the form of the sonnet. So, an alternative history of England and also an alternative history of the sonnet, where subjects are replaced by citizens and self-expression by public discourse.

Or if these alternatives are not, in the end, possible, an England that is monarchist, anti-republican and insular but all of those things quite otherwise. Modernity displaced, ruined and out of time, what Geoffrey Hill, in his sonnet sequence on the Wars of the Roses, 'Funeral Music', calls 'restless / Habitation, no man's dwelling place.' In the second sonnet of the sequence, he brings up the impossibility of a future as happy ending, reconciled as if at the end of a Shakespearean tragicomedy:

(Suppose all reconciled
By silent music; imagine the future
Flashed back at us, like steel against sun,
Ultimate recompense.)

Hill places in parenthesis this romance vision of 'ultimate recompense' realised in an imagined future; the romance of an impossible future is quickly reversed by a reminder of history's recall:

Recall the cold
Of Towton on Palm Sunday before dawn,
Wakefield, Tewkesbury: Fastidious trumpets
Shrilling into the ruck; some trampled
Acres, parched, sodden or blanched by sleet,
Struck with strange-postured dead. Recall the wind's
Flurrying, darkness over human mire.

This turn towards a 'recall' of history, of a Jamesonian 'Real' of history, is what I see as characteristic of some instances of the sonnet form and provides me, for the moment, with a way of thinking about the relationship between form and history in the late sixteenth century, as the sonnet form emerges alongside the arrival of a specific English nationhood that is, after all, monarchical, anti-republican, insular subject-bound.

I am drawing some of my critical inspiration from recent calls within Renaissance studies for a return to considering form in our understandings of text, textuality, culture and history. This could never be a return to a narrow formalism that simply re-inhabits the critical space left by the long dead New Criticism, but a formalism that pays full attention to the developments in literary criticism and cultural studies from the 1980s onwards that have asked us to attend to the material production and productivity of cultural artefacts.

These latter developments have, however, typically avoided tracing the historical specificity of that aspect of culture designated 'literary' that is, literary form itself. Stephen Cohen argues that whilst the study of extra-literary culture has benefited from the application of the literary technique of close reading and that, at the same time, the study of literature has been enhanced by an engagement with cultural studies' politically charged materialism, the study of 'literary form as a cultural practice has fallen into disfavour and neglect.'

Cohen calls instead for a 'historical formalism' which may emerge as 'both a measure and a means of historical change.' Such historical formalism will have, at its heart, Frederic Jameson's concept of an 'ideology of form' (The Political Unconscious, 98) in which the form of literary texts is understood to emerge from historically specific modes of production and ideological conflicts, the individual text 'crisscrossed and intersected by a variety of impulses from contradictory modes of cultural production all at once.' I would like, within this broad notion of an ideology of form, to put forward an alternative history of the English sonnet. This would not seek to eclipse the part this poetic form is seen to have played in the emergence of a modern self-consciousness, but would place that development within a political context where self-reflexivity in lyric verse is not solely part of a developing modernity. Instead, poetic forms that turn back in on themselves, self-regarding like the English sonnet, are produced by political pressures placed on transparent communication and by the potential that poetic form has to register a resistance to those pressures.

The three sonnets from 1599 that I pay particular attention to are two sonnets from the preface to Lewkenor's English translation of Contarini, an account of the governmental structures of Venice, and the sonnet that forms the final chorus to Shakespeare's Henry V. These poems instantiate the tension that is evident in all lyric poetry between the passing of a particular moment and the striving for the eternal.

By focussing on the idea of the 'ruin', explicitly present in two of these sonnets and available as a subtext to the other, I hope to demonstrate an historicised formalism, a formalism that is attendant to circumstance and historical change, even as it acknowledges the impulse towards stasis that is a feature of the sonnet form. At the same time, I will offer an understanding of the early modern English sonnet that departs from the more common study of that form in the light of its production of subjectivity effects.

I will argue that the form of these poems can be read as a product of the ideological conflicts that emerge in the breakdown of consensus surrounding monarchical authority in the late years of Elizabeth's reign. The ironies of the ruinous and anachronistic nature of these poems' narrations of national history will be seen to work in tandem with the form of the early modern English sonnet. Examining this relation will provide some understanding of the limited and restricted nature of political expression in Elizabeth's 'second reign'.

The literary, historical and mythical material that English writers of the sixteenth and seventeenth centuries draw on in their development of a sense of nation is littered with ruins, both real and symbolic. Amongst these ruins are the ransacked citadel of Troy, the plundered remains of the Roman Empire, the fallen Tower of Babel and the empty shells of the English and Welsh medieval abbeys 'Bare ruined choirs, where late the sweet birds sang.' (Shakespeare, Complete Sonnets 527) Ruins in this period are, almost necessarily, ironic.

They disclose failure in the place of achievement. Our idea of the Renaissance is rightly taken up by developments in architecture, building and construction, but these great works are always shaded by an awareness of destruction destruction that both precedes and succeeds them. The fragments of classical civilisations act as a foundation for the achievements of the Renaissance throughout Europe, yet the awareness of distance between the ancient and the modern produces a profound sense of anachronism, of irony, and of mortality.

Similarly, the presence of medieval religious buildings in the British national landscape calls forth an awareness of an ancient history, but one that is lost, broken and ruined. This paper will examine the emergence of these ironies within the formal structures of the sonnet its rhetoric and verbal patterning whilst insisting on a historicised understanding of the individual poems.

In the literature of the sixteenth and seventeenth centuries, the figure of the ruin is deployed as a means to discuss the public world. The image of the ruined wall or building connects the piece of writing to the world of historical change and of political shifts and aspirations. Buildings and architecture constitute the public realm of human achievement and political interaction.

Although undoubtedly political in its own way, the Romantic literary ruin of the late eighteenth and nineteenth centuries is very different from this. A similar emphasis may be placed on the futility of human ambition, such as you might find in Shelley's famous 'Ozymandias' sonnet, but the Renaissance literary ruin does not engender a feeling of contact with 'the sublime' in quite the same way.

Instead, the Renaissance ruin connects the poetic task of memorialising with political and religious histories of "ruin and reform". With the anachronistic and untimely figure of the early modern ruin we gain an insight into the relationship between the emergence of the discrete nation-space as a horizon against which people make sense of their political identity and the conflicting histories of classical retrieval and religious reformation that underpin this development.

In 1599, questions of political identity for English writers inevitably drew them into discussions of alternative political configurations to that currently headed by an ailing and arguably despotic monarch. It was, in 1599, possible to see hereditary monarchy as a failure on two fronts as inherently problematic in that it might allow a disastrously inadequate leader to assume power and as immediately problematic when, as was the case with Elizabeth, a country had run out of clear successors to the throne.

Nevertheless, it is also true to say that the articulation of such ideas was difficult in a politically oppressive and increasingly paranoid atmosphere. The sonnets that I look at here testify, both in form and content, to these two trends a need to imagine alternative political configurations for the nation and the difficulties of articulating this.

In their textual relations the preface to an account of the Venetian republic and the epilogue to an epic national drama they also enact the process of transmission for these ideas. Their particular rhetoric might offer us, then, something of a 'measure of historical change', if not an obvious 'means' (Cohen 33).

The antique Babel, Empresse of the East,
Upreard her buildings to the threatened skie:
And Second Babell tyrant of the West,
Her ayry Towers upraised much more high.
But with the weight of their own surquedry [pride],
They both are fallen, that all the earth did feare,

And buried now in their own ashes ly,
Yet shewing by their heapes how great they were.
But in their place doth now a third appeare,
Fayre Venice, flower of the last worlds delight,
And next to them in beauty draweth neare,
But farre exceedes in policie of right.
Yet not so fayre her buildings to behold
As Lewkenors stile that hath her beautie told.
(Lewkenor, 3v)

Spenser's sonnet is part of the prefatory material to Lewis Lewkenor's 1599 translation of Contarini's 1543 book which describes the Venetian republican political system. Contarini's detailed account of Venice is a celebration of the Venetian constitution and its longevity. Its translation into English by Lewis Lewkenor has been associated with a growth of interest in alternative forms of government during the difficult 'second reign' of Elizabeth.

Andrew Hadfield has argued that, 'It is surely no coincidence that [Contarini] . . . should be translated into English in 1599 when criticism of Elizabeth was reaching epidemic proportions.' (Hadfield 41) Lewkenor's apparent connections with the Essex and Sidney circles further indicate the potential for this text to participate, not only in the factional politics of the late Elizabethan court, but in the political debate that emerged in the difficult years of the 1590s.

The year, 1599, was itself a moment of climax for political tensions that had been gathering since the late 1580s and the year that court factionalism emerged on the international stage. The Earl of Essex was sent to Ireland to combat Hugh O'Neill's extensive and militarily successful rebellion against English rule. Essex understood this as a form of political exile, engineered by his opponents at court, and his campaign in Ireland was largely uninspired, ending up in a secret truce brokered with the Earl of Tyrone, O'Neill himself.

The two men, on horseback, waded into the centre of a river on the Ulster border and, without anybody overhearing, negotiated some kind of deal. This deal, whatever it was, was treated with a great deal of speculation and suspicion in the

English court. It was widely believed that Essex was, with O'Neill, planning for a world without Elizabeth, a world in which Ulster and the English were no longer at odds, where Essex held sway over an England that had liberated itself from the Tudor grip on power.

This episode provides, for me, an image of the Jamesonian 'Real', a history that our interpretations of text should be oriented towards but that is only available in the traces of textuality a silence at the heart of our histories that provides for speculation on alternatives.

It is into this atmosphere of political instability, fraught with the possibilities of regime change, that Lewkenor's republican manifesto was launched. In his prefatory poem, Spenser describes the ruin of two ancient edifices Babel and Rome. He draws on commonly-made connections between Babel, the archetypal tyrannous empire, Babylon, and both ancient and contemporary Rome. These comparisons come from Protestant apocalyptic readings of the bible.

The Geneva Bible made these comparisons explicit in its annotations to the story of Babel in Genesis, to the apocalyptic narratives in the Book of Daniel and to the Book of Revelations itself. The implicit comparison in the poem is between Babel, the ancient Roman Empire and the contemporary state of Rome, itself often called the 'whore of Babylon' in Protestant polemic. Venice, though, has now emerged to replace these former cities, and to outdo them in her 'policie of right'.

Her republicanism will, perhaps, save her from the fate of Babel, Babylon and Rome who had all 'upreard' their buildings, threatening the skies and were brought down by the weight of their own pride ('surquedry'). I say 'perhaps', because there is, here, a sense in which modern Venice might be expected to follow suit. 'But in their place doth now a third appeare,' does not predict unequivocal glory for the real Venice.

However, it is in the writings of Lewkenor that she will survive in her idealised form, the real city coming a poor second. Lewkenor was read in England by those interested in the possibilities of political configurations that offered an alternative to the tyrannous monarchy that they believed themselves to be living under. He was popular amongst the Essex circle and Spenser, as part of this political circle, is here stating his own sympathies for an anti-tyrannical stance. The Venice that is being celebrated in this volume, and introduced by Spenser's poem, actively competes against and transcends the tyrannies of the past.

The role of the writer is, though, crucial and Venice can seemingly only be idealised in written form. It is the task of the writer to undo the ruins of fallen beauty and to reconstruct them in our memories. Spenser's poem suggests that it is only on paper that such a faultless political state can exist and that human endeavours for perfection are doomed to failure even Venice herself. But yet . . . but yet . . . the form of Spenser's writing here, and the rhetoric of the sonnet, renders ironic the potentially optimistic links being made here between an apocalyptic view of the world and the search for a new way of doing things in the 1590s.

It is precisely in the writing of this poem that pessimism about the potential for this message is revealed. What I want to call the recessive rhetoric of the sonnet works in tandem with the ironies of the ruin to stifle the expression of any opportunity for political development potentially implied in the publication of this English translation of what is, essentially, a republican tract.

One way of characterising traditional sonnet structures what I am calling their 'recessive rhetoric' is to understand them within the rhetorical figure of metanoia. George Puttenham refers to this figure as 'the penitent' or 'the repentant' in The Art of English Poesy in that it indicates a turning back from an original statement (Puttenham 215). In searching for a definitive statement, sonnets refine their own definitions through refutation and counter-refutation.

The insertion of the 'turn' or caesura at the start of the ninth line of the English sonnet is the most characteristic example of this. The 'But' of Shakespeare's sonnet 18, 'But thy eternal summer shall not fade' is merely the best known example of a trait that structures a wide range of early modern sonnet-writing in which topics are defined through negation and through 'repenting' of, and turning back from, earlier definitions (Shakespeare, Complete Sonnets 417). Spenser's own Amoretti can be included in this, with the 'But' in the ninth line of the second sonnet announcing the participation of this sequence in the recessive logic of the sonnet (Spenser, The Yale Edition 601).

The sonnet that Spenser writes for the opening material of Lewkenor, however, takes the recessive rhetoric of the sonnet to extensive lengths. It is not just that each change of fortune for the world's succeeding empires is met with a 'yet' or a 'but'; Spenser's attitudes to the vicissitudes of history also go through several reversals. The first 'but' follows the narrative pattern of this sonnet in which pride comes before a fall, the 'ayry' towers of Babel and Rome collapsing, with the second quatrain of the sonnet beginning, 'But with the weight of their own surquedry, / They both are fallen'.

This repeated narrative of circumstances is itself reinterpreted by the end of the second quatrain with, 'Yet shewing by their heapes how great they were.' The 'yet' here could have two implications either as an alternative for 'but', or indicative of a continuing sense of their power into the present 'Still showing by their heaps how great they were.'

Even this line, with its apparent move towards reinterpreting the ruins not as symbols of moral degeneration, but as emblems of human achievement, is rendered ironic through Spenser's use of the word 'heapes'. This word has negative connotations elsewhere in Spenser's writing. However, Venice itself arrives in the expected position of the sonnet's turn presumably to resolve the fluctuations and refutations of the octave: 'But in their place now a third appeare'. This description of Venice is, though, staggered by further qualifications; it is not so beautiful as either Rome or Babel, whilst ('But') exceeding them 'in policie of right'.

These qualifications are still further qualified as Spenser, repenting of this celebration of Venice, tells us that the city is further outdone by Lewkenor's writing in the book which this sonnet prefaces. Venice, itself, will not be able to resolve the processes of historical decay that have been traced in the form of the sonnet but Lewkenor's beautiful writing may offer some aesthetic and political compensation for these losses. In most other prefatory poems, such hyperbolic comparisons could be read as merely conventional but in a poem which exploits the penitential rhetoric of the sonnet form to such a high degree, this final qualification only adds to the irony rather than providing the closure that is always, at least notionally, on offer in the English sonnet's last rhyming couplet.

Elsewhere in Spenser's writing notably the complaint poem, The Ruines of Time, and translations of du Bellay in Ruines of Rome, Visions of Bellay and A Theatre for Worldlings the succession of apocalyptically ruined cities is linked to a search for firm grounds on which to base claims for England's emergence as an imperial successor, part of the translatio imperii in which the mantle of empire is passed steadily west from Troy, through Rome and on to England.

Spenser's own writing, translating these texts into the English language and into an English context, enacts the processes of translation. Andrew Escobedo has identified this search for historical origins in sixteenth and seventeenth-century writing with an accompanying sense of loss, associating this particularly with the 'monument', a general term referring to remains from the past:

The figure of the monument, as antiquaries often referred to the physical remains of the past, produces a double effect: it reminds the English nation of its history, closing the gap between past and present, but its materiality assures that it will itself disappear some day, signalling the loss or death of history.

Although addressing this question of the 'monument', the relationship of Spenser's sonnet to the formation of a sense of the English nation as nation is different. The implication that England is part of this ongoing line of ruined empires whose histories are revealed as always lost, behind them, is certainly there in this sonnet. However, its relationship to a project for the potential future political configuration of the English nation is more interesting. As the sonnet closes, it invites us to consider the place of writing within historical change and to think about Lewkenor's ability to effect political discussion amongst his readers. In doing so, it just barely articulates the otherwise unstated political context within which Lewkenor's translation of Contarini might have been received.

In his recent book, Shakespeare and Republicanism, Andrew Hadfield acknowledges that he may have overstated the case for the presence of republican discourse in early modern England and that if his detailed picture of the scope of republicanism within English sixteenth-century political theory produces the impression that such writing 'was ubiquitous and that it could not be avoided' then 'this would be wrong.' (Hadfield 47)

One of the things that is missing from Hadfield's otherwise important and welcome rewriting of the political contexts in which Shakespeare's writings should be understood is an appropriate understanding of literary form and, as a result, he misses an opportunity to trace ideological conflict in the particular forms of writing that he deals with.

Paying more attention to questions of form, genre and rhetoric might allow us to see not just what was being written, but offers insight into how that writing relates to the historical circumstances from which it emerged and in which it was received particularly into what assumptions might be made about the potential for favourable reception that such ideas might have.

As I have argued elsewhere, in relation to Shakespeare's Lucrece, the poetry of the 1590s features rhetorical formations which highlight particular difficulties of expression. The recessive rhetoric of the sonnet is, I believe, part of this tendency. Its definitions and redefinitions move towards clarity that is then rendered ironic in the awkwardness of its expression.

The 'penitent' and self-cancelling nature of the Elizabethan sonnet can be read as a product of the ideological conflicts that emerge in the breakdown of consensus surrounding monarchical authority in the late years of Elizabeth's reign. The occluded nature of its rhetorical forms mediates a culture that itself finds it difficult to articulate forms of government or representation that exist outside of hereditary forms of dynastic monarchy, at the same time as successive political crises render it necessary to attempt just such a formulation.

The anachronisms of the ruin that interrupt the timely progression of a teleological narrative of national origins can be seen as analogous to the turning back from easy progression that is a feature of the sonnet form itself, a movement towards a unity that is revealed as specious. The radical untimeliness of the ruin, as it relates to an emerging sense of nationhood, is realised in sonnet form.

This may, at least, be one reason for Shakespeare's choice of the sonnet form at the close of his ironic national epic, Henry V. This sonnet, or this play, may not mention ruins at all but, as with the trope of the ruin, it deals with the revelation of defeat in the place of national triumph, turning back in its closing moments from the overt celebration of English victory over France to a reminder that this trophy was lost within a generation:

Thus farre with rough, and all-unable Pen,
Our bending Author hath pursu'd the Story,
In little roome confining mightie men,
Mangling by starts the full course of their glory.
Small time: but in that small, most greatly lived
This Starre of England. Fortune made his Sword;
By which, the Worlds best Garden he atchieved:
And of it left his Sonne Imperiall Lord.
Henry the Sixt, in Infant Bands crown'd King
Of France and England, did this King succeed:
Whose State so many had the managing,
That they lost France, and made England bleed:
Which oft our Stage hath showne; and for their sake,
In your faire minds let this acceptance take.
(Epilogue. 1-14)

Patricia Parker, in Shakespeare From the Margins, has written very influentially on the 'preposterous' nature of Shakespeare's English histories, including Henry V a play which reminds its audience of English loss and failure at the end of a story of apparent national success. Whilst acknowledging the careful and pioneering work that Parker has done to make us aware of the importance of form and rhetoric in our historicist analyses of early modern texts, I would like to offer an extension of this historical formalism through an investigation of the form in which this reminder takes place the sonnet.

None of the Chorus's speeches are included in the First Quarto text of the play but are inserted into the 1623 Folio, a text that is presumed to be based on Shakespeare's foul papers. In this final speech, the Chorus speaks a perfect English sonnet with rhyme pattern and iambic pentameter intact. The references in the first two lines of this final Chorus to an 'Author' and a 'pen' seem to refer an audience or reader beyond the dramatic context and into the scene of writing, a more conventional location for the formation of a sonnet.

These references to the material practices of writing indicate a particular self-consciousness about literary form in this speech. Again, though, the sonnet's rhetoric is not the locus for the development of a particular form of subjectivity. Rather, the recessive nature of the sonnet is a further extension of the play's ironies and links the form both of the drama and this chorus-sonnet to late Elizabethan receptions of political narrative. Ruinous anachronism meets up with the self-cancelling nature of the sonnet to reveal, through irony, the difficulties for transparent political communication in the 1590s.

The political contexts for Shakespeare's Henry V are well established. Written and performed in 1599, at a time of heightened anxiety for the nation's security, Henry V is not so much a celebration of English history as a response to a number of contemporary crises: the problem of succession for an ageing Elizabeth, the Irish rebellion and growing discontent and factionalism in the English court. However, it also has to be said that the articulation of these contemporary concerns in this play is far from straightforward.

Yet, the search for alternative political configurations that is increasingly seen as a feature of the 1590s and particularly of writing that is related to the Sidney and Essex circles, is also present in Henry V. The ambiguities of Shakespeare's attitudes towards the role of the king throughout the English history plays have been the subject of critical interest for some time.

In Shakespeare and Republicanism, Andrew Hadfield has argued for seeing the first tetralogy as Shakespeare's version of Lucan's Pharsalia. An interest in the Pharsalia has been identified both by Hadfield and others, especially David Norbrook, as indicative of an emerging republican discourse in the late sixteenth and early seventeenth centuries.

Henry V may seem like a move away from the more radical interrogations of kingship that are a feature of the history plays from earlier in the 1590s. However, in its equivocal portrayal of Henry himself, in the various complaints of his troops throughout the course of the play, in the references contained within the play to contemporary concerns such as Ireland and the royal succession and in the Chorus's reminder of Henry VI's failure and hence the failure of monarchy by succession, Henry V may play more of a role in the 1590s' search for alternative forms of government than might, at first, be thought.

This, though, is not clearly stated in the play. If Henry V toys with republicanism, as I think it does, this can only ever be an occluded republicanism, a product of the difficult and paranoid political circumstances of the 1590s.

These difficulties can be traced in the form of this final sonnet and may, indeed, have guided Shakespeare's choice for this particular chorus. There is, of course, a major turn in this sonnet which comes with the arrival of 'Henry the Sixt' at the start of the ninth line. However, the ironies of this sonnet's conclusions about Henry V's French success have already appeared earlier on in the poem.

The octave is taken up with the ongoing argument of the chorus that the stage is an inadequate medium for the portrayal of such heroic events. As the play has gone on up until this point, these kinds of statement from the Chorus have been open to an increasingly ironic reading, as Henry's actions have been seen on occasions not always to match up to the apparent optimism of the Chorus's depiction of him as a national hero.

In the fourth line of this final Chorus 'Mangling by starts the full course of their glory' the subject of the verb, 'mangling' is left ambiguous. The primary meaning of this line is clearly that the pen of the author has 'mangled by starts' the glory of the men depicted. However, a secondary interpretation must also be allowed in which it is the men themselves who 'mangled by starts' their initially heroic enterprise.

The ironies of the 'full course' of these men's actions not being allowed to play out either through their own faults or those of the dramatist are initially reversed by the praise of Henry in the second quatrain but the self-cancelling rhetoric of the sonnet comes fully into play with the arrival of Henry's son at the 'turn'. The apparent narrative of national progress that has been seen throughout the play and that is partly echoed in the octave of the final sonnet is turned towards anticlimax in the sestet of this last chorus.

The trope of the ruin, in early modern writing, renders narratives of national destiny ironic. It reveals inevitable failure in the place of the greatest achievement; it provides a history of conflict in the place of unity and peace. The presence of ruins in the national landscape makes the historicist project of forming a discrete nation-space, rendered present through linear narrative, seem untenable. Homi Bhabha, in the influential essay, 'DissemiNation: Time, Narrative and the Margins of the Modern Nation' writes that, 'The linear equivalence of event and idea that historicism most commonly proposes, signifies a people, a nation, or a national culture as an empirical sociological category or a holistic cultural entity.' (Bhabha 140)

The time of the nation as linear narrative, achieved within the discrete horizon of the nation-space, cannot be sustained beyond the discovery of the ruin.

The two occasional sonnets that I have looked at so far in this essay both present narratives of nationhood which turn back on themselves, refrain from moving towards a telos of political clarity and national destiny. The Spenser sonnet seems to offer an endorsement of a political future in which a debate over forms of government, and particularly over forms of republicanism, may contribute to the formation of the nation. However, its recessive and metanoiac rhetoric seems, at the same time, to reveal the impossibility of any such debate. The Chorus at the end of Henry V, apparently concluding a glorious chapter of English history, nevertheless reveals the collapse of any progressive narrative of nationhood.

The marginal nature of these sonnets one being part of a book's prefatory material and the other a speech from a Chorus that does not participate in the main action of the play offers us ways of thinking about the communication of historical narrative and political debate.

The function of these two poems is, purportedly, to facilitate the wider dissemination of the political knowledge contained within the main bodies of the texts. However, they both highlight the difficulties that such dissemination might face. An examination of the form of these sonnets structured through the self-cancelling rhetoric of metanoia may point us in the direction of how these poems mediate the political circumstances in which they are produced.

Recognising the nature of these sonnets' rhetoric allows us to understand the circumstances in which they are produced as propitious neither to the transparent communication of alternatives to hereditary monarchy, nor conversely to a straightforward celebration of the status quo. Henry V is conventionally read as a celebration of monarchy, however vexed that celebration might be. Lewkenor's account of Venice is a text that, on first publication, actively pursued the promotion of alternatives to hereditary monarchy.

That these two texts share rhetorical strategies of reversion and self-cancellation is both illustrative of, and a product of, the circumstances of their production. Furthermore, it shows that some of the particular characteristics of late sixteenth-century poetry its self-reflexiveness, its peculiarly articulate inarticulacy might not always be sufficiently understood through references to the emergence of a modern sense of selfhood. Rather, Jameson's concept of an 'ideology of form' may alert us to the conflicting ideological motivations that work to produce the sonnet form in the late sixteenth century.

Spenser's sonnet dedication to Lewkenor's translation is one of four short poems, three of them sonnets, that precede the dedications proper. The sonnet that comes immediately after the Spenser sonnet, written by 'I.Ashley' is a much more negative depiction of Venice's virtues and beauties. It also exhibits the use of explicitly Petrarchan tropes, common to Elizabethan sonnet-writing but which might normally be confined to discussions of love, desire and subjectivity:

Fayer mayden towne that in rich Thetis armes,
Hath still been fostered since thy first foundation.
Whose glorious beauty cals unnumbered swarmes
Of rarest spirits from each forrein nation,
And yet (sole wonder to all Europes eares,
Most lovely Nimph, that ever Neptune got)
In all this space of thirteene hundred yeares,
Thy virgins state ambition nere could blot.
Now I prognosticate thy ruinous case,
When thou shalt from thy Adriatique seas,
View in this Ocean Isle thy painted face,
In these pure colours coyest eyes to please,
Then gazing in thy shadowes peereles eye,
Enamour'd like Narcissus thou shalt dye.
I.Ashley.
(Lewkenor 3v)

Ashley imagines Venice as a type of Petrarchan mistress, pursued by suitors a 'Fayer mayden' and a 'Most lovely Nimph'. The turn of the poem, though, presents a different view of Venice. Moving from an eternity of beauty in which Venice has sustained its virginity, 'In all this space of thirteene hundrede yeares' to a situation, 'Now', when the poet prognosticates Venice's 'ruinous case'.

This sonnet is again structured through recessive rhetoric and by metanoia. The praise of Venice as an example of the perfect city state is positioned within a reversal in which time has caught up with her. Ashley is less equivocal than Spenser in his attitude towards Venice's ruin. He sees it as inevitable and does not gesture towards Lewkenor's or Contarini's text as compensation.

What is also interesting about this is the language within which Ashley depicts the ruinous future that he is predicting for Venice. The lyric tension between the fleeting moment and the eternal all turns on Ashley's 'Now'. But, in this he steers away from Protestant apocalyptic and, instead, rewrites Venice as a Narcissus-figure, something straight out of the conventions of Petrarchan sonnet-writing. Venice moves from cruel virginal mistress to narcissistic self-regarding lover, staring at her own reflection until she drowns in the Adriatic.

The one lingering suggestion of apocalypse or, at least, of judgement, is in the reference to Venice's 'painted face'. In that 'now' a moment for an English republicanism is passing, has passed. Ashley uses Petrarchan language, imagery and poetic structure that would not be out of place in a sequence of love sonnets. The self-regarding, self-cancelling structure of the sonnet is both narcissistic and indicative of a particular political context in which republicanism might, now, be discussed but now or yet only in ways that can be repented of by the writer.

It might seem odd to have prefaced this discussion of three occasional late sixteenth-century sonnets with a brief foray into the complex writing of the contemporary poet, Geoffrey Hill. This might be doubly unexpected as Hill's politics are more frequently identified with that national destiny I see being resisted in the recessive rhetoric of these sonnets monarchical, insular and conservative.

And yet, in the forms of 'Funeral Music', Hill's 1968 sonnet sequence, there is a sense, too, that history is being told otherwise, crossed by multiple voices that can not be fully enclosed within the form. The final sonnet of the sequence is narrated in the voices of three 'soldier-martyrs', executed in the course of the Wars of the Roses, all by different, successive Kings Henry VI, Edward IV and Richard III. The three, speaking as 'we' in this final sonnet, move towards a bitter understanding of their role in history, beyond their own subjectivity 'Set apart in timeless colloquy: / So it is required;

so we bear witness'. But then, the sonnet 'turns', as they see the inadequacy of their deaths as historical allegory:

If it is without
Consequence that we vaunt and suffer, or
If it is not, all echoes are the same
In such eternity. Then tell me, love,
How should that comfort us or anyone
Dragged half-unnerved out of this worldly place,
Crying to the end 'I have not finished'.

In its impossible conjunctions of apocalyptic vision and precise historical concerns, Hill's sonnet and the sequence from which it comes, evokes the untimely trope of the ruin as I understand it presenting us with the need to rethink our histories, to inhabit them differently and to approach that through careful work on the mediating forms in which that thinking might take place.

Chapter 4

The Forms of Desire in Shakespeare's Venus and Adonis

Recent articles by Catherine Belsey, Richard Halpern, and James Schiffer have shifted the critical focus of Shakespeare's Venus and Adonis from questions of what the poem means, to how it means, from its moral allegory to its erotic and literary effects. For Belsey, this transition arose from her sense that readers of Shakespeare's epyllion who seek a "moral centre that would furnish the work with a final meaning, a conclusion, a definitive statement" tend to be interpreted by the poem in the very effort made to interpret it.

Venus and Adonis, Belsey contends, "prompts in the reader a desire for action it fails to gratify. Meanwhile, the critical tradition in its turn, tantalized by the poem's lack of closure, has sought to make something happen, at least at the thematic level". Likewise, Halpern asserts that "Venus and Adonis is not only a poem about female sexual frustration; it is meant to produce such frustration.

Just as Adonis' beauty arouses Venus but refuses to satisfy her, so Shakespeare's poem aims to arouse and frustrate the female reader". Similarly, Schiffer argues that the poem dramatizes a Lacanian conception of desire to the extent that it reveals "desire can never be truly satisfied, because desire is always for absence, for lack, for what is not there".

Although I agree that the poem aims to inspire a sense of frustration in its reader through its unrealized promise of satisfying closure, I do not think adequate attention has been paid to the rhetorical and intertextual elements that work to effect a reader's frustration. This paper aims, then, to demonstrate that the poem's frustrating effects are largely a product of its rhetorical design, the fact that a substantial portion of the narrative's comic-tragic trajectory is constructed through patterns of opposition, resolution, and subsequent disunion.

Moreover, a closer rhetorical and intertextual analysis of Venus and Adonis reveals that the poem's "erotic ontology" (Halpern 383) does not, as Halpern suggests, restrict its frustrating effects to early modern female readers. Instead, the poem's reversal of gender norms enables a complex and unstable series of identifications that betray any straightforward assertion that a male reader is less likely to sympathize with Venus's cause than is a female reader; or, on the other hand, that a female reader is necessarily prone to identify with Venus over and against Adonis.

Indeed, one of the primary effects of the poem's gender reversal is to complicate the process of identification so essential to literary response, making the identificatory process itself an issue for the reader, rather than something operating in terms of gender alone.

Part of the complexity involved in how a reader responds to the poem's use of reversals results from the way that Shakespeare organizes the symbolic oppositions through which the text is constructed. S. Clark Hulse understands the iconographic and imagistic oppositions in the poem less in terms of sustained narrative deferral, than as an expression of the poem's mythic and existentially mediating design:

Shakespeare's sophisticated reworking of a literary myth [in Venus and Adonis] comes suprisingly close to recovering the function that Levi-Strauss suggests for primary myth: 'to bridge the gap between conflicting values through a series of mediating devices, each of which generates the next one by a process of opposition and correlation.' (Hulse 172-3, Levi-Strauss 213-23)

For Hulse, "Shakespeare's manner of paradox making has

the characteristics of a persistent personal syntax. Indeed, if we think of myth as a conceptual form rather than as a content, we might call it Shakespeare's personal myth, a way of perceiving and reconciling the paradoxes of experience" (173). Although the poem's imagistic and rhetorical design, its "mediating devices" as it were, clearly orbit the mythic concerns of existential and ideological antagonisms, Shakespeare's text makes no claim, as does primary myth, to "explanatory totality" (Levi-Strauss 213-23).

Venus and Adonis, in other words, has no pretensions of reconciling "the paradoxes of experience"; it dramatizes such paradoxes and, as Belsey argues, it problematizes certain conflicting values but it offers no answers. To this extent, Shakespeare's poem makes explicit what Jacques Derrida sees as the latent unending deferral operating in all mythic structures of thought. For Derrida the themes [in myth] duplicate themselves to infinity.

When we think we have disentangled them from each other and can hold them separate, it is only to realise that they are joining together again, in response to the attraction of unforeseen affinities. In consequence, the unity of myth is only tendential and projective; it never reflects a state or moment of the myth.

Unlike primary myth, which aims explicitly towards a complete mediation of existential and ideological oppositions, Venus and Adonis purposefully resists the state of closure, the point of full reconciliation of opposites. In this sense, Shakespeare's poem makes dramatically explicit what Derrida locates as an implicit feature of mythic thought in general.

By choosing the sixain form of Thomas Lodge's epyllion Scillaes Metamorphosis over the heroic couplets of Marlowe's minor epic Hero and Leander, Shakespeare is able to create a sense of narrative deferral through the use of repetition offered by the smaller narrative units of the sixain pattern.

Indeed, when we compare the opening stanza of Venus and Adonis with the opening of Marlowe's poem, for instance, we notice that Shakespeare emphasizes action and movement rather than description and imagistic detail. The sense of movement achieved in the opening of Shakespeare's poem occurs through a series of implied similes that are contiguously linked. Marlowe, on the other hand, begins by describing the Ovidian world of Hero and Leander.

In particular he draws on the Ovidian ekphrastic tradition in his description of Hero's garments. Such extended detail so early in the poem focuses less on dramatic action than on the narrator's witty rhetorical displays and his capacity for evoking lush visual imagery:

At Sestos, Hero dwelt; Hero the faire . . .
The outside of her garments were of lawne
The lining, purple silke, with guilt starres drawne,
Her wide sleeves greene, and bordered with a grove
Where Venus in her naked glory strove. (7-11)

In Shakespeare's poem, however, we get neither extended physical description nor anything approaching narrative aside until the ekphrasis at line 259 when Adonis fails to mount his "trampling courser." Instead, we are immediately presented with Venus' wooing of Adonis through a series of contiguous images that creates tension and movement:

Even as the sun with purple-colored face
Had ta'en last leave of the weeping morn,
Rose-cheeked Adonis hied him to the chase;
Hunting he loved, but love he laughed to scorn.
Sick-thoughted Venus makes amain unto him,
And like a bold-faced suitor 'gins to woo him. (1-6)

These opening six lines present the reader with three movements of pursuit and one clear instance of abandonment. The larger narrative movement of pursuit and abandonment in the poem is thus encapsulated in this opening stanza as the first six lines initiate a movement towards resolution but conclude by simply emphasizing further pursuit.

The proleptic image of the sun leaving the "weeping morn" frames both Adonis's and Venus' respective pursuits, establishing the poem's pattern of endless seeking, a pattern which fails to cease even at Adonis' death. In this case the pattern evolves through a series of contiguously associated implied similes that develop from the sun and morn to Adonis and the chase, to Venus and her erotic hunt. Shakespeare spends little time describing the mythic world that his characters inhabit; instead, he employs the image of the sun to establish the theme of temporality and the cycle of loss and dissatisfaction to which Venus and Adonis are prisoners.

The chiasmus in line four introduces a rhetorical reversal that mirrors the gender reversal of the sexual combatants; such reversals, and the oxymoronic rhetoric they are often figured through, are central to establishing the sense of opposition characteristic of the poem and the subsequent sense of postponement such opposition inspires.

From the very beginning of the poem the key axis upon which the narrative moves is not the totalizing motion of metaphor, but a series of delayed and incomplete contiguous or metonymic relationships. The beginning of Venus and Adonis, which already alludes to its own unsatisfying end, begins a pattern or cycle of unfulfillment that repeats throughout the text.

This repetition of unfulfillment constitutes the narrative's postponement or detour which sustains the sense of tension that is usually accented by the "middle section" of the narrative and then resolved at the end. In Venus and Adonis, however, the beginning, middle, and end all play a role in enhancing the sense of postponement and delay. By dividing the first 810 lines of the poem into four narrative movements each constituting (with the exception of the ekphrasis) a pattern of pursuit, ostensible resolution and subsequent opposition, it becomes clear that the poem is experienced as an over-determined series of unresolved patterns of sexual pursuit intertwined with moments of apparent, but finally unrealized union. Lines 1-258 constitute the first main narrative pattern which is followed by the "breeding jennet" episode.

Subsequently, lines 325-545 renew Venus' momentum lost at the end of the first section. This third movement concludes with the kiss at 545, but rather than satiating Venus the kiss leads to yet another intensification of her desire: "Now quick desire hath caught the yielding prey/ And glutton like she feeds, yet never filleth". This intensification of desire and the unbearable sense of frustration it inspires reaches its climax at the poem's centre when it becomes apparent to the reader, if not to Venus, that "All is imaginary. . . / He will not manage her, although he mount her". Venus follows this with an impassioned, if "over-handled," speech that Adonis be ruled by her rather than Cynthia and Cynthia's subordinate, the boar.

This takes us up to the tragic movement of the poem which furthers Venus' sense of loss and dissatisfaction through Adonis' death and the eventual "cropping" of the anemone. These larger narrative units within the first section of the poem contain a series of smaller narratives, as well as imagistic and metynomic patterns that develop the pattern of cyclic unfulfillment. Such sequences of images and the intertexts they evoke work in combination to develop the ceaseless detour and postponement of sexual and narrative resolution.

Lines 1-254 constitute the first extended narrative pattern of pursuit, imaginary resolution, and subsequent opposition. This narrative segment begins with the opening stanza that initiates Venus' hunt of Adonis and it moves towards the imaginary resolution of her attempt to "hemm [Adonis] here/ Within the circuit of this ivory pale". Venus' desire to imaginatively alter Adonis' perception of the world in her favour is then foiled when the narrator intervenes: "her words are done, her woes the more increasing/ The time is spent, her object will away/ And from her twining arms doth urge releasing".

Adonis then breaks from her arms and chases after his "trampling courser," allowing the major narrative cycle to repeat while the sub-plot of the horses portrays the quenching of previously thwarted desire. The primary sequence of pursuit and failure is over-determined within this first narrative unit through a series of imagistic and intertextual patterns that repeat the narrative cycle of unfulfillment. Between lines 55-90, for instance, the narration moves from the predatory eagle imagery of stanza 10 to Adonis' coy escape when "her lips were ready for his pay/ He winks, and turns his lips another way".

This movement away from Venus breaks the ostensible union established through the imaginary "truce" where "one sweet kiss shall pay this comptless debt". This early and failed attempt at seduction initiates a common rhetorical play on paradoxical images that insinuate incommensurability while ostensibly expressing a sense of sensual reciprocity.

Although the narrator indicates the possibility of union through the anxiously awaited kiss, his use of market language reveals that such desire is "comptless," hence unpayable. This rhetoric of monetary exchange accentuates the incommensurability between a Goddess and a human; its irony and humour arise through an unlikely figure in which Adonis is presented as infinitely wealthy and Venus as an impoverished investor in the market of love.

Although the narration seems to sympathize with Venus to the extent that "she cannot choose but love" while Adonis remains uninterested, the patterning of imagery consistently implies a constitutional sense of dissension set between them. Line 81, for instance, introduces another proleptic image that looks forward to Venus' lament for Adonis when he is prosopopeically figured by the anemone: "And by her fair immortal hand she swears/ From his soft bosom never to remove".

This image is reversed at the poem's tragic end when she holds the flower in the "hollow cradle" of her breast. Venus' desire never to be removed from Adonis' breast, and the previous image of Adonis "fastened" in her net, evoke the false, or in Northrop Frye's terms, demonic union of Ovid's "Salamacis and Hermaphrodite." Salamacis, like Venus, grapples her lover/foe as she

catches him fast betweene hir armes for ought that he could do
Yea maugre all his wrestling and his struggling to and fro
She held him still, and kissed him a hundred times and mo
And willde he nillde he with hir handes she toucht his naked breast
And now on this side now on that (for all he did resist
And strive to wrest him from hir gripes) she clung unto him fast

And wound about him like a Snake, which snatched up in hast
And being by the Prince of Birdes borne lightly up aloft
Doth writhe hir selfe about his necke and griping talants oft,
And cast hir taile about his wings displayed in the winde.
(Golding trans. 442-52)

The dramatization of this violent union leads up to the poem's tragic finale in which "Salamacis and Hermaphrodite" merge "in one form and face," completing Hermaphrodite's emasculation. The intertextual relationship between Salamacis and Venus is ambiguous at this point because on the one hand Venus is the Goddess of love and thus she offers Adonis the possibility of manhood rather than posing any threat to his masculinity, yet on the other a clear parallel is drawn between her and Salamacis through the similarity of their predatory images.

What is unambiguous about the Ovidian intertext at this point is that it indicates a sense of unresolved or at least unsatisfying union. Indeed, Venus and Adonis' relationship is aligned very early on with the negative Ovidian transformations of dissension and false union rather than narratives which dramatize full reciprocity.

If we trace the imagistic patterning of lines 55-90 we notice that they follow our sequence of opposition, imaginary union, and subsequent conflict. In stanza 10 Venus is figured as an "empty eagle" gluttonously feeding on her prey. The final couplet of the stanza plays on the Sisyphian or Tantalean nature of her desire: "Even so she kissed his brow, his cheek, his chin/ And where she ends she doth anew begin".

The end couplet of the next stanza momentarily resolves this oppositional image of predatorial feeding by representing Venus' imaginary and hypothetical hope for satisfaction. Just as Venus will ostensibly resolve this first major narrative pattern through images of potential reciprocity in which she imagines her body as a park that contains Adonis who is transformed into a deer, she resolves this minor sequence by "Wishing her cheeks were gardens full of flowers/ So they were dewed with [his breath's] distilling showers".

Here again the imaginary and hypothetical nature of

Venus' imagery of reciprocation masks the predatory action which the narration had just presented. In the following stanza the narrator reverses Venus' wish full-filling flower and rain imagery into its dialectical opposite, turning the garden full of flowers into a "river that is rank/ Perforce will force it overflow the bank".

Thus we move from an image of opposition that the narrator presents in stanza 10, to an image of reciprocation that comes from Venus in the following stanza, back to an image of opposition that reverses Venus' hope for union. The same pattern then repeats over the next two stanzas as lines 73-8 introduce the oppositional colour motif of red and white which is momentarily resolved in the couplet of the following stanza where "one sweet kiss shall pay this comptless debt".

The sense of sexual combat and the tension which provokes it is bodied forth through the narrator's heavy use of medial caesura and the repetition of terms such as "still" and "entreats" which overtly express a sense of frustration:

Still she entreats, and prettily entreats
For to a pretty ear she tunes her tale
Still is he sullen, still he low'rs and frets
Twixt crimson shame and anger ashy-pale.
Being red, she loves him best; and being white
Her best is bettered with a more delight. (73-8)

The colour imagery which expresses Adonis' combination of fear and anger recalls us again to a similar passage in Golding's translation of "Salamacis and Hermaphroditus":

This sed, the Nymph did hold hir peace, and therewithall the boy
Waxt red : he wist not what love was : and sure it was a joy
For in his face the colour fresh appeared like the same
That is in Apples which doe hang upon the Sunnie side :
Or Ivorie shadowed with a red : or such as is espide
Of white and scarlet colours mixt appearing in the Moone.
(Golding 400-6)

One of the most distinguishing features of Shakespeare's variation on this Ovidian passage results from the metrical patterning of the sixain stanza which naturally lends itself to a closing couplet that develops or reverses the sense of the previous lines.

The closing couplet of stanza 13, for instance, plays on the sense of desire's incapacity for fulfillment that closed out the previous stanza with the river imagery. This sense of Venus' insatiability is then repeated in the following stanza through the trope of the comptless debt. Such imagistic patterning and rhetorical reversals, which are usually accomplished in the final couplet of the sixain, are more fully exploited in Shakespeare than in Ovid.

Moreover, within this minor narrative and imagistic unit of lines 55-90 we see that the closing couplets of stanzas 10, 12, 13, and 15 express the constitutional impossibility of Venus satisfying her desire for Adonis, while stanzas 11 and 14 present an imaginary sexual resolution. Shakespeare thus adopts much of Ovid's imagery in order to dramatize the sexual combat between Venus and Adonis at the same time as he exploits a series of rhetorical reversals in order to create the sense of an irreconcilable gap between the characters' perception of one another.

Because Venus' sensuality is highly verbal as well as deeply physical, she has far greater success achieving a union of words than of bodies. Her failure to entice Adonis reaches a brief and comic climax in lines 85-9 which completes this minor narrative pattern while developing the water and flood imagery that re-appears when Adonis sets off to meet the boar mid-way through the poem.

Line 86 embellishes the flood imagery introduced in the couplet of stanza 11 as Adonis "like a divedapper peering through a wave. . ./ ducks as quickly in:/ So offers he to give what she did crave, But when her lips were ready for his pay/ He winks, and turns his lips another way" (86-9). This comic disappearing act is tragically replayed at line 819 as Adonis vanishes in the waves of a "merciless and pitchy night." The flood imagery takes on more profoundly tragic dimensions as the shift in tone from the comic to the mournful is initiated with the image of Adonis being swallowed into the darkness of approaching death:

after him she darts, as one on shore
Gazing upon a late-embarked friend
Till the wild waves will have him seen no more
Whose ridges with the meeting clouds contend.
So did the merciless and pitchy night
Fold in the object that did feed her sight.
Whereat amazed, as one that unaware
Hath dropped a precious jewel in the flood. . . (816-34)

The imagery of the rising and devouring waves contending with the limits of sky expresses a sense of tragic foreboding that extends beyond Adonis' particularity. This sense of the world becoming increasingly tragic in tone is realized more fully when Venus bewails the loss of true beauty that dies with Adonis. "Alas, poor world, what treasure hast thou lost/ What face remains alive that's worth the viewing?/ . . . The flowers are sweet, their colors fresh and trim,/ But true sweet beauty lived and died with him" (1075-80).

The patterning of flood imagery embellishes and repeats the cycle of loss and unfulfillment throughout the smaller narrative sequences as well as the larger shift from the comic to the tragic. This pattern over determines the profound sense of frustration that Venus eloquently, if unsuccessfully, strives to resolve.

The erotic rhetoric intensifies towards the end of the first major narrative pattern (lines 1-258) as Adonis arouses greater and greater frustration in his pursuer. The carnal and even violent crescendo of the narrative at this point is marked by a cyclic movement of metonymic images which propels the sense of narrative and sexual postponement. The sequence of images from lines 240-53 moves through a metonymic logic that concludes as it began, taking us through an imagistic variation of the cyclic pattern of incommensurability, union, and subsequent opposition.

These lines immediately follow Venus' wish-fulfilling and imaginary transformation into a park; they begin by reversing the sense of union proposed by the park imagery and then re-introduce it, only to undo it yet again:

At this Adonis smiles as in disdain

That in each cheek appears a pretty dimple;
Love made those hollows, if himself were slain
He might be buried in a tomb so simple
Foreknowing well, if there he came to lie
Why, there love lived, and there he could not die.
These lovely caves, these round enchanting pits,
Opened their mouths to swallow Venus' liking
Being mad before, how doth she now for wits?
Struck dead at first, what needs a second striking?
Poor queen of love, in thine own law forlorn,
To love a cheek that smiles at thee in scorn! (241-53)

The patterning of images in these two stanzas illustrates the sort of narrative negotiation between Venus' desire and the reality principle of Adonis' refutations that constitutes much of the poem's structural motion.

The metonymic sequence begins with Adonis' dimple metamorphosing into a "tomb so simple" where Cupid may lie "if himself were slain." Here again, the poem's paradoxical rhetoric balances a latent sense of impending tragedy while manifestly expressing the young boy's remarkable beauty. As the narrative focus shifts from Cupid to Venus, Adonis' tomb like dimples transform again into "lovely caves round enchanting pits. . . [which] opened their mouths to swallow Venus' liking".

This transformation introduces one of the most explicit and sensual images of Venus' masculine position in the poem. The highly charged euphemism of Venus penetrating Adonis' "dimple" gives way as the narrative shifts from Venus' perception of the situation to the actual distance placed between her and Adonis: "Poor queen of love, in thine own law forlorn/ To love a cheek that smiles at thee in scorn." Here the narrative moves away from Venus' perception of Adonis' dimple as a sexualized and penetrable object to a more sobre and less erotic view of the situation.

The patterning of imagery, here, is cyclic in motion, moving from dimple to tomb, to cave, to pit, to mouth, to cheek again. Such patterning creates a sense of movement towards quiescence while continually frustrating its realization.

Moreover, Venus' imaginary and metaphoric transformations are continually undermined by the narration's re-deployment of her own rhetoric, revealing that there is not "relief enough" within her limits.

The reversal of gender roles in Venus and Adonis, as in Ovid's "Salamacis and Hermaphrodite", plays an integral role in the necessarily frustrating conclusion the relation is driven towards. Venus' masculine role bodied forth in lines 55-90 is complemented in the third narrative section (lines 325-545) as Adonis unwittingly tropes himself in effeminate and emasculating terms. In an attempt to counter Venus' carpe diem argument, Adonis displays wisdom beyond his years, at the same time as he expresses an unwitting effeminacy and immature narcissism that undermines his argument:

'Who wears a garment shapeless and unfinished
Who plucks the bud before one leaf put forth?
If springing things be any jot diminished
They wither in their prime, prove nothing worth.
The colt that's backed and burdened being young
Loseth his pride, and never waxeth strong.
You hurt my hand with wringing; let us part
And leave this idle theme, this bootless chat;
Remove your siege from my unyielding heart;
To love's alarms it will not ope the gate.
Dismiss your vows, your feigned tears, your flatt'ry;
For where a heart is hard they make no batt'ry.' (415- 26)

In line 417 Adonis implicitly reintroduces the absent and/ or flaccid phallus theme with unintentionally humorous results. Then in line 423, through another unfortunate choice of images, he portrays himself as the assailed virgin striving to keep the female phallus from his unyielding gate. Finally he adds insult to his own injury when he reveals that the only "hard" thing about him is his unbattered heart.

Adonis' self-emasculating choice of images weakens his position in the poem, indicating an unnatural fear of intimacy that leads some readers to sympathize with Venus' reproach of the coy and unyielding boy. It is the insistent absence of a satisfying male presence in Venus and Adonis, according to

Halpern and Schiffer, which accounts for much of the poem's frustrating effect. Halpern reads this absence in the context of the poem's misogynistic and male centered vision of Venus' sexuality.

Challenging the assumption that Shakespeare's audience was predominantly male, Halpern cites a variety of sources from the period to show that Venus and Adonis was often characterized as the reading material of "courtesans, lascivious nuns, adulterous housewives, or libidinous young girls" rather than the "sophisticated" readers alluded to in the Ovidian epigraph. Halpern's case regarding the poem's misogyny and its intention to frustrate primarily female readers is overstated to the extent that it underestimates the poem's capacity to titillate readers representing any number of gender and sexual differences, as is indicated by Titan's position in the poem:

By this the lovesick queen began to sweat
For where they lay the shadow had forsook them
And Titan, tired in the midday heat
With burning eye did hotly overlook them
Wishing Adonis had his team to guide
So he were like him, and by Venus' side. (175-80)

Titan's evocation here accentuates the poem's lack of a satisfying male presence, and his wish parallels that of a male reader frustrated with Adonis's coyness. Titan manifests a heterosexual male reader's desire within the poem, marking out a definite textual site that invites a reader to play out his desire through identification with a powerful, yet finally absent, male presence in the narrative. Such passages indicate that Shakespeare's text does not discriminate in its capacity to titillate and amuse as well as frustrate its readers; if it did, its popularity in the sixteenth and early seventeenth centuries would be even more difficult to explain than is already the case.

As we saw in the poem's first narrative sequence (1-259), the poem's Tantalean structure moves through a series of images that express an apparent but unrealized union. This initial sequence establishes the imagistic and structural basis upon which the rest of the poem is then based. Within the larger narrative patterns of the poem there are smaller imagistic sequences, intertextual elements, and rhetorical forms that develop the dissension between Venus and Adonis while manipulating the reader's desire for a resolution to this dissension.

These patterns also constitute the structural form of the third narrative pattern (lines 325-545) which begins by making explicit the Ovidian theme that unexpressed desire leads to dire consequences. Developing on the river and flood imagery introduced in lines 70-90, the narration moves from the ekphrasis which expresses the fulfillment of desire to the mounting tension of Venus' lust and Adonis' growing impatience:

An oven that is stopped, or river stayed,
Burneth more hotly, swelleth with more rage;
So of concealed sorrow may be said
Free vent of words love's fire doth assuage;
But when the heart's attorney once is mute
The client breaks, as desperate in his suit. (331-6)

The narrator establishes the ensuing debate (lines 368-450) between Venus and Adonis through a complementary set of images that ostensibly compare the two while further distancing them. Lines 331-6 imply that Venus burns to express her desire for Adonis, while in line 338 Adonis is figured as a burning coal whose anger revives with her return. "He sees her coming and begins to glow/ Even as a dying coal revives with wind". This imagistic chiasmus concludes with another illusory union between Venus and Adonis as "Taking no notice that she is so nigh/ For all askance he holds her in his eye".

The erotic distance between the two becomes even more palpable in this momentary unification in which Adonis "holds her in his eye" while he tries to hide from her in a solipsistic gesture of concealment. The gaze according to Renaissance theories based in Plato's Phaedrus saw staring as the beginning of intimacy; in this case it signifies a reluctant beginning that moves nowhere. This indication of a potential sexual union without its realization complements the patterning of imagery surrounding it which also evokes the sense of sexual union while suspending its actualization. Thus, action and image, plot and rhetoric, form and content move in analogous patterns of opposition and ostensible union, teasing but never fulfilling the text's and the subsequently the reader's desire for closure and completion.

The dialectic play of colour imagery in lines 353-364 shifts into a series of rhetorical and conversational reversals that begin the intense verbal combat of lines 368-450. The rhetorical chiasmuses which begin this sequence give the debate a dynamic, dramatic quality that retains a clear sense of playfulness, while at the same time developing Venus' increasing frustration:

Would thou wert as I am, and I a man,
My heart all whole as thine, thy heart my wound!
Give me my hand' saith he. 'Why dost thou feel it?'
Give me my heart,' saith she, 'and thou shalt have it.
O, give it me lest thy hard heart do steel it,
And being steeled, soft sighs can never grave it.
Then love's deep groans I never shall regard
Because Adonis' heart hath made mine hard." (369-78)

Venus here develops the earlier image of Adonis' imprinted cheek. This motif of "engravement" plays proleptically on Adonis' death in which the boar's tusk will "trench" itself in his thigh; when Venus laments that she will not witness "love's deep groans" she unwittingly parallels the "groans" of love with the "groans" of pain during Adonis' agonized and violent demise. For further on at line 950 when Venus chides death she ironically, and tragically asks "What may a heavy groan advantage thee?" thus returning our focus to the absent and long awaited coitus scene passed over in favour of the "hard hunt."

Shakespeare ends the third sequence with a unique and highly ironic variation on Adonis' death, which in traditional mythic readings tends to signify the "dead time of the year, whether winter or the late summer drought" (Frye Code 69). Shakespeare sets up a comic play on the mythic death and rebirth element underlying the narrative by having Venus faint and then quickly revive with expectations for sexual gratification. This variation further develops the ontological and erotic distance between the two as we see Adonis comically kissing and poking Venus in an attempt to arouse her from her feigned sleep. "He bends her fingers, holds her pulses hard/ He chafes her lips; a thousand ways he seeks/ To mend the hurt that his unkindness marred./ He kisses her; and she, by her good will,/ Will never rise, so he will kiss her still".

These unsatisfying kisses finally lead to the very thing Venus has been waiting for: "Her arms do lend his neck a sweet embrace; Incorporate then they seem; face grows to face; . . ./ Till breathless he disjoined, and backward drew/. . . He with her plenty pressed, she faint with dearth,/ Their lips together glued, fall to the earth". These lines offer the clearest example of the poem's capacity to tease a reader with a sense of fulfillment while sustaining a dramatic sense of incompleteness. The ostensibly sensuous term "Incorporate" indicating the possibility of full physical union is qualified and thus undone by the disappointing "seem." Following the term "incorporate" Shakespeare alludes to the imagery of Corinthians I 13:12, expressing a sense of reciprocity which is consistently undermined: "For now we see through a glass, darkly; but then face to face: now I know in part; but then shall I know even as also I am known".

This passage expresses precisely the sense of intimacy and knowledge of the other the poem seems to move towards without ever achieving. Finally, after drawing on this powerful Pauline image of reciprocity the narrator teases us further, relating how, "Their lips together glued." Even this moment of apparent union is permeated with comic and ironic overtones as the word "glued" indicates the struggle Venus had to undergo and which she must sustain in order to simply kiss the elusive boy-hunter.

The proximity the two achieve in the end of the third section is dramatically undone in the first three stanzas of the fourth sequence. In the first of these stanzas the narration repeats three of the main rhetorical images of incommensurability we saw developed in the first sequence between lines 55-90.

The first two lines of the stanza return us to the bird of prey motif indicating the unequal and predatory nature of the sexual rapport: "Now quick desire hath caught the yielding prey/ And glutton-like she feeds, yet never filleth". The third line repeats the military or combative image of master and slave implicit throughout much of the poem: "Her lips are conquerors, his lips obey,". And the fourth line returns us to the rhetoric of monetary exchange: "Paying what ransom the insultor willeth". The repetition of such images indicates that Venus and Adonis have returned to their original state of disunion.

The most indicative feature of Shakespeare's concern with expressing the frustration and antinomies of passion, rather than any sense of symbolic union achieved through Adonis' death, is the way that Shakespeare reconfigures the significance of the anemone as it appears in Ovid. In Shakespeare's version, Adonis' body does not undergo the sort of active and ritualistic metamorphosis into an enduring reminder that we see in Ovid; instead, it is transformed by a power that remains unspecified and it is then quickly "cropped" by Venus in another aggressive act that perpetuates rather than resolves her desire. In Book X of Ovid's Metamorphoses Venus reproaches the fates and then immediately transforms Adonis' body into an anemone:

She rent her garments. . .
. . . and springing down
Reproached the fates: "Even so, not everything
Shall own your sway. Memorials of my sorrow
Adonis, shall endure; each passing year
Your death repeated in the hearts of men
Shall re-enact my grief and my lament. . . .
And with these words she sprinkled nectar
Sweet scented, on his blood, which at the touch
Swelled up, as on a pond when showers fall. (Melville trans. 724-37)

Shakespeare's ending is decidedly lacking the theme of recurrence and resurrection that characterizes Ovid's version, placing in its stead, a continued sense of dissension:

By this the boy that by her side lay killed
Was melted like a vapour from her sight
And in his blood, that on the ground lay spilled,
A purple flower sprung up, check'red with white,
Resembling well his pale cheeks and the blood
Which in round drops upon their whiteness stood.
Comparing it to her Adonis' breath,
And says within her bosom it shall dwell, . . ./
She crops the stalk, and the breach appears
Green-dropping sap which she compares to tears. (1165-76)

Some critics, most notably Robert Merrix, have ignored or overlooked the term "crops", which clearly implies a sense of being "cut short", in order to read the ending in more Ovidian terms of union and resurrection. Merrix cites lines 1183-5, "Here was thy father's bed, here in my breast;/ Thou art next of blood, and 'tis thy right. Lo in this hollow cradle take thy rest;" in order to show that "[w]ith the transformation of Adonis into the anemone. . . the two composites are united, forming a sexual resolution, a synthesis in which the major attributes of each are embodied in the other". Yet, even here we are invited to read against Venus' choice of images at the same time we are encouraged to sympathize with her.

First of all, the image of the hollow cradle recalls us to her intense and insatiable desire that propels the poem's narrative motions; it indicates a sense of emptiness that has not yet been filled; and second by drawing attention to her throbbing heart we do not get a sense that she feels any release or resolution; but rather we sense a feeling of deepening sadness. We might also recall that at line 945 Venus accuses death of the very thing she is later guilty of, introducing an unintentional and unfortunate proleptic warning of the eternal dissension set between her and Adonis: "The Destinies will curse thee for this stroke/ They bid thee crop a weed; thou pluck'st a flower". In Shakespeare's version Venus becomes the procurer of her own worst fears.

It is also important to notice that the only line indicating close proximity between the ill fated two is spoken indirectly by Venus herself, creating a gap between the actual event as it is narrated and her own interpretation of it: "Comparing it to her Adonis' breath, and says within her bosom it shall dwell".

William Keach has noted that the repetition of the word "compares" and the shock of the word "crops" in this final sequence makes it clear that the flower functions prosopopeiacally, rather than indicating the promise of return. Venus, Keach notes, realizes that "Adonis is not reincarnated in the flower. . . She. . . 'crops' the stalk and 'compares'. . . the drops of sap to the tears which came to Adonis' eyes. Venus' realization that the flower is not Adonis contributes to the pathos of her comparisons and, in a sense, mitigates the shock of her 'cropping' the flower".

Part of the narrative dynamic of frustration being played out in this fourth narrative sequence, as well as the poem as a whole, consists of what Catherine Belsey, following Lacan, terms the trompe l'oeil motif. Because the poem constructs what Belsey refers to as a "promise of . . . presence it fails to deliver", it is structurally analogous to the scopic or visual effect known as trompe l'oeil.

Just as a visual representation might appear to be the thing-as-such, Shakespeare's poem represents an apparent but finally unrealized union. This withholding of aesthetic fulfillment suggests that the poem is based on an "erotic rather than philosophic ontology". Both Halpern and Belsey point to the poem's allusion to Pliny's story of artistic competition between Zeuxis and Parrhasius, based as it is on the principle of the trompe l'oeil, as a lucid example of this erotically charged aesthetic:

Even so poor birds, deceived with painted grapes
Do surfeit by the eye and pine the maw;
Even so she languisheth in her mishaps
As those poor birds that helpless berries saw.
The warm effects which she in him finds missing
She seeks to kindle with continual kissing. (601-6)

This passage, which occurs directly after the allusion to Tantalus, offers a pictorial analogy for the dynamic of frustrated desire the poem dramatizes. This "pictorial" analogy not only offers a meta-commentary on Venus' unrealized desire, it also reflects the aesthetic ontology with which the reader is engaged. For the reader, like Venus, is tantalized by a promise of narrative and sexual fulfillment that remains unfulfilled. Catherine Belsey summarizes Lacan's insights into the deceitful pleasures this trompe-l'oeil dynamic offers a reader or viewer:

In order to enjoy the trompe-l'oeil we have to be convinced by it in the first instance and then to shift our gaze so that, seeing the object resolve itself into lines on a canvas, we are no longer convinced; we have to be deceived and then to acknowledge our own deception.

For Lacan, the essence of tragic anagnorisis is the recognition of one's lack-of-being (manque-a-etre). Venus is driven to such a recognition through her failed attempts to have Adonis return her desire. She expresses this negative recognition with a combination of humour and pathos, tragedy and melodrama we have come to expect from Shakespeare's Queen of love. "O, where am I? . . . in earth or heaven/ Or in the ocean drenched, or in the fire?/ What hour is this? or morn or weary even?/ Do I delight to die, or life desire?/ . . ./ O, thou didst kill me, kill me once again!" The pun on sexual satisfaction, mixed as it is with cosmological references, expresses a sense of total absence, loss, and lack. Venus' agonized recognition of her emptiness is appropriately expressed as a question, indicating the deep uncertainty she feels as a result of Adonis' refusals. This passage sets up the even more dramatic moment when she falls to the ground with Adonis on top of her only to realise "he will not manage her, although he mount her".

Venus' recognition of her lack stems from her perception of Adonis as being full and complete unto himself. This same structural relation exists between the reader of the poem and the text; for just as Venus feels herself absent before a self-sufficient Adonis, the reader experiences a sense of lack in relation to a text that appears complete. Richard Halpern articulates the paradoxical nature of the poem's desire-based ontology by recognizing that to reveal [an] image's emptiness is precisely to confirm its power. . . . Indeed, a kind of metamorphic inversion occurs between viewer and object, for the unsatisfied hunger of the birds indicates their own emptiness in relation to the image, which is complete.

This "metamorphic inversion," in which the viewer feels empty in the presence of an object that appears full and self-sufficient, occurs throughout the poem in a number of varying forms. The first instance of this occurs at lines 211-16 when Venus alludes to Pygmalion as she bewails Adonis: "Fie, lifeless picture, cold and senseless stone/ Well-painted idol, image dull and dead,/ Statue contenting but the eye alone,/ Thing like a man, but of no woman bred!" Here, as in the Pliny allusion, Venus' psychosexual struggle is expressed through an aesthetic analogy in which the object viewed inspires a heightened sense of lack in the viewer.

Her object contents "but the eye alone", evoking rather than fulfilling desire. Where the reader is confronted with the fact that "the signifier precisely defers, supplants, relegates the imagined presence it sets out to name" (Belsey Desire 64), Venus is confronted with the fact that her object is unattainable and unrealizable. Venus' growing frustration over this intolerable situation expresses itself through her aggressive and cruel allusion to Adonis' unnatural origins. "Thing like a man, but of no woman bred!"

This erotic/aesthetic ontology in which Adonis is full and self-sufficient while Venus languishes in her lack is reversed in lines 235-40 when Venus imagines herself as a park upon which Adonis feeds himself. The fulfillment that Venus seeks thus demands a reversal of the unreciprocal mode of perceiving presented in lines 211-16: in order to achieve a sense of momentary fulfillment she imagines being self-sufficient, full, and generative.

The same dynamic occurs even more explicitly at line 370, "Would thou wert as I am, and I a man/ My heart all whole as thine, thy heart my wound!" Venus' only power against Adonis' refusals lies in such rhetorical gestures; for as Richard Halpern observes, Venus "must content herself with 'venerian speculation'". Halpern, moreover, sees an analogy between Venus' plight and the reader's relation to the text insofar as "[t]he theological gap that separates Venus from the merely mortal Adonis stands in for the ontological gap between the. . . reader and the empty imaginations generated by the poem". Thus part of the process of reading the poem consists of imaginatively re-enacting or reproducing its dramatization of unfulfilled desire.

A further example of the trompe l'oeil dynamic occurs during the ekphrasis, when Adonis' horse is described in complete detail, playing on this ontological relationship between viewer and object:

Look when a painter would surpass the life
In limning out a well proportioned steed
His art with nature's workmanship at strife
As if the dead the living should exceed
So did this horse excel a common one
In shape, in courage, colour, pace and bone . . .
Look what a horse should have he did not lack
Save a proud rider on so proud a back.
(my emphasis 290-300)

The density of this passage lies in its long, careful description of the horse which functions like the close and mimetically accurate brush-strokes of a Renaissance painter filling in every conceivable detail in order to convey a sense of totality and completeness within the image:

Round-hoofed, short-jointed, fetlocks shag and long,
Broad breast, full eye, small head and nostril wide
High crest, short ears, straight legs and passing strong,
Thin mane, thick tail, broad buttock, tender hide. (295- 300)

Although some readers may find this passage somewhat tedious, its unusually dense and exaggerated description paradoxically reminds us as viewers that it is description and not real.

Shakespeare's description presents a kind of wholeness while at the same time making it clear to a reader that the fullness is an effect and not the thing itself. Passages such as this offer a complex and subtle meta-commentary on the relationship between the reader and the text; for just as the description of the horse is a "full-representation" and not the thing itself, the text is an "unresponsive artwork" intended to "generate some kind of sexual thrill or tension" without being able to actually fulfill the desire it is capable of evoking. Thus Shakespeare's poem presents an unusual self-awareness of the relationship between the text and the reader, revealing the ways in which the text is the site upon which the reader's own desires are manipulated, frustrated, and enjoyed.

As much of the critical history of the poem reveals, it is extraordinarily difficult, perhaps even impossible, to interpret the poem without repeating some of the dramatic motions it represents. To see the text as an allegory against lust is to repeat Adonis' position in the poem; to unabashedly enjoy its erotic and verbal play is to align oneself with Venus; to become frustrated with Adonis' refusals is to take up Titan's place in the poem. Thus the structure of the poem with its repetition of ostensible moments of resolution, enticing and humorous rhetorical displays and its highly erotic aesthetic ontology opens up an interpretive space that allows a reader to identify his or her own desires within its frame.

Chapter 5

Old and Young Bodies in Shakespeare's Sonnets

Beginning in the year 1665, the English doctor Richard Lower conducted a series of experiments involving the transfusion of animal blood. In a few years he had developed an effective technique and began observing the effects of a series of transfusions, usually involving either two dogs or a dog and another domestic animal. His work excited international interest. Soon scholars in France and Italy began to report similar experiments, and for a moment it looked as though transfusion might offer extraordinary promise. This, at least, is how medical historians traditionally understand these events.

For them, this work is invoked as the beginning of modern transfusion, a sign of the tremendous power of Harvey's earlier discovery of the circulatory system. But like many of the scientific accounts of the seventeenth century, these experiments look as far backward as they do forward. Consider Lower's report of a fairly typical experiment conducted in 1668, not by himself but by colleagues in Italy, as recorded in the Philosophical Transactions of the soon-to-be Royal Society:

At S. Griffoni's at Udine, the Blood of a Lamb was transfused into the Vein of a Spaniel, if a middle Size of that Kind, 13 years old, who had been altogether deaf for above three Years ... He walked very little, and was so feeble, that being unable to lift up his Feet, all he did was to trail his Body forward. After the Transfusion... leaping down, he went to find his Masters that were in other Chambers. Two Days after he went abroad, and ran up and down the Streets with other Dogs, without trailing his Feet, as he did before. His Stomach also returned to him, and he began to eat more, and more greedily than he had done before. But that which is more surprizing is, that from that time he gave Signs that he began to hear ... The thirteenth of June, he was almost quite cured of his Deafness, and he appear'd without comparison more jocund than he was before the Operation.

On the one hand, this account seems to reflect an intense desire that the new technique be helpful (at least to the recipient) rather than simply curious. To this extent it is a medical experiment and one that anticipates the development of later techniques applied to humans. On the other hand, like many of the experiments of the period, this one was not really conducted to see if transfusion was a viable surgical technique but rather to confirm existing notions about the body, in this case the ageing body.

It is no accident that the recipient of the transfusion was an old dog and a dog whose symptoms are carefully represented as the traditional accidentia senectute of human life. The whole series of experiments reflects this interest in ageing. In one of his early experiments, Lower says, "I procured an Old Mungrel Cur all over-run with the Mange, of a middle Size ... Then I took a Young Land-Spaniel of about the same bigness and prepared his jugular vein, as is usually done..."

Soon after, he reports, his colleague Mr. Gayant "transfusd the Blood of a Young Dog into the Veins of an Old, which two Hours after did leap and frisk; whereas he was almost blind with Age, and could hardly stir before." French experimenters also focused on age: "Mr Denys writes from Paris, that they had lately transmitted the Blood of 4 Weathers into a Horse of 26 Years old, and that this Horse had thence received as much Strength, and more than ordinary Stomach". Today we tend to think of transfusion as a kind of mechanical replacement, quickly restoring lost fluid to a system that would, given time, be able to repair itself. Lower and his colleagues, however, were operating on the classical notion of life as the union of "radical heat" and "radical moisture," substances whose gradual disappearance corresponded to the ageing and mortality of the body. It was natural for them to think of transfusion in terms of longevity. Youth, for them, was a physical substance contained within young bodies. Their very decision to pursue transfusion, while in hindsight it seems to herald a new kind of medicine, actually reflects traditional notions of the ageing humoral body.

Lower's work also reflects an interest in the ageing body that had become particularly intense by the late sixteenth century. Youth itself served as something of a cultural locus in the period. As Phillippe Ariès has pointed out, every period has a "privileged age," and youth, rather than childhood or adolescence, is the privileged age of early modern Europe. But the privileging of youth has as its corollary an interest in avoiding or alleviating old age, and longevity was also something of an obsession in early modern Europe.

As a result, the medical works of the period are frequently concerned with youth and age, and particularly with the physical contents of young bodies. This concern is not a result of any changes in actual longevity. European demographics of the period indicate that the number of aged people was about as limited in the Renaissance as it was in the late Middle Ages. Rather, the early modern discussions of longevity constituted a coherent pattern of thought, a way of theorizing the relationship between youth and age in the context of growing interest in the body itself.

As in much of the medical theory of the period, the most characteristic feature of discussions of ageing is the tendency to combine mental and physical aspects of the subject. Discussions of longevity frequently merged with discussions of the passions, also a subject of equal interest in the period. In part the associations seem to be related to the popular iconography of the life cycle, which as Philippe Ariès points out, connected the "ages of man" with specific social functions (the young man is frequently a soldier, for instance) and hence with their associated passions. But the connection is often more explicit. Sometimes the passions are thought to affect the ageing process. Thus, Francis Bacon argues that excessive passions such as joy, grief and fear shorten life but that moderate passions extend life by restraining and strengthening the spirits. Du Laurens warns old men in particular to beware of violent passions. And many writers, including the entire "hygienic" tradition, agree that lust shortens life. Sometimes, on the other hand, the ageing process is thought to affect the passions. In fact, most discussions of youth and age include some reference to the characteristic passions of each.

These discussion arise from the assumption that maturity, or what we could call middle age, is characterized by the ability to restrain the passions. Youth and age are unable to do so. But the discussions are frequently explicitly medical. Bacon argues that "The vices of old mens minds [have] some correspondence and [are] parallel to the putrefactions of their bodies". More broadly, the interest in youth and age seems to pervade works otherwise entirely devoted to the passions.

Thomas Wright's The Passions of the Minde in General concludes with an appendix on the climactericall years, ostensibly generated by the debate surrounding Elizabeth's death, but also based on the assumption that "those humors which alter the bodie, and dispose it to sicknesse, and death; the same bend the soul to take inordinate affections and passions".

These patterns of thought, combining an obsession with age and a growing interest in the passions, can help us understand a literary work like Shakespeare's Sonnets, a work deeply concerned both with age and with the passions. The subject positions of the three main characters of the Sonnets (the young man, the dark lady, and the poet) have always presented problems for critics. In the past, scholars struggled to assign these roles to real people from the historical record. Even more recent criticism, although not as concerned with autobiography and ostensibly more interested in historical specificity, still often assumes that Shakespeare's depiction of the self is either unique or at least highly distinctive.

Such criticism often has difficulty confronting the role of

the body in the poems, and its reliance on the poems' thematic material to explain the physical types results in potentially circular arguments. One cannot entirely explain the ageing Poet, for instance, by saying that the Sonnets are obsessed with mortality (or time) because the Poet's age is itself crucial to that theme. Only slightly less dissatisfying are arguments that explain the poet by pointing to the pose of superannuation as a petrarchan convention. This convention is rarely as emotionally or physically insistent as it is in Shakespeare's poems. The medical literature of the period, however, opens up another avenue of explanation, revealing the extent to which the subject positions of the three main characters of the Sonnets may be connected with the poems' representation of their humoral bodies.

Early modern works on longevity suggest not only that the three-way drama of young man, young woman, and older poet would have been considered an appropriate subject for any early modern author interested in the passions, but also that what is often perceived as the poems' unique mental pathology is really an expression of the relationship between early modern physical regimes of health and the ageing body. What one finds if one looks at early modern medical and psychological works is that the three characters of the Sonnets-old man, young man, and woman (her age being, as we shall see, in crucial ways less important)-come up again and again, particularly in discussions of the passions and of the scholarly life.

In humoral terms at least, the relationship that these poems appear to describe is not unique. It is not that lots of people engaged in exactly these kind of relationships, nor that Shakespeare was somehow directly influenced by the medical literature. Instead, I argue, the process by which early modern culture imagined the passions constantly called up the image of old man, young man, and woman. If one was interested in the passions, and Shakespeare's Sonnets certainly appear to be, then this trio would be a natural scenario for representing them. As a whole, these patterns of early modern thought help demystify subject positions that have frequently been perceived as either enigmatic or idiosyncratic.

Although the triangular relationship between two men and a woman has been crucial to recent interpretations of the Sonnets, the way that critics have deployed erotic triangles has frequently obscured much of the early modern cultural context. Most notably, Eve Sedgwick, in Between Men, has argued that the homoerotic aspects of the Sonnets are set firmly within a structure of institutionalized social relations that are carried out via women: marriage, name, family, loyalty. Sedgwick's arguments resemble those of René Girard in Violence and the Sacred.

When two men compete over a woman, desire circulates between them in a process that he calls "mimetic": one man's desire is imitated by the other. For Sedgwick, this desire is ultimately neither heterosexual nor homosexual but, as she so famously has put it, "homosocial." Sedgwick's arguments manage to unify the psychology of desire with a kind of Straussian anthropological approach that sees heterosexual relationships as a way of cementing power relationships between men.

More recently, Jonathan Dollimore has extended Sedgwick's arguments to cover other aspects of early modern literature. In Sexual Dissidence, Dollimore uses drama to show that the man-man-woman triangle is evidence of "that always unstable disjunction between identification and desire upon which male bonding depends".

Men are supposed to identify with other men but desire women. Drawing on Freud, Dollimore argues that such homoerotic passages are "not the eruption of repressed homosexual desires so much as the fantasized, fearful convergence of identification and desire". When applied to Shakespeare's Sonnets, these kind of arguments are, of course, fundamentally ahistorical. Sedgwick comments directly on this problem, admitting that her arguments are "synchronic," "ahistorical," and "deracinated".

As license for this treatment, she argues that the Sonnets themselves obscure a specific context, as generations of diverse scholarship testify. Therefore, she implies, if the Sonnets don't demonstrate a highly particularized individuality, they do at least serve as a "pattern" for the broad phenomenon of male homosocial desire. Now it is possible that the Sonnets may serve as such a transcendent pattern, but the pattern seems to have a very specific place in early modern thought. The trio of characters that recent critics have explored in the Sonnets is not unique to them.

In fact, this trio appears repeatedly in connection with discussions of the passions. One early and fairly popular work is Thomas Wright's The Passions of the Minde In Generall. This was reprinted several times after 1604. It is even possible (although not necessary for this argument) that Shakespeare may have known of Wright's work. Wright's aim is both to define and to explain the passions. Of course, the passions here are not entirely the same as what we would call emotions, although they are close.

Wright accepted the common view of the passions as largely external to the self. They were one of the six non-naturals, which included diet, air, exercise, sleep, and repletion. Ideally, one was supposed to be able to control one's passions much as one would control one's diet. But Wright also recognizes that people are naturally passionate and some more passionate than others. And he devotes an entire chapter to the topic of "What sort of persons be most passionate." His answer? Young men, old men, and women.

Not only are Wright's categories strikingly reminiscent of the subject positions of the Sonnets, but the whole thrust of his work reflects a similar interest in identifying passions, both in others and in oneself, and ultimately in controlling these passions. In his introductory chapter, Wright argues that through his book "every man may ... come to a knowledge of himself, which ought to be preferred before all treasures and riches." At the same time, however, he advertises a knowledge of the passions as a means of exploiting others, both by recognizing their inclinations and by actively persuading them. Among the potential audience he lists lawyers, magistrates, orators, and "prudent politicians."

This division is reflected in the kind of language Wright uses to talk about the passions themselves. At times they are simply that which must be controlled or suppressed. He calls them "thorny bryars sprung from the infected root of originall sine" or " Serpents, and Basilisks, who suck out the sweet blood of [a man's] soule".

At other times, however, the passions are essential parts of the human fabric. After all, he asks, "Who would attend to eating or drinking, to the act of generation, if Nature had not joyned thereunto some delectation?" To solve this dilemma Wright suggests that the passions are "not unlike the foure humours of our bodies." When out of balance, they cause disease, but if kept in due proportion they are "the preservative of health, & perhaps health itself".

His reliance on a specifically medical metaphor for the passions suggests the extent to which he wants them to be the object of a complex and active series of interventions. The passions were not something to be condemned or approved but something to be treated, modified, and employed for profitable ends. Given this attitude, it is understandable that one of Wright's main goals is to locate excessive passion in particular kinds of people.

Wright's interests in the mutability of the passions are also part of a larger cultural pattern By his own admission, Wright's conclusions about old men, young men, and women are not unique. "Many thing more might be said of this matter," he remarks near the end of his chapter on particularly passionate people, "but I finde all bookes and commonplaces, so stuffed with these discourses, that I thought it superfluous to write any more".

Indeed, the connection between the extremes of passion and the extremes of age was conventional. It underlies works like Edward Calver's dialogue, Passion and Discretion in Youth and Age, in which the two extremes are mirror images of potentially dangerous desire. Young men, seduced by their own beauty and strength, incontinently waste their bodily resources. Old men, conscious that they are about to leave the good things of the world, are grasping and miserly.

This view of the arc of human life ultimately derives from humoral physiology, which sees balance as the source of health. Young bodies and old bodies, by virtue of being at the extremes, are necessarily more prone to excess. As for the third member of Wright's group, women, the connection between them and the passions in the early modern period has been well documented.

Almost all medical writers attribute excessive passions to women. They were not necessarily thought to have such passions because of their constitutions which, supposedly tending to the cold and moist phlegm, would not be inclined to passion, but because of the weakness of their minds. According to Helkiah Crooke's Microcosmographia, for example,

[That] Females are more wanton and petulant then Males, wee thinke hapneth because of the impotencie of their minds; for the imaginations of lustfull women are like the imaginations of bruite beastes which have no repugnancie or contradiction of reason to restraine them.

Women's passions, too, were perceived more slightly different than men's. Crooke tries to distinguish between anger (female) and wrath (male), between fierceness (female) and stoutness (male). For men, youth and age were the times of extreme passion, while women of all ages were liable to be stigmatized as excessively passionate. More unusual than Wright's categories themselves is the extent to which the qualities he attributes to old men, young men, and women mirror the attributes of the poet, the young man, and the dark lady in Shakespeare's Sonnets.

According to Wright, for example, young men's hot blood makes them arrogant, proud, prodigall, incontinent, given to all sorts of pleasure. Their pride proceedeth from lacke of experience; for they will vaunt of their strength, beauty, and witts, because they have not yet tried sufficiently, how farre they reach, how fraile they are. Their prodigality is caused by confidence they have in their owne strength and ability, wherby they thinke they shall be able to get more.

In the Sonnets, the poet begins by censuring the young man's prodigality and narcissism (as part of the attempt to convince him to marry). Although he moves to praise, he also faults him for his heedless and arrogant pursuit of pleasure, especially when this leads him to ignore the poet. The poet also recognizes that the young man's faults spring from age:

Those pretty wrongs that liberty commits,
When I am somtime absent from thy heart,
Thy beauty and thy years full well befits,
For still temptation follows where thou art.

Old men, on the other hand, according to Wright, are:

subject to sadness, caused by coldnesse of blood: to suspect ill, by reason of long experience, wherein they have often been deceived; to lament, to be fastidious, teastie, froward, and never contented... Old age is a perpetuall sicknesse: wherefore, as sick men are ever whining, so old men are never satisfied.

Shakespeare's poet has almost all of these qualities, sometimes all at once, as in Sonnet 30 when the remembrance of things past makes him "sigh the lack of many a thing I sought, / And with old woes new wail my dear time's waste". He is all too aware that he is "With what I most enjoy contented least". As for women, like many of his contemporaries Wright attributes many passions to them, but primarily inconstancy. Needless to say, her inconstancy is one of the poet's primary objections to the dark lady in the Sonnets, particularly when she seduces the young man:

... all my honest faith in thee is lost,
For I have sworn deep oaths of thy deep kindness,
Oaths of thy love, thy truth, thy constancy.

Finally, inconstancy is also supposed to be typical of young men, and Wright says that it springs from the same root in both women and young men. In the Sonnets, the poet often perceives the dark lady and the young man as in league with one another or as sharing something that he is excluded from. This only increases the old man's suspicion. He may "suspect... yet not directly tell" whether the young man has really been seduced.

This correspondence between Wright's categories and the characters of Shakespeare's Sonnets is neither coincidental nor the result of direct influence. Wright's three categories make a great deal of sense in a broad early modern context. They are inclusive rather than exclusive. Because women's bodies in the period were more likely to be defined and limited by sex while men's bodies were usually thought of as limited only by age, there were, one might say, only three kinds of bodies in early modern England: old bodies, young bodies, and female bodies.

It is not that women's ages were unimportant (quite the contrary), but that their age could not be considered apart from their sex ageing in men, on the other hand, was often treated as a gender-neutral topic, and ageing has frequently been one of the few events for which men are represented as limited or defined by their bodies. This distinction is supported by a wide variety of early modern medical literature. Women's medicine most frequently concentrated on sex and reproduction; men's medicine concentrated on ageing.

To some extent, therefore, Wright's categories of "most passionate" people cover everyone except the middle aged male. And his body, as we shall see in the medical literature, occupies a vanishingly small space at the intersection of youth and age.

These attitudes are reflected in the Sonnets to some extent. A sonnet like 138, for example, hinges on the comparison of the poet's age with the dark lady's sexual infidelity: "When my love swears that she is made of truth," he says, "I do believe her, though I know she lies, / That she might think me some untutor'd youth." Later in the same sonnet the speaker asks, "wherefore says she not she is unjust? / And wherefore say not I that I am old?"

The poet's fault is age; the dark lady's fault is inconstancy. If these faults do not seem to have the same ontological status, the reason is that the poet is setting up an opposition between an unlike pair. Inconstancy is frequently represented as a consequence of femininity in early modern medical literature, so the dark lady's infidelity is linked to her gender. But while we might see the two characters as neatly opposed: age/youth, man/woman, the poet is only partially representing the opposition. The result is more nearly age/woman. The poet has age; the dark lady has gender. Although the dark lady may be younger than the speaker, youth, in the Sonnets, is mostly reserved for the young man. To this extent, the trio of characters in the Sonnets fits well into wider conceptions about the kinds of bodies people can inhabit.

The medical literature also helps make sense of the Sonnets' division of masculine identity into youth and age. As was the case for so many fields of philosophical endeavor in the Renaissance, prolongevity was obsessed with taxonomy. Treatises on ageing in the period frequently began by explaining the different ages. There were many different schemes. The most general medical works tended to put ages into four categories.

Thomas Elyot, for example, in The Castell of Helth, designates the ages as "adolescenscie," the first 25 years, "juventute," to age 40, "senectute," to age 60, and "age decrepit," which lasts "until the last tyme of life. Although the names and chronology attached to the categories were variable, the fourfold pattern always mirrored the Galenic humors. Thomas Walkington's Optick Glasse of Humours begins with a diagram calling youth choleric, "adolescence" sanguine, "vergeus aetas" phlegmatic, and age melancholic. Actual treatises on ageing tended to be more detailed, allowing for five or more categories.

Du Laurens describes five ages: infancy (age 0-13 months), adolescence, youth, manhood and old age. But old age was usually further divided into three parts, "green," middle, and "decrepit," so the number of separate categories was frequently seven, the number covered by Jaques in the famous passage from As You Like It.

Two things stand out when one considers the ages in years attached to these various categories. First, simple adulthood or "manhood" seems to be vanishingly small, sometimes a mere decade sandwiched in among categories each of which, apart from infancy, is far longer. As a result, this medical taxonomy tends to reinforce the polarization between youth and age that dominates so much other discourse at the time. The simpler fourfold schemes made this polarization even more apparent. Second, the taxonomic interest in the category of old age itself, with its three subsidiary divisions, argues a greater medical interest in this age and in its complications (the accidentia senectute) than for some of the other ages. Consequently, it makes sense that representations of mortality should centre on the opposition between youth and old age, and that old age should be the more important of the two. Even more fundamental to the old man-young man-woman triad is the connection between age and passion.

Age is, above all, a process. Thus while medical theory of the period tended to taxonomize age, dividing it into ever more finely defined categories, medical writers were also acutely aware that the same person would, barring disease or accident, traverse all the categories, perhaps more or less quickly but nevertheless inevitably. And while older people may have been thought to be more susceptible to certain kinds of passion, the passions themselves were also thought to be dangerous to the aged. According to Du Laurens, older men should be particularly wary of violent passions:

Olde men more then any other must beware, both because they are ordinarily more subject to feare, taking of offence, and waywardness, because of their cold distemperature: as also because of the weaknes of their braine. And other men must indevour to take from them all occasion of feare and sadness.

Strong passions were also implicated in the ageing process itself. Among the various things that can accelerate ageing, Arnaldus de Villanova lists sorrow, desperation, and fear. The last two, he says, are particularly dangerous because they cause the humors to turn inward and become adust.

These passions are all reflected in the poet's self-depiction in the Sonnets. Sorrow, of course, is traditional for a petrarchan poet, but this poet's sense of "how hard true sorrow hits", seems to go beyond his resentment of the way he is treated in love. Fortune itself causes the poet sorrow, and he has cause to compare the "other petty griefs" caused by the rest of the world with the sorrow caused by his beloved's behaviour. The poet also calls himself "desperate". But it is fear which most dominates him: fear of offending the young man, fear of rivals, fear of dying, fear that the young man will die. And fear comes to seem basic to the poet's constitution.

At one point he contrasts "mine own fears" with "the prophetic soul / Of the wide world dreaming on things to come". Neither, he says, has the power to control the "lease" of his true love, but the juxtaposition gives his fear tremendous stature. Fear is constitutive of the personal, insofar as it looks to the future, just as the soul of the world constitutes the same attitude in its public manifestation. By the medical standards of the day, this poet's ageing body should be at risk, not just of sudden crises but of premature ageing.

Now, the medical literature of the period shows that the Sonnets may be drawing on well-established traditions in describing the passions, or that for a writer interested in the passions, the trio of characters in the Sonnets would have seemed natural, but it doesn't explain why the poet should be an old man rather than one of the other two members of the trio. To understand the poet's age, it is necessary to look more closely at the prolongevitists, those who took the ageing (and usually male) body as their subject.

The most famous of these is the Italian Marsilio Ficino, whose De Triplici Vita (Three Books on Life) is notable as the first health manual intended specifically for those interested in the scholarly life. Ficino devotes much of the book to treatments designed to extend life. Of these, the most remarkable is as follows. When one ages, one's vital moisture dries up and must be replenished:

Immediately after the age of seventy and sometimes after sixty-three, since the moisture has gradually dried up, the tree of the human body often decays. Then for the first time this human treee must be moistened by a human youthful liquid in order that it may revive.

The old man has two options. First, "choose a young girl who is healthy, beautiful, cheerful, and temperate, and when you are hungry and the Moon is waxing, suck her milk; immediately eat a little powder of sweet fennel properly mixed with sugar." Second, Ficino asks, "Why shouldn't our old people [men]... likewise suck the blood of a youth? a youth, I say, who is willing, healthy, happy, and temperate, whose blood is of the best but perhaps too abundant. They will suck, therefore, like leeches, an ounce or two from a scarcely opened vein of the left arm". It is characteristic of Ficino that while the youth in question must be willing, the woman need only be cheerful (although one doubts she would remain cheerful). Here is the trio once again in a more explicitly medical context, although also in more bizarre and predatory circumstances.

These circumstances, however, are helpful because they make clear not only why old men, young men, and women are categories that belong together, but also how these categories might relate to each other. For authors like Wright, these types of people simply share a tendency to extreme passion. Someone like Ficino, however, imagines the potential for connecting young and old bodies. And as it happens, Ficino's De Triplici Vita systematically portrays the managment of the ageing male body in terms of its relationship with other kinds of bodies.

To begin with, Ficino's exacting physical regime puts the ageing male scholar at the centre of a network of unusually extensive care-giving, necessarily administered by others. Every aspect of the scholar's physical life, all the six non-naturals, are to be carefully orchestrated and controlled, yet the scholar himself is to be left free to contemplate. He is to be kept free from such dangers as wakefulness, fasting, thirst, fatigue of body and mind, solitude, and grief. And intellectuals are by nature particularly needy:

Their sharp and hot intelligence and the constant activity of their imagination seem to threaten them with resolution, but their body's inactivity and indigestion seem to threaten them with suffocation. Hence there is no case in which the physicians labour harder than in the care of such people.

The cheerful young mother presented at the precisely appropriate moment (astronomically and physically) is only one of the many people who must minister to the scholar's needs. But Ficino's language also implies a constant anxiety about the possibility of inappropriate ministration. While the mother's milk may seem happy enough, for example, women are elsewhere in Ficino's work a deadly threat. As sexual partners they represent another kind of predation. The problem, of course, is that the procreative functions are directed not to the preservation of the present body but to the creation of a future one.

Hence Ficino speaks of "Venus," as someone who "drains her victim, little by little... as it were through a secret pipe, filling and procreating another thing with your fluid and leaving you finally as if you were an old skin of a cicada drained upon the ground." This colorful imagery helps us understand why Ficino's positive regimes sometimes involve another kind of predation. Youth and life are actually physical substances to be preserved if possible and obtained if not. Ficino also sees bodily fluids as intrisically communicable, a fact that makes the relationship between youth and age potentially dynamic. "There is a power in human blood to both attract and, in turn, to follow human blood," he says. Consequently "the blood of a youth drunk by an old person can be drawn to the veins and the bodily parts and can do a lot of good there".

With the exception of breast milk, a treatment widely recommended until the middle of the eighteenth century, Ficino's longevity treatments are not frequently repeated in other texts. But the principle behind them is. Such beliefs were made almost inevitable by the Galenic account of the ageing body, an account which saw both age and disease as potentials already contained within the body. As Ariès puts it "disease, old age, and death are merely eruptions out of the bodily envelope of the rottenness within".

Michael Neill has tracked these attitudes into Vesalian anatomy, arguing that the entire memento mori tradition depends upon a notion of inward corruption. Above all, however, ageing was described as a dynamic process, not a sudden eruption but a progressive deterioration. Du Laurens, whose piece on ageing was widely repeated, describes the process as follows. The two mainsprings of life are radical heat and radical moisture. The first feeds upon the last. But because the body's imperfect concoction of food provides an imperfect moisture, the body ages, getting progressively colder and dryer. The process is speeded by the body's intrinsic humoral imbalances, the "jarre... in our complexion" which "is the principal cause of our old age".

If old men do not always appear dry, it is because they possess a superfluous moisture, not radical, but as Tobias Whitaker puts it in another work on ageing, "excrementitious" (Whitaker 1638 42). Such moisture was more dangerous than helpful. One of the explanations for memory loss in the aged is that an increase in phlegm blocks the necessary passages in the brain (Lessius 1743 76). Both Galen and Avicenna perceived the ageing process as both inevitable and normal, not pathological. Later writers, however, and the prolongevitists in particular, often proceeded from the assumption that old age is a disease even if, as for many, it is a disease the seeds of which we all have within us (Du Laurens 172).

Consequently, ageing and death were not necessarily inevitable, although scholars disagreed on the question of how long one could prolong life and what the virtues of such preservation would be (Gruman 1966). The key, for these writers, is the replenishment either of radical moisture or of radical heat, and the problem is that these substances have an almost mystical quality. One school of theorists, dominated by the work of Luigi Cornaro, argued that one could never actually replace radical moisture, only retard its dissipation by regulating the six non-naturals, particularly diet.

As Du Laurens says, "all the precious liquors that are, Aurum Potabile, conserves of rubies and emeralds, elixir vitae, or the fained and fabulous fountaine of restored youth cannot withstand but that our heate muste at length grow weake and feeble". The metaphor of the old man as a fire burning low through natural causes had classical roots. Cicero likened the death of an old man to "the gradual, utterly gentle and spontaneous flickering out of a fire that has used up its fuel" (Cicero 1967 36), like the poet in the Sonnets who resembles "the glowing of such fire / That on the ashes of his youth doth lie" (73.9-10). Even those writers who thought ageing inevitable, however, thought bodily substances such as milk and blood might at least retard the process because they most closely resembled the innate moisture of the ageing patient.

Wine, which Whitaker recommends above all else, was called "The old man's milk" and milk, of course, is blood "dealbated or thrice concocted" (Whitaker 30, Du Laurens 187). A strong red wine was preferable because it most resembled blood. When blood or substances resembling it were not directly available, foods that were thought to be blood-forming were recommended (Villanova 9ff).

Others interested in prolongevity, however, like Ficino, thought that a substance could be found that would actually replace one's radical heat or moisture. Not surprisingly, the most likely place to find the perfect moisture and heat was in another human being. The oblique ways in which such writers describe these medicines betray their potentially scandalous nature. The medieval alchemist Roger Bacon, one of the earliest proponents of a medical cure for old age, is hesitant to name the actual substance. "I have read many volumes of the wise, he says, and I find few things in physick, which restore the natural heat, weakened by dissolution of the innate moisture, or increase of a foreign one."

Nevertheless, he says, certain wise men have tacitly made mention of some medicine. This medicine is like "Youth itself" (Bacon 1683 99). Later, Roger Bacon argues that "the infirmity of a man passeth into man; and so doth Health because of likeness" and then suggests that this medicine "will very much recreate an Old Man, and change him to a kind of Youth." Further, he says, "There is such a heat in this thing, as is in Young men of a sound complexion." Although at this point the nature of the medicine seems obvious, Bacon insists on keeping its name secret "lest the Incontinent should offend their Creator". Finally, in the subsequent chapter heading he acknowledges at least some of the reader's potential suspicions by denying that the medicine is derived from man's blood.

Instead he offers as an example of the treatment "more plainly which is here more obscurely described" the familiar story of the old king David (1 Kings, 1.2-4) in which close, but not sexual, contact with the body of a beautiful young virgin cures the king (temporarily) of age. Thus Bacon manages to obliquely offer the body of a young man as a kind of model apothecary shop and then, abruptly removing this body, replace it with the body of a young woman. The man-man-woman trio appears here in a kind of alchemical shell game. Sir Francis Bacon plays a similar game, and a central ambiguity pervades his History naturall and experimentall of life and death (1638), perhaps the best summation of prolongevitist tradition in the early modern period. On the one hand Bacon wants to discredit what he considers to be outlandish attempts to "cure" old age.

He blames Cornaro, the hygienist who advocated a specific regime of diet and lifestyle, for requirements such as living in caves, constant baths in liquor, special clothing or painting of the body, or overprecise ordering of diet. Instead, Bacon, says, he wishes to have remedies that don't interfere with normal life. On the other hand, Bacon eventually returns to some of these same ideas more positively. He ends up recommending astringent baths and painting the skin in order to keep out the "predatory" air. Likewise he advocates exotic substances like nitre and opiates, which are supposed to help refrigerate and calm the spirits respectively. And of course Bacon has plenty to say about diets, which he divides into two types: "liberal" and "spare."

Bacon's interest in comparative longevity also reveals the extent to which youth itself can be tied to substance. Drawing on the tradition by which longevity is associated with particular animals, such as stags, Bacon embarks on a list of the qualities that make an animal live long. In part their long life is represented as tied to their diet. Thus carnivores are supposed to live longer than herbivores and seed eaters longer than grass eaters. Bodily structure is also supposed to play a part. Because the head contains so many animal spirits (and Bacon, dismissing the tripartite division of spirits common in the period, calls the animal spirits the "all-in-all") and because the spirits "do most of all waste and prey upon the body" so animals with small heads live longer. But most important is the quality of an animal's flesh itself.

Creatures with darker flesh, for example, live longer because "it showeth that the Juyce of the body is more firme and lesse apt to dissipate". To a great extent the "substance" of the body is a matter of ontogeny. Birds are long lived chiefly because they "are made more of the substance of the Mother, than of the Father; whereby their Spirit is not so eager and hot," and human children who spend longest in the womb or who resemble their mother (as does Shakespeare's Young Man, who is his "mother's glasse") partake most of her substance and so are longer lived. Youth, for Bacon, is clearly deeply material.

Bacon's materialism pervades his analysis of ageing human bodies as well. At issue for him is not so much the accidentia of age (wrinkles, trembling, loss of eyesight and hearing, etc.) as its internal evidence. In comparing old and young men he frequently refers to the quality of their bodily fluids. "A young man's bowels are soft and succulent," he says, "an old mans salt, and parched." In a young man "the juyces of his bodie are more roscide [dewy], in an old man more crude and watrish". Later, in explaining the existence of fat old men, an apparent contradiction given the supposed dessicating action of age, he argues that old men improve in fatness only because their bodies "doe neither Perspire well, nor assimilate well".

Their fluids therefore stagnate within them, building up an unhealthy mass. Bacon is also preoccupied with the connection between internal bodily fluids and the outside of the body. In surveying the traditional cures for old age, he clearly prefers those which can be applied externally over those which are taken internally (diet and medicines). Since old men's concoction (digestion) is supposed to be weak, Bacon reasons that the best nourishment would be from without, a nourishment that might even restore old men's ability to digest food properly.

External remedies of course lead Bacon back to internal substances. He surveys traditional remedies such as the bath of infant's blood supposed to cure leprosy and putrefaction, the use of kittens' blood to cure St. Anthony's fire, and the external application of split pigeons. As Bacon's discussion nears the scandalous cures advocated by writers like Roger Bacon and Ficino, a significant ambiguity returns to his text. At one point he calls bloody baths " Sluttish and Odious", but elsewhere he refers positively to "the warm cherishings of living bodies".

He approves Ficino's advice about the external application of a maid, adding only she should be annointed with Myrrh, and he mentions cases such as Barbarossa who "did continually apply young boys to his stomach and belly" and men who lay with whelps. Bacon eventually mentions Ficino's treatment directly, in the section of the book dealing with "mallasification" or the suppling of the body. At first he dismisses Ficino's ideas "Touching the Sucking of Bloud out of the Arme of a wholesome young Man" as "frivolous." But the reason he distrusts it hinges on the same distinction between internal and external medication. Internal nourishment should be achieved by "inferior" substances which can be converted to higher ones.

External medicine, on the other hand, works by "consent" and requires substances as much like the patient as possible. So young men's blood is still a valuable medicine; it just needs different kind of labelling. Still hedging, Bacon disparages the legend of Artephius, the twelfth century alchemist, "who when hee found his spirit ready to depart, drew into his Body the Spirit of a certaine young Man; And thereby made him Breathlesse; But Himselfe lived many years by another man's spirit". Later, however, he acknowledges the principle behind this legend:

If any man could procure that a young mans spirits could be conveyed into an old mans body; it is not unlikely, but this great wheele of the spirits, might turne about the lesser wheele of the parts; And so the Course of Nature become Retrograde.

These early modern discussions of youth and age help us to understand why the speaker in the Sonnets is positioned as an ageing man. The Sonnets, of course, are equally obsessed with ageing. Initially, this concern feeds the poet's insistence that the young man marry.

In the first sonnets he threatens the young man with age, asking him to imagine himself "When forty winters shall besiege thy brow, / And dig deep trenches in thy beauty's field." The reference to "forty winters" here has sometimes puzzled critics since the phrase is frequently glossed as "when you reach the age of forty." Some critics use this interpretation as evidence that age in the Sonnets is the self-consciously subjective and conventional weariness of the petrarchan poet (Klause 1983).

Others have wondered if at a time of low life expectancy, forty might not actually be old. The latter, as we have seen, is not supported by the medical literature of the period, nor is it necessarily true that life expectancy determines categories of ageing (Smith 1976 236). The former is probably true at least to some extent-certainly we know that the poet's age is fictional rather than autobiographical-but it is not the only way of explaining the passage. If the young man is already in his late teens or early twenties ("adolescent" in most contemporary taxonomies), then forty winters will certainly bring him well into old age by contemporary standards and even by modern standards.

At this early stage in the sequence, the poet's advice is fairly conventional. In Calver's somewhat later Passion and Discretion in Youth and Age, Discretion advises Youth to think of the future, not to be seduced by his own beauty, strength, and to hold age before his eyes (Calver 1641 11). The solution in the Sonnets, at first, is a child who will mean new life. But the young man's imagined dotage eventually becomes a reflection of the poet's own state. In Sonnet 63, for instance, the poet also looks for an antidote,

Against my love shall be, as I am now,
With Time's injurious hand crush'd and o'erworn;
When hours have drain'd his blood and fill'd his brow
With lines and wrinkles. . . . (63.1-4)

In this sonnet, of course, the solution to the young man's mortality turns out to be no longer a child but the literary work of the poet. But the image of age itself has focused on the poet and has become even more insistently bodily. As in contemporary medical accounts, age dries the body, draining its vital moisture and cooling its heat, here imagined, as so frequently in medical texts, as being located in the blood.

The Sonnets also frequently depict the process of revitalization in terms of the exchange of blood. In one early passage, the poet describes the imagined child as containing the blood of the young man:

As fast as thou shalt wane, so fast thou grow'st
In one of thine, from that which thou departest;
And that fresh blood which youngly thou bestow'st
Thou mayst call thine when thou from youth convertest. (11.1-4)

In part the word blood here is used in the sense of family relationship (OED 8), but the words "fresh" and "youngly" gives it a more physical dimension. The child is fresh because it was created from fresh blood. The adverb "youngly" could mean simply vigorously, but in connection with fresh it also carries the implication that the blood transferred from a youth is more powerful than the blood that might be transferred from an old man. This passage also suggests that the blood of a youth will actually benefit an old man. The imagined child's blood will belong to the young man (he will call it his own) when he himself grows old. This imagined transference will make him grow as fast as he wanes.

Throughout the Sonnets, Shakespeare flirts with the physical qualities of youth and age, and with the notion of an exchange between them. He alerts us to the possibility of a deeply embodied connection between the aged poet and the young man but never fully commits to the physical side. In Sonnet 22, for example, the poet begins by suggesting that the youth is an antidote to his own age: "My glass shall not persuade me I am old," the poet begins, "So long as youth and thou are of one date". As the poem progresses, however, youth almost becomes a liability: so much depends on the young man not ageing. By the middle of the poem, the relationship becomes an exchange of hearts; the poet speaks of "my heart / Which in thy breast doth live, as thine in me". This image is fairly conventional. Yet lest we think that this exchange is entirely metaphorical, the poet reminds us of the connection between hearts and age.

Since he has a young man's heart inside him, he asks, "How can I then be elder than thou art?" But the more insistently physical the exchange becomes, the more problematic it is. In the final lines, the poet is thinking of exchange mainly as a way of talking about the foreseen end to the relationship. "Presume not on thy heart when mine is slain, / Thou gav'st me thine not to give back again".

Here the exchange is final. What the poet has been given from the young man is now his forever, regardless of what happens to his own heart in the young man's possession. These lines manage to twist the question of ageing, which is the main threat to the hearts in the first part of the poem, into a question of disloyalty in love. Because the notion of moveable hearts is so conventional in love poetry of this period, however, the final couplet realigns the poem with the petrarchan tradition, suggesting that the whole exchange was only a poetic conceit. Like Roger Bacon's elliptical hints at the nature of the medicine that will cure old men, the Sonnets only hint that the young man's body is a source of youth for the poet.

The sonnets to the dark lady complicate this situation. Into the early hints of literary anti-senescence she introduces a note of uncertainty. On the one hand, since she is younger than the poet she ought to be good for him. Like Ficino's young mother, cheerfully yielding up her milk for the old man, the dark lady ought to be potentially curative. Yet the closest the poet comes to representing such a cure is in Sonnet 138, where the dark lady flatters him by pretending not to notice his age even though she is perfectly aware of it. The poet is left in the dubious position of "vainly thinking that she thinks me young," willing to buy her flattery at the cost of not referring to her inconstancy.

This humorous situation is far from the kind of physical transformation hinted at in the young man poems. It resembles only the milder kind of prophylaxis suggested by Du Laurens, who argues that to prevent accidents, "old men must be held up with such discourses as they like of; they must be praised, they must be flattered, they must not be gainsayd in anything". The only transformation possible in the world of Sonnet 138 is through a willing suspension of disbelief.

Longevity in Sonnet 138 is socially contingent. And as might be expected, age itself is not as prevalent a subject in this section of the Sonnets. Sonnet 138 is the only one in which the poet even mentions his advanced age. Thus while the contrast between speaker and beloved in the young man poems may be between youth and age, in the dark lady poems it is between man and woman. Yet the poet's physical anxieties and the interest in mortality do not vanish in the dark lady poems. The woman in the triangle just plays a very different role than the man. As in Ficino's account, she represents the kind of physical predation that can be summed up in the well known "expense of spirit in a waste of shame."

Of course, these ideas about the danger of intercourse are extremely widespread in the period. Lust almost always shortens life. The health of the celebrated Thomas Parr, who was supposed to have lived more than 152 years, was attributed by one writer partly to diet, but more to his avoidance of any kind of lasciviousness. Consequently the less radical prolongevitists like Leonardus Lessius made sexual moderation one of the main ingredients in their "sobre diet". Ideally, such moderation was supposed to ensure that "malignant" passions themselves would be less likely to occur.

In the dark lady sonnets such anxieties emerge from the conventions of lovesickness. In Sonnet 147 the poet calls his love a "fever" that feeds "on that which doth preserve the ill." Such an image has a long poetic history in the period, but this particular sonnet develops the conceit more literally than most, and the poet is left to contemplate how "Desire is death, which physic did except." The poet's self-representation in these sonnets is also tinged with a less abstract notion of the passage of time. He sees himself, in Sonnet 146, as using up his inner strength and resources in order to make his "fading mansion" appear fine. In the end, he wonders, "Shall worms, inheritors of this excess, / Eat up thy charge? Is this thy body's end?" In this way, while the young man in the Sonnets holds out the possibility of amelioration for the poet's ageing body, the dark lady threatens that body with an obsession that will hasten mortality.

These connections between the medical discourse of longevity and the subject positions of the Sonnets ultimately help explain some of the more puzzling features of the collection. The role of the body in Shakespeare's Sonnets has frequently created problems for critics. Certainly the age of the poet has always been a problem for those who wanted to see the Sonnets as autobiographical. Since they pre-date 1609, they must have been written before Shakespeare reached 45, an age which according to contemporary classification was the prime of life.

To make sense of this, one would have to rely on arguments such as Du Lauren's warning that "there are very many which old men at fortie become," but of course he also says that "there are an infinit sort, which are young men at sixtie". More recent critics, who are not as concerned with autobiography, can assume that the Poet's pose of extreme age is either part of a thematically appropriate persona or a reflection of lyric traditions. But even these critics have to confront what seems to be a peculiar combination of distinct physical types. An using thematic material to explain the physical types results in potentially circular arguments.

Such arguments also have a tendency to take the fictional quality of age in the Sonnets as grounds for a claim that the poet is making an almost entirely abstract statement about the "human fate". The medical literature opens up another possibility. Given the Sonnets' reliance on a trio of characters that appears so frequently in early modern medical discussions, it seems likely that the complex themes of Shakespeare's Sonnets emerge in part from a fairly conventional relationship between early modern physical regimes of health and the ageing body.

Chapter 6

On "Romeo and Juliet"

Romeo and juliet is the only tragedy which Shakespear has written entirely on a love-story. It is supposed to have been his first play, and it deserves to stand in that proud rank. There is the buoyant spirit of youth in every line, in the rapturous intoxication of hope, and in the bitterness of despair. It has been said of Romeo and juliet by a great critic, that "whatever is most intoxicating in the odour of a southern spring, languishing in the song of the nightingale, or voluptuous in the first opening of the rose, is to be found in this poem." The description is true; and yet it does not answer to our idea of the play. For if it has the sweetness of the rose, it has its freshness too; if it has the languor of the nightingale's song, it has also its giddy transport; if it has the softness of a southern spring, it is as glowing and as bright.

There is nothing of a sickly and sentimental cast. Romeo and Juliet are in love, but they are not love-sick. Every thing speaks the very soul of pleasure, the high and healthy pulse of the passions: the heart beats, the blood circulates and mantles throughout. Their courtship is not an insipid interchange of sentiments lip-deep, learnt at secondhand from poems and plays,—made up of beauties of the most shadowy kind, of "fancies wan that hang the pensive head," of evanescent smiles and sighs that breathe not, of delicacy that shrinks from the touch and feebleness that scarce supports itself, an elaborate vacuity of thought, and an artificial dearth of sense, spirit, truth, and nature! It is the reverse of all this. It is Shakespear all over, and Shakespear when he was young.

We have heard it objected to Romeo and juliet, that it is

founded on an idle passion between a boy and a girl, who have scarcely seen and can have but little sympathy or rational esteem for one another, who have had no experience of the good or ills of life, and whose raptures or despair must be therefore equally groundless and fantastical. Whoever objects to the youth of the parties in this play as "too unripe and crude" to pluck the sweets of love, and wishes to see a first-love carried on into a good old age, and the passions taken at the rebound, when their force is spent, may find all this done in the Stranger and in other German plays, where they do things by contraries, and transpose nature to inspire sentiment and create philosophy.

Shakespear proceeded in a more strait-forward, and, we think, effectual way. He did not endeavour to extract beauty from wrinkles, or the wild throb of passion from the last expiring sigh of indifference. He did not "gather grapes of thorns nor figs of thistles." It was not his way. But he has given a picture of human life, such as it is in the order of nature. He has founded the passion of the two lovers not on the pleasures they had experienced, but on all the pleasures they had not experienced. All that was to come of life was theirs.

At that untried source of promised happiness they slaked their thirst, and the first eager draught made them drunk with love and joy. They were in full possession of their senses and their affections. Their hopes were of air, their desires of fire. Youth is the season of love, because the heart is then first melted in tenderness from the touch of novelty, and kindled to rapture, for it knows no end of its enjoyments or its wishes. Desire has no limit but itself. Passion, the love and expectation of pleasure, is infinite, extravagant, inexhaustible, till experience comes to check and kill it. Juliet exclaims on her first interview with Romeo—

"My bounty is as boundless as the sea,
My love as deep."

And why should it not? What was to hinder the thrilling tide of pleasure, which had just gushed from her heart, from flowing on without stint or measure, but experience which she was yet without? What was to abate the transport of the first sweet sense of pleasure, which her heart and her senses had just tasted, but indifference which she was yet a stranger to? What was there to check the ardour of hope, of faith, of constancy, just rising in her breast, but disappointment which she had not yet felt? As are the desires and the hopes of youthful passion, such is the keenness of its disappointments, and their baleful effect. Such is the transition in this play from the highest bliss to the lowest despair, from the nuptial couch to an untimely grave.

The only evil that even in apprehension befalls the two lovers is the loss of the greatest possible felicity; yet this loss is fatal to both, for they had rather part with life than bear the thought of surviving all that had made life dear to them. In all this, Shakespeare has but followed nature, which existed in his time, as well as now. The modern philosophy, which reduces the whole theory of the mind to habitual impressions, and leaves the natural impulses of passion and imagination out of the account, had not then been discovered; or if it had, would have been little calculated for the uses of poetry.

It is the inadequacy of the same false system of philosophy to account for the strength of our earliest attachments, which has led Mr. Wordsworth to indulge in the mystical visions of Platonism in his Ode on the Progress of Life. He has very admirably described the vividness of our impressions in youth and childhoods and how "they fade by degrees into the light of common day," and he ascribes the change to the supposition of a pre-existent state, as if our early thoughts were nearer heaven, reflections of former trails of glory, shadows of our past being. This is idle. It is not from the knowledge of the past that the first impressions of things derive their gloss and splendour, but from our ignorance of the future, which fills the void to come with the warmth of our desires, with our gayest hopes, and brightest fancies.

It is the obscurity spread before it that colours the prospect of life with hope, as it is the cloud which reflects the rainbow. There is no occasion to resort to any mystical union and transmission of feeling through different states of being to account for the romantic enthusiasm of youth; nor to plant the root of hope in the grave, nor to derive it from the skies. Its root is in the heart of man: it lifts its head above the stars. Desire and imagination are inmates of the human breast. The heaven "that lies about us in our infancy" is only a new world, of which we know nothing but what we wish it to be, and believe all that we wish. In youth and boyhood, the world we live in is the world of desire, and of fancy: it is experience that brings us down to the world of reality. What is it that in youth sheds a dewy light round the evening star? That makes the daisy look so bright? That perfumes the hyacinth? That embalms the first kiss of love? It is the delight of novelty, and the seeing no end to the pleasure that we fondly believe is still in store for us. The heart revels in the luxury of its own thoughts, and is unable to sustain the weight of hope and love that presses upon it.—The effects of the passion of love alone might have dissipated Mr. Wordsworth's theory, if he means any thing more by it than an ingenious and poetical allegory.

That at least is not a link in the chain let down from other worlds; "the purple light of love" is not a dim reflection of the smiles of celestial bliss. It does not appear till the middle of life, and then seems like "another morn risen on mid-day." In this respect the soul comes into the world "in utter nakedness." Love waits for the ripening of the youthful blood. The sense of pleasure precedes the love of pleasure, but with the sense of pleasure, as soon as it is felt, come thronging infinite desires and hopes of pleasure, and love is mature as soon as born. It withers and it dies almost as soon!

This play presents a beautiful coup-d'oeil of the progress of human life. In thought it occupies years, and embraces the circle of the affections from childhood to old age. Juliet has become a great girl, a young woman since we first remember her a little thing in the idle, prattle of the nurse, Lady Capulet was about her age when she became a mother, and old Capulet somewhat impatiently tells his younger visitors,

I've seen the day,
That 1 have worn a visor, and could tell
A whispering tale in a fair lady's ear,
Such as would please; 'tis gone, 'tis gone, 'tis gone."

Thus one period of life makes way for the following, and one generation pushes another off the stage. One of the most striking passages to shew the intense feeling of youth in this play is Capulet's invitation to Paris to visit his entertainment.

"At my poor house, look to behold this night
Earth-treading stars that make dark heaven light;
Such comfort as do lusty young men feel
When well-apparel'd April on the heel
Of limping winter treads, even such delight
Among fresh female-buds shall you this night
Inherit at my house."

The feelings of youth and of the spring are here blended together like the breath of opening flowers. Images of vernal beauty appear to have floated before the author's mind, in writing this poem, in profusion. Here is another of exquisite beauty, brought in more by accident than by necessity. Montague declares of his son smit with a hopeless passion, which he will not reveal—

"But he, his own affection's counsellor,
Is to himself so secret and so close,
So far from sounding and discovery,
As is the bud bit with an envious worm,
Ere he can spread his sweet leaves to the air;
Or dedicate his beauty to the sun."

This casual description is as full of passionate beauty as when Romeo dwells in frantic fondness on "the white wonder of his Juliet's hand." The reader may, if he pleases, contrast the exquisite pastoral simplicity of the above lines with the gorgeous description of Juliet when Romeo first sees her at her father's house, surrounded by company and artificial splendour.

"What lady's that which cloth enrich the hand
Of yonder knight?
O she doth teach the torches to burn bright;
Her beauty hangs upon the cheek of night,
Like a rich jewel in an Aethiop's ear."

It would be hard to say which of the two garden scenes is the finest, that where he first converses with his love, or takes leave of her the morning after their marriage. Both are like a heaven upon earth: the blissful bowers of Paradise let down upon this lower world. We will give only one passage of these well known scenes to shew the perfect refinement and delicacy of Shakespear's conception of the female character. It is wonderful how Collins, who was a critic and a poet of great sensibility, should have encouraged the common error on this subject by saying—"But stronger Shakespear felt for man alone."

The passage we mean is Juliet's apology for her maiden boldness.

"Thou know'st the mask of night is on my face;
Else would a maiden blush bepaint my cheek
For that which thou hast heard me speak to-night.
Fain would I dwell on form, fain, fain deny
What I have spoke—but farewel compliment:
Dost thou love me? I know thou wilt say, ay,
And I will take thee at thy word—Yet if thou swear'st,
Thou may'st prove false; at lovers' perjuries
They say Jove laughs. Oh gentle Romeo,
If thou dost love, pronounce it faithfully;
Or if thou think I am too quickly won,
I'll frown and be perverse, and say thee nay,
So thou wilt woo: but else not for the world,
In truth, fair Montague, I am too fond;
And therefore thou may'st think my 'haviour light;
But trust me, gentleman, I'll prove more true
Than those that have more cunning to be strange.
I should have been more strange, I must confess,
But that thou over-heard'st, ere I was ware,
My true love's passion; therefore pardon me,
And not impute this yielding to light love,
Which the dark night hath so discovered."

In this and all the rest her heart fluttering between pleasure, hope, and fear, seems to have dictated to her tongue, and "calls true love spoken simple modesty." Of the same sort, but bolder in virgin innocence, is her soliloquy after her marriage with Romeo.

"Gallop apace, you fiery-footed steeds,
Towards Phoebus' mansion; such a waggoner
As Phaëton would whip you to the west,
And bring in cloudy night immediately.
Spread thy close curtain, love-performing night;
That run-aways' eyes may wink; and Romeo
Leap to these arms, untalked of, and unseen!—
Lovers can see to do their amorous rites
By their own beauties: or if love be blind,
It best agrees with night.—Come, civil night,
Thou sobre-suited matron, all in black,
And learn me how to lose a winning match,
Play'd for a pair of stainless maidenhoods:
Hood my unmann'd blood bating in my cheeks,
With thy black mantle; till strange love, grown bold,
Thinks true love acted, simple modesty.
Come night!—Come, Romeo! come, thou day in night;
For thou wilt lie upon the wings of night
Whiter than new snow on a raven's back.—
Come, gentle night; come, loving, black-brow'd night,
Give me my Romeo: and when he shall die,
Take him and cut him out in little stars,
And he will make the face of heaven so fine,
That all the world shall be in love with night,
And pay no worship to the garish sun.—
O, I have bought the mansion of a love,
But not possess'd it; and though I am sold,
Not yet enjoy'd: so tedious is this day,
As is the night before some festival
To an impatient child, that hath new robes,
And may not wear them."

We the rather insert this passage here, inasmuch as we have no doubt it has been expunged from the Family Shakespear. Such critics do not perceive that the feelings of the heart sanctify, without disguising, the impulses of nature. Without refinement themselves, they confound modesty with hypocrisy. Not so the German critic, Schlegel. Speaking of ROMEO AND JULIET, he says, "It was reserved for

Shakespear to unite purity of heart and the glow of imagination, sweetness and dignity of manners and passionate violence, in one ideal picture." The character is indeed one of perfect truth and sweetness. It has nothing forward, nothing coy, nothing affected or coquettish about it;—it is a pure effusion of nature. It is as frank as it is modest, for it has no thought that it wishes to conceal.

It reposes in conscious innocence on the strength of its affections. Its delicacy does not consist in coldness and reserve, but in combining warmth of imagination and tenderness of heart with the most voluptuous sensibility. Love is a gentle flame that rarefies and expands her whole being. What an idea of trembling haste and airy grace, borne upon the thoughts of love, does the Friar's exclamation give of her, as she approaches his cell to be married—

"Here comes the lady. Oh, so light of foot
Will ne'er wear out the everlasting flint:
A lover may bestride the gossamer,
That idles in the wanton summer air,
And yet not fall, so light is vanity."

The tragic part of this character is of a piece with the rest. It is the heroic founded on tenderness and delicacy. Of this kind is her resolution to follow the Friar's advice, and the conflict in her bosom between apprehension and love when she comes to take the sleeping poison. Shakespeare is blamed for the mixture of low characters. If this is a deformity, it is the source of a thousand beauties. One instance is the contrast between the guileless simplicity of Juliet's attachment to her first love, and the convenient policy of the nurse in advising her to marry Paris, which excites such indignation in her mistress. "Ancient damnation! oh most wicked fiend," &c.

Romeo is Hamlet in love. There is the same rich exuberance of passion and sentiment in the one, that there is of thought and sentiment in the other. Both are absent and self-involved, both live out of themselves in a world of imagination. Hamlet is abstracted from every thing; Romeo is abstracted from every thing but his love, and lost in it. His "frail thoughts dally with faint surmise," and are fashioned out of the suggestions of hope, "the flatteries of sleep." He is himself only in his Juliet; she is his only reality, his heart's true home and idol. The rest of the world is to him a passing dream. How finely is this character pourtrayed where he recollects himself on seeing Paris slain at the tomb of Juliet!

"What said my man when my betossed soul
Did not attend him as we rode? I think
He told me Paris should have married Juliet."

And again, just before he hears the sudden tidings of her death—

"If I may trust the flattery of sleep,
My dreams presage some joyful news at hand;
My bosom's lord sits lightly on his throne,
And all this day an unaccustom'd spirit
Lifts me above the ground with cheerful thoughts.
I dreamt my lady came and found me dead,
(Strange dream! that gives a dead man leave to think)
And breath'd such life with kisses on my lips,
That I reviv'd and was an emperour.
Ah me! how sweet is love itself possess'd,
When but love's shadows are so rich in joy!"

Romeo's passion for Juliet is not a first love: it succeeds and drives out his passion for another mistress, Rosaline, as the sun hides the stars. This is perhaps an artifice (not absolutely necessary) to give us a higher opinion of the lady, while the first absolute surrender of her heart to him enhances the richness of the prize. The commencement, progress, and ending of his second passion are however complete in themselves, not injured, if they are not bettered by the first.

The outline of the play is taken from an Italian novel; but the dramatic arrangement of the different scenes between the lovers, the more than dramatic interest in the progress of the story, the development of the characters with time and circumstances, just according to the degree and kind of interest excited, are not inferior to the expression of passion and nature. It has been ingeniously remarked among other proofs of skill in the contrivance of the fable, that the improbability of the main incident in the piece, the administering of the sleeping-potion, is softened and obviated from the beginning by the introduction of the Friar on his first appearance culling simples and descanting on their virtues.

Of the passionate scenes in this tragedy, that between the Friar and Romeo when he is told of his sentence of banishment, that between Juliet and the Nurse when she hears of it, and of the death of her cousin Tybalt (which bear no proportion in her mind, when passion after the first shock of surprise throws its weight into the scale of her affections) and the last scene at the tomb, are among the most natural and overpowering.

In all of these it is not merely the force of any one passion that is given, but the slightest and most unlooked-for transitions from one to another, the mingling currents of every different feeling rising up and prevailing in turn, swayed by the master-mind of the poet, as the waves undulate beneath the gliding storm. Thus when Juliet has by her complaints encouraged the Nurse to say, "Shame come to Romeo," she instantly repels the wish, which she, had herself occasioned, by answering—

"Blister'd be thy tongue
For such a wish, he was not born to shame.
Upon his brow shame is ashamed to sit,
For 'tis a throne where honour may be crown'd
Sole monarch of the universal earth!
O, what a beast was I to chide him so?
Nurse. Will you speak well of him that killed your cousin?
Juliet. Shall I speak ill of him that is my husband?
Ah my poor lord, what tongue shall smooth thy name,
When I, thy three-hours' wife, have mangled it?"

And then follows on the neck of her remorse and returning fondness, that wish treading almost on the brink of impiety, but still held back by the strength of her devotion to her lord, that "father, mother, nay, or both were dead," rather than Romeo banished. If she requires any other excuse, it is in the manner in which Romeo echoes her frantic grief and disappointment in the next scene: at being banished from her.—Perhaps one of the finest pieces of acting that ever was witnessed on the stage, is Mr. Kean's manner of doing this scene and his repetition of the word, Banished. He treads close indeed upon the genius of his author.

A passage which this celebrated actor and able commentator on Shakespear (actors are the best commentators on the poets) did not give with equal truth or force of feeling was the one which Romeo makes at the tomb of Juliet, before he drinks the poison.

"Let me peruse this face—
Mercutio's kinsman! noble county Paris!
What said my man, when my betossed soul
Did not attend him as we rode! I think,
He told me, Paris should have marry'd Juliet!
Said he not so? or did I dream it so?
Or am I mad, hearing him talk of Juliet,
To think it was so?—O, give me thy hand,
One writ with me in sour misfortune's book!
I'll bury thee in a triumphant grave—
For here lies Juliet.
—O, my love! my wife!
Death that hath suck'd the honey of thy breath,
Hath had no power yet upon thy beauty:
Thou art not conquer'd; beauty's ensign yet
Is crimson in thy lips, and in thy cheeks,
And Death's pale flag is Dot advanced there.—
Tybalt, ly'st thou there in thy bloody sheet?
O, what more favour can I do to thee,
Than with that hand that cut thy youth in twain,
To sunder his that was thine enemy?
Forgive me, cousin! Ah, dear Juliet,
Why art thou yet so fair! I will believe
That unsubstantial death is amorous;
And that the lean abhorred monster keeps
Thee here in dark to be his paramour.
For fear of that, I will stay still with thee;
And never from this palace of dim night
Depart again: here, here will I remain
With worms that are thy chamber-maids; O, here
Will I set up my everlasting rest;

And shake the yoke of inauspicious stars
From this world-wearied flesh.—Eyes, look your last!
Arms, take your last embrace! and lips, O you
The doors of breath, seal with a righteous kiss
A dateless bargain to engrossing death!—
Come, bitter conduct, come unsavoury guide!
Thou desperate pilot, now at once run on
The dashing rocks my sea-sick weary bark!
Here's to my love!—[Drinks.] O, true apothecary!
Thy drugs are quick.—Thus with a kiss I die."

The lines in this speech describing the loveliness of Juliet, who is supposed to be dead, have been compared to those in which it is said of Cleopatra after her death, that she looked "as she would take another Antony in her strong toil of grace;" and a question has been started which is the finest, that we do not pretend to decide.

We can more easily decide between Shakespeare and any other author, than between him and himself.—Shall we quote any more passages to shew his genius or the beauty of ROMEO AND JULIET? At that rate, we might quote the whole. The late Mr Sheridan, on being strewn a volume of the Beauties of Shakespeare, very properly asked—"But where are the other eleven?" The character of Mercutio in this play is one of the most mercurial and spirited of the productions of Shakespeare comic muse.

Chapter 7

On "Lear"

We wish that we could pass this play over, and say nothing about it. All that we can say must fall far short of the subject; or even of what we ourselves conceive of it. To attempt to give a description of the play itself or of its effect upon the mind, is mere impertinence: yet we must say something.—It is then the best of all Shakespeare's plays, for it is the one in which he was the most in earnest. He was here fairly caught in the web of his own imagination. The passion which he has taken as his subject is that which strikes its root deepest into the human heart; of which the bond is the hardest to be unloosed; and the cancelling and tearing to pieces of which gives the greatest revulsion to the frame.

This depth of nature, this force of passion, this tug and war of the elements of our being, this firm faith in filial piety, and the giddy anarchy and whirling tumult of the thoughts at finding this prop failing it, the contrast between the fixed, immoveable basis of natural affection, and the rapid, irregular starts of imagination, suddenly wrenched from all its accustomed holds and resting-places in the soul, this is what Shakespeare has given, and what nobody else but he could give.

So we believe.—The mind of Lear staggering between the weight of attachment and the hurried movements of passion is like a tall ship driven about by the winds, buffetted by the furious waves, but that still rides above the storm, having its anchor fixed in the bottom of the sea; or it is like the sharp rock circled by the eddying whirlpool that foams and beats against it, or like the solid promontory pushed from its basis by the force of an earthquake. The character of Lear itself is very finely conceived for the purpose. It is the only ground on which such a story could be built with the greatest truth and effect. It is his rash haste, his violent impetuosity, his blindness to every thing but the dictates of his passions or affections, that produces all his misfortunes, that aggravates his impatience of them, that enforces our pity for him.

The part which Cordelia bears in the scene is extremely beautiful: the story is almost told in the first words she utters. We see at once the precipice on which the poor old king stands from his own extravagant and credulous importunity, the indiscreet simplicity of her love (which, to be sure, has a little of her father's obstinacy in it) and the hollowness of her sisters' pretensions. Almost the first burst of that noble tide of passion, which runs through the play, is in the remonstrance of Kent to his royal master on the injustice of his sentence against his youngest daughter—"Be Kent unmannerly, when Lear is mad!"

This manly plainness which draws down on him the displeasure of the unadvised king is worthy of the fidelity with which he adheres to his fallen fortunes. The true character of the two eldest daughters, Regan and Gonerill (they are so thoroughly hateful that we do not even like to repeat their names) breaks out in their answer to Cordelia who desires them to treat their father well—"Prescribe not us our duties"—their hatred of advice being in proportion to their determination to do wrong, and to their hypocritical pretensions to do right. Their deliberate hypocrisy adds the last finishing to the odiousness of their characters. It is the absence of' this detestable quality that is the only relief in the character of Edmund the Bastard, and that at times reconciles us to him.

We are not tempted to exaggerate the guilt of his conduct, when he himself gives it up as a bad business, and writes himself down "plain villain." Nothing more can be said about it. His religious honesty in this respect is admirable. One speech of his is worth a million. His father, Gloster, whom he has just deluded with a forged story of his brother Edgar's designs against his life, accounts for his unnatural behaviour and the strange depravity of the times from the late eclipses in the sun and moon.

Edmund, who is in the secret, says when he is gone—"This is the excellent coppery of the world, that when we are sick in fortune (often the surfeits of our own behaviour) we make guilty of our disasters the sun, the moon, and stars: as if we were villains on necessity; fools by heavenly compulsion; knaves, thieves, and treacherous by spherical predominance; drunkards, liars, and adulterers by an enforced obedience of planetary influence; and all that we are evil in, by a divine thrusting on.

An admirable evasion of whore-master man, to lay his goatish disposition on the charge of a star! My father compounded with my mother under the Dragon's tail, and my nativity was under Ursa Major: so that it follows, I am rough and lecherous. I should have been what I am, had the maidenliest star in the firmament twinkled on my bastardizing."—The whole character, its careless, light-hearted villainy, contrasted with the sullen, rancorous malignity of Regan and Gonerill, its connection with the conduct of the under-plot, in which Gloster's persecution of one of his sons and the ingratitude of another, form a counterpart to the mistakes and misfortunes of Lear,—his double amour with the two sisters, and the share which he has in bringing about the fatal catastrophe, are all managed with an uncommon degree of skill and power.

It has been said, and we think justly, that the third act of Othello and the three first acts of LEAR, are Shakespear's great master-pieces in the logic of passion: that they contain the highest examples not only of the force of individual passion, but of its dramatic vicissitudes and striking effects arising from the different circumstances and characters of the persons speaking. We see the ebb and flow of the feeling, its pauses and feverish starts, its impatience of opposition, its accumulating force when it has time to recollect itself, the manner in which it avails itself of every passing word or gesture, its haste to repel insinuation, the alternate contraction and dilatation of the soul, and all "the dazzling fence of controversy" in this mortal combat with poisoned weapons, aimed at the heart, where each wound is fatal. We have seen in Othello, how the unsuspecting frankness and impetuous passions of the Moor are played upon and exasperated by the artful dexterity of Iago. In the present play, that which aggravates the sense of sympathy in the reader, and of uncontroulable anguish in the swoln heart of Lear, is the petrifying indifference, the cold, calculating, obdurate selfishness of his daughters.

His keen passions seem whetted on their stony hearts. The contrast would be too painful, the shock too great, but for the intervention of the Fool, whose well-timed levity comes in to break the continuity of feeling when it can no longer be borne, and to bring into play again the fibres of the heart just as they are growing rigid from over-strained excitement. The imagination is glad to take refuge in the half-comic, half-serious comments of the Fool, just as the mind under the extreme anguish of a surgical operation vents itself in sallies of wit.

The character was also a grotesque ornament of the barbarous times, in which alone the tragic ground-work of the story could be laid. In another point of view it is indispensable, inasmuch as while it is a diversion to the too great intensity of our disgust, it carries the pathos to the highest pitch of which it is capable, by strewing the pitiable weakness of the old king's conduct and its irretrievable consequences in the most familiar point of view. Lear may well "beat at the gate which let his folly in," after, as the Fool says, "he has made his daughters his mothers."

The character is dropped in the third act to make room for the entrance of Edgar as Mad Tom, which well accords with the increasing bustle and wildness of the incidents; and nothing can be more complete than the distinction between Lear's real and Edgar's assumed madness, while the resemblance in the cause of their distresses, from the severing of the nearest ties of natural affection, keeps up a unity of interest. Shakespear's mastery over his subject, if it was not art, was owing to a knowledge of the connecting links of the passions, and their effect upon the mind, still more wonderful than any systematic adherence to rules, and that anticipated and outdid all the efforts of the most refined art, not inspired and rendered instinctive by genius.

One of the most perfect displays of dramatic power is the first interview between Lear and his daughter, after the designed affronts upon him, which till one of his knights reminds him of them, his sanguine temperament had led him to overlook. He returns with his train from hunting, and his usual impatience breaks out in his first words, "Let me not stay a jot for dinner; go, get it ready." He then encounters the faithful Kent in disguise, and retains him in his service; and the first trial of his honest duty is to trip up the heels of the officious Steward who makes so prominent and despicable a figure through the piece.

On the entrance of Gonerill the following dialogue takes place:

"Lear. How now, daughter? what makes that frontlet on?
Methinks, you are too much of late i' the frown.

Fool. Thou wast a pretty fellow, when thou had'st no need to care for her frowning; now thou art an O without a figure: I am better than thou art now; I am a fool, thou art nothing.—
—Yes, forsooth, I will hold my tongue; To Gonerill. so your face bids me, though you say nothing. Mum, mum.

He that keeps nor crust nor crum,
Weary of all, shall want some:
That's a sheal'd peascod! Pointing to Lear. Gonerill.
Not only, sir, this your all-licens'd fool,
But other of your insolent retinue
Do hourly carp and quarrel; breaking forth
In rank and not-to-be-endured riots.
I had thought, by making this well known unto you,
To have found a safe redress; but now grow fearful,
By what yourself too late have spoke and done,
That you protect this course, and put it on
By your allowance; which if you should, the fault
Would not 'scape censure, nor the redresses sleep,

Which in the tender of a wholesome weal,
Might in their working do you that offence,
(Which else were shame) that then necessity
Would call discreet proceeding.
Fool. For you trow, nuncle,
The hedge sparrow fed the cuckoo so long,
That it had its head bit off by its young.
So out went the candle, and we were left darkling.
Lear. Are you our daughter?
Gonerill. Come, sir,
I would, you would make use of that good wisdom
Whereof I know you are fraught; and put away
These dispositions, which of late transform you
From what you rightly are.
Fool: May not an ass know when the cart draws the horse?—
—Whoop, Jug, I love thee.
Lear. Does any here know me? Why, this is not Lear:
Does Lear walk thus? speak thus? Where are his eyes?
Either his notion weakens, or his discernings
Are lethargy'd Ha! waking? 'Tis not so.
Who is it that can tell me who I am?—Lear's shadow?
I would learn that: for by the marks
Of sov'reignty, of knowledge, and of reason,
I should be false persuaded I had daughters.——
Your name, fair gentlewoman?
Gonerill. Come, sir:
This admiration is much o' the favour
Of other your new pranks. I do beseech you
To understand my purposes aright:
As you are old and reverend, you should be wise:
Here do you keep a hundred knights and squires;
Men so disorder'd, so debauch'd, and bold,
That this our court, infected with their manners,
Shews like a riotous inn: epicurism and lust
Make it more like a tavern, or a brothel,
Than a grac'd palace. The shame itself doth speak
For instant remedy: be then desir'd
By her, that else will take the thing she begs,

A little to disquantity your train;
And the remainder, that shall still depend,
To be such men as may besort your age,
And know themselves and you.
Lear. Darkness and devils!— —
Saddle my horses; call my train together.— —
Degenerate bastard! I'll not trouble thee;
Yet have I left a daughter.
Gonerill. You strike my people; and your disorder'd rabble
Make servants of their betters.
Enter ALBANY.
Lear. Woe, that too late repents—O, sir, are you come?
Is it your will? speak, sir.—Prepare my horses.— — [To Albany.
Ingratitude! thou marble-hearted fiend,
More hideous, when thou shew'st thee in a child,
Than the sea-monster!
Albany. Pray, sir, be patient.
Lear. Detested kite! thou liest. [To Gonerill.
My train are men of choice and rarest parts,
That all particulars of duty know;
And in the most exact regard support
The worships of their name.— —O most small fault,
How ugly didst thou in Cordelia shew!
Which, like an engine, wrench'd my frame of nature
From the fixt place; drew from my heart all love,
And added to the gall. O Lear, Lear, Lear!
Beat at the gate, that let thy folly in, [Striking his head.
And thy dear judgment out!— —Go, go, my people!
Albany. My lord, I am guiltless, as I am ignorant
Of what hath mov'd you.
Lear. It may be so, my lord— —
Hear, nature, hear! dear goddess, hear!
Suspend thy purpose, if thou didst intend
To make this creature fruitful!
Into her womb convey sterility;
Dry up in her the organs of increase;
And from her derogate body never spring
A babe to honour her! If she must teem,

Create her child of spleen: that it may live,
To be a thwart disnatur'd torment to her!
Let it stamp wrinkles in her brow of youth;
With cadent tears fret channels in her cheeks;
Turn all her mother's pains, and benefits,
To laughter and contempt; that she may feel
How sharper than a serpent's tooth it is
To have a thankless child!——Away, away! [*Exit.*
Albany. Now, gods, that we adore, whereof comes this?
Gonerill. Never afflict yourself to know the cause;
But let his disposition have that scope
That dotage gives it.

Re-enter LEAR.

Lear. What, fifty of my followers at a clap!
Within a fortnight!
Albany. What's the matter, sir?
Lear. I'll tell thee; life and death! I am asham'd
That thou hast power to shake my manhood thus: [To Gonerill.
That these hot tears, which break from me perforce,
Should make thee worth them.——Blasts and fogs upon thee!
The untented woundings of a father's curse
Pierce every sense about thee!——Old fond eyes
Beweep this cause again, I'll pluck you out;
And cast you, with the waters that you lose,
To temper clay.——Ha! is it come to this?
Let it be so:——Yet have I left a daughter,
Who, I am sure, is kind and comfortable;
When she shall hear this of thee, with her nails
She'll flee thy wolfish visage. Thou shalt find,
That I'll resume the shape, which thou dost think

I have cast off for ever. [Exeunt Lear, Kent, and Attendants."

This is certainly fine: no wonder that Lear says after it, "O let me not be mad, not mad, sweet heavens," feeling its effects by anticipation: but fine as is this burst of rage and indignation at the first blow aimed at his hopes and expectations, it is nothing near so fine as what follows from his double disappointment, and his lingering efforts to see which of them he shall lean upon for support and find comfort in, when both his daughters turn against his age and weakness.

It is with some difficulty that Lear gets to speak with his daughter Regan, and her husband, at Gloster's castle. In concert with Gonerill they have left their own home on purpose to avoid him. His apprehensions are first alarmed by this circumstance, and when Gloster, whose guests they are, urges the fiery temper of the Duke of Cornwall as an excuse for not importuning him a second time, Lear breaks out,

"Vengeance! Plague! Death! Confusion!
Fiery? What fiery quality? Why, Gloster,
I'd speak with the Duke of Cornwall and his wife."

Afterwards, feeling perhaps not well himself; he is inclined to admit their excuse from illness, but then recollecting that they have set his messenger (Kent) in the stocks, all his suspicions are roused again, and he insists on seeing them.

"Enter CORNWALL, REGAN, GLOSTER, and Servants.
Lear. Good-morrow to you both.
Cornwall. Hail to your grace! [Kent is set at liberty.
Regan. I am glad to see your highness.
Lear. Regan, I think you are; I know what reason
I have to think so: if thou should'st not be glad,
I would divorce me from thy mother's tomb,
Sepulch'ring an adultress.— —O, are you free? [To Kent.
Some other time for that.— —Beloved Regan,
Thy sister's naught: O Regan, she hath tied
Sharp-tooth'd unkindness, like a vulture, here— — [Points to his heart.
I can scarce speak to thee; thou'lt not believe,
Of how deprav'd a quality— —O Regan!
Regan. I pray you, sir, take patience; I have hope
You less know how to value her desert,
Than she to scant her duty.
Lear. Say, how is that?
Regan. I cannot think my sister in the least
Would fail her obligation; if, sir, perchance,
She have restrain'd the riots of your followers,
'Tis on such ground, and to such wholesome end,

As clears her from all blame.
Lear. My curses on her!
Regan. O. sir, you are old;
Nature in you stands on the very verge
Of her confine: you should be rul'd, and led
By some discretion, that discerns your state
Better than you yourself: therefore, I pray you,
That to our sister you do make return;
Say, you have wrong'd her, sir.
Lear: Ask her forgiveness?
Do you but mark how this becomes the use?
Dear daughter, I confess that I am old;
Age is unnecessary; on my knees I beg,
That you'll vouchsafe me raiment, bed, and food.
Regan: Good sir, no more; these are unsightly tricks:
Return you to my sister.
Lear: Never, Regan:
She hath abated me of half my train;
Look'd blank upon me; struck me with her tongue,
Most serpent-like, upon the very heart:—
All the stor'd vengeances of heaven fall
On her ungrateful top! Strike her young bones,
You taking airs, with lameness!
Cornwall. Fie, sir, fie!
Lear: You nimble lightnings, dart your blinding flames
Into her scornful eyes! Infect her beauty,
You fen-suck'd fogs, drawn by the powerful sun,
To fall, and blast her pride!
Regan: O the blest gods!
So will you wish on me, when the rash mood is on.
Lear: No, Regan, thou shalt never have my curse;
Thy tender-hefted nature shall not give
Thee o'er to harshness; her eyes are fierce, but thine
Do comfort, and not burn: 'Tis not in thee
To grudge my pleasures, to cut off my train,
To bandy hasty words, to scant my sizes,
And, in conclusion, to oppose the bolt
Against my coming in: thou better know'st

The offices of nature, bond of childhood,
Effects of courtesy, dues of gratitude;
Thy half o' the kingdom thou hast not forgot,
Wherein I thee endow'd.
Regan: Good sir, to the purpose. [Trumpets within.
Lear: Who put my man i' the stocks?
Cornwall. What trumpet's that?

Enter Steward.

Regan: I know't, my sister's: this approves her letter,
That she would soon be here.—Is your lady come?
Lear: This is a slave, whose easy-borrow'd pride
Dwells in the fickle grace of her he follows:——
Out, varlet, from my sight!
Cornwall: What means your grace?
Lear: *Who stock'd my servant? Regan, I have good hope*
Thou did'st not know on't.
Who comes here? O heavens,

Enter Gonerill.

If you do love old men, if your sweet sway
Allow obedience, if yourselves are old,
Make it your cause; send down, and take my part!—
Art not asham'd to look upon this beard ?—[To Gonerill.
O, Regan, wilt thou take her by the hand?
Gonerill. Why not by the hand, sir? How have I offended?
All's not offence, that indiscretion finds,
And dotage terms so.
Lear: O, sides, you are too tough!
Will you yet hold?—How came my man i' the stocks?
Cornwall: I set him there, sir: but his own disorders
Deserv'd much less advancement.
Lear: You! did you?
Regan: I pray you, father, being weak, seem so.
If, till the expiration of your month,
You will return and sojourn with my sister,
Dismissing half your train, come then to me;
I am now from home, and out of that provision
Which shall be needful for your entertainment.
Lear: Return to her, and fifty men dismiss'd?

No, rather I abjure all roofs, and choose
To be a comrade with the wolf and owl——
To wage against the enmity o' the air,
Necessity's sharp pinch!——Return with her!
Why, the hot-blooded France, that dowerless took
Our youngest born, I could as well be brought
To knee his throne, and squire-like pension beg
To keep base life afoot. Return with her!
Persuade me rather to be slave and sumpter
To this detested groom. [Looking on the Steward.
Gonerill: At your choice, sir.
Lear. Now, I pr'ythee, daughter, do not make me mad;
I will not trouble thee, my child; farewell:
We'll no more meet, no more see one another:——
But yet thou art my flesh, my blood, my daughter;
Or, rather, a disease that's in my flesh,
Which I must needs call mine: thou art a bile,
A plague-sore, an embossed carbuncle,
In my corrupted blood. But I'll not chide thee;
Let shame come when it will, I do not call it:
I did not bid the thunder-bearer shoot,
Nor tell tales of thee to high-judging Jove:
Mend, when thou canst; be better, at thy leisure:
I can be patient; I can stay with Regan,
I, and my hundred knights.
Regan. Not altogether so, sir;
I look'd not for you yet, nor am provided
For your fit welcome: Give ear, sir, to my sister;
For those that mingle reason with your passion
Must be content to think you old, and so——
But she knows what she does.
Lear: Is this well spoken now?
Regan. I dare avouch it, sir: What, fifty followers?
Is it not well? What should you need of more?
Yea, or so many? Sith that both charge and danger
Speak 'gainst so great a number? How, in one house,
Should many people, under two commands,
Hold amity? 'Tis hard; almost impossible.

Gonerill. Why might not you, my lord, receive attendance
From those that she calls servants, or from mine?
Regan: Why not, my lord? If then they chanc'd to slack you,
We would controul them: if you will come to me
(For now I spy a danger) I entreat you
To bring but five-and-twenty; to no more
Will I give place, or notice.
Lear: I gave you all——
Regan: And in good time you gave it.
Lear: Made you my guardians, my depositaries;
But kept a reservation to be follow'd
With such a number: what, must I come to you
With five-and-twenty, Regan! said you so?
Regan. And speak it again, my lord; no more with me.
Lear: Those wicked creatures yet do look well-favour'd,
When others are more wicked; not being the worst,
Stands in some rank of praise: I'll go with thee; [To Gonerill.
Thy fifty yet doth double five-and-twenty,
And thou art twice her love.
Gonerill. Hear me, my lord;
What need you five-and twenty, ten, or five,
To follow in a house, where twice so many
Have a command to tend you?
Regan: What need one?
Lear: O, reason not the need: our basest beggars
Are in the poorest thing superfluous:
Allow not nature more than nature needs,
Man's life is cheap as beast's: thou art a lady;
If only to go warm were gorgeous,
Why, nature needs not what thou gorgeous wear'st;
Which scarcely keeps thee warm. But, for true need
You heavens, give me that patience which I need!
You see me here, you gods; a poor old man,
As fun of grief as age; wretched in both!
If it be you that stir these daughters' hearts
Against their father, fool me not so much
To bear it tamely; touch me with noble anger!
O, let no woman's weapons, water-drops,

Stain my man's cheeks! No, you unnatural hags,
I will have such revenges on you both,
That all the world shall I will do such things
What they are, yet I know not; but they shall be
The terrors of the earth. You think, I'll weep:
No, I'll not weep:
I have full cause of weeping; but this heart
Shall break into a hundred thousand flaws,
Or e'er I'll weep: O, fool, I shall go mad!
[Exeunt Lear, Gloster, Kent, and Fool."

If there is any thing in any author like this yearning of the heart, these throes of tenderness, this profound expression of all that can be thought and felt in the most heart rending situations, we are glad of it; but it is in some author that we have not read. The scene in the storm, where he is exposed to all the fury of the elements, though grand and terrible, is not so fine, but the moralising scenes with Mad Tom, Kent, and Gloster, are upon a par with the former.

His exclamation in the supposed trial-scene of his daughters, "See the little dogs and all, Tray, Blanch, and Sweetheart, see they bark at me," his issuing his orders, "Let them anatomize Regan, see what breeds about her heart," and his reflection when he sees the misery of Edgar, "Nothing but his unkind daughters could have brought him to this," are in a style of pathos, where the extremest resources of the imagination are called in to lay open the deepest movements of the heart, which was peculiar to Shakespear. In the same style and spirit is his interrupting the Fool who asks, "whether a madman be a gentleman or a yeoman," by answering "A king, a king!"

The indirect part that Gloster takes in these scenes where his generosity leads him to relieve Lear and resent the cruelty of his daughters, at the very time that he is himself instigated to seek the life of his son, and suffering under the sting of his supposed ingratitude, is a striking accompaniment to the situation of Lear. Indeed, the manner in which the threads of the story are woven together is almost as wonderful in the way of art as the carrying on the tide of passion, still varying and unimpaired, is on the score of nature.

Among the remarkable instances of this kind are Edgar's meeting with his old blind father; the deception he practices upon him when he pretends to lead him to the top of Dover-cliff—"Come on, sir, here's the place," to prevent his ending his life and miseries together; his encounter with the perfidious Steward whom he kills, and his finding the letter from Gonerill to his brother upon him which leads to the final catastrophe, and brings the Wheel of Justice "full circle home" to the guilty parties.

The bustle and rapid succession of events in the last scenes is surprising. But the meeting between Lear and Cordelia is by far the most affecting part of them. It has all the wildness of poetry, and all the heartfelt truth of nature. The previous account of her reception of the news of his unkind treatment, her involuntary reproaches to her sisters, "Shame, ladies, shame," Lear's backwardness to see his daughter, the picture of the desolate state to which he is reduced, "Alack, 'tis he; why he was met even now, as mad as the vex'd sea, singing aloud," only prepare the way for and heighten our expectation of what follows, and assuredly this expectation is not disappointed when through the tender care of Cordelia he revives and recollects her.

"Cordelia. How does my royal lord? How fares your majesty!
Lear: You do me wrong, to take me out o' the grave:
Thou art a soul in bliss; but I am bound
Upon a wheel of fire, that mine own tears
Do scald like molten lead.
Cordelia: Sir, do you know me?
Lear: You are a spirit I know: when did you die?
Cordelia. Still, still, far wide!
Physician: He's scarce awake; let him alone awhile.
Lear: Where have I been? Where am I? Fair daylight?
I am mightily abus'd.—I should even die with pity,
To see another thus.—I know not what to say.——
I will not swear these are my hands:—let's see;
I feel this pin prick. 'Would I were assur'd
Of my condition.
Cordelia: O, look upon me, sir,

And hold your hands in benediction o'er me:——
No, sir, you must not kneel.
Lear: Pray, do not mock me:
I am a very foolish fond old man,
Fourscore and upward;
Not an hour more, nor less: and, to deal plainly,
I fear, I am not in my perfect mind.
Methinks, I shou'd know you, and know this man;
Yet I am doubtful: for I am mainly ignorant
What place this is; and all the skill I have
Remembers not these garments; nor I know not
Where I did lodge last night: do not laugh at me;
For, as I am a man, I think this lady
To be my child Cordelia.
Cordelia: And so I am, I am!"

Almost equal to this in awful beauty is their consolation of each other when, after the triumph of their enemies, they are led to prison.

"Cordelia. We are not the first,
Who, with best meaning, have incurr'd the worst.
For thee, oppressed king, am I cast down;
Myself could else out-frown false fortune's frown.——
Shall we not see these daughters, and these sisters?
Lear: No, no, no, no! Come, let's away to prison:
We two alone will sing like birds i' the cage:
When thou dost ask me blessing, I'll kneel down,
And ask of thee forgiveness: so we'll live,
And pray, and sing, and tell old tales, and laugh
At gilded butterflies, and hear poor rogues
Talk of court news; and we'll talk with them too—
Who loses, and who wins; who's in, who's out;—
And take upon us the mystery of things,
As if we were God' spies: and we'll wear out,
In a walled prison, packs and sects of great ones,
That ebb and flow by the moon.
Edmund. Take them away.
Lear: Upon such sacrifices, my Cordelia,
The gods themselves throw incense."

The concluding events are sad, painfully sad, but their pathos is extreme. The oppression of the feelings is relieved by the very interest we take in the misfortunes of others, and by the reflections to which they give birth. Cordelia is hanged in prison by the orders of the bastard Edmund, which are known too late to be countermanded, and Lear dies broken-hearted, lamenting over her.

"Lear: And my poor fool is hanged! No, no, no life:
Why should a dog, a horse, a rat, have life,
And thou no breath at all? O, thou wilt come no more,
Never, never, never, never, never!
Pray you, undo this button: thank you, sir."

He dies, and indeed we feel the truth of what Kent says on the occasion

"Vex not his ghost: O, let him pass! he hates him,
That would upon the rack of this rough world
Stretch him out longer."

Yet a happy ending has been contrived for this play, which is approved of by Dr. Johnson and condemned by Schlegel. A better authority than either, on any subject in which poetry and feeling are concerned, has given it in favour of Shakespeare, in some remarks on the acting of Lear, with which we shall conclude this account.

"The LEAR of Shakespeare cannot be acted. The contemptible machinery with which they mimic the storm which he goes out in, is not more inadequate to represent the horrors of the real elements than any actor can be to represent Lear. The greatness of Lear is not in corporal dimension, but in intellectual; the explosions of his passions are terrible as a volcano: they are storms turning up and disclosing to the bottom that rich sea, his mind, with all its vast riches. It is his mind which is laid bare.

This case of flesh and blood seems too insignificant to be thought on; even as he himself neglects it. On the stage we see nothing but corporal infirmities and weakness, the impotence of rage; while we read it, we see not Lear, but we are Lear;—we are in his mind, we are sustained by a grandeur, which baffles the malice of daughters and storms; in the aberrations of his reason, we discover a mighty irregular power of reasoning, immethodised from the ordinary purposes of life, but exerting its powers, as the wind blows where it listeth, at will on the corruptions and abuses of mankind. What have looks or tones to do with that sublime identification of his age with that of the heavens themselves, when in his reproaches to them for conniving at the injustice of his children, he reminds them that "they themselves are old!"

What gesture shall we appropriate to this? What has the voice or the eye to do with such things? But the play is beyond all art, as the tamperings with it shew: it is too hard and stony: it must have love-scenes, and a happy ending. It is not enough that Cordelia is a daughter, she must shine as a lover too.

Tate has put his hook in the nostrils of this Leviathan, for Garrick and his followers, the shewmen of the scene, to draw it about more easily. A happy ending! as if the living martyrdom that Lear had gone through, the flaying of his feelings alive, did not make a fair dismissal from the stage of life the only decorous thing for him. If he is to live and be happy after, if he could sustain this worlds burden after, why all this pudder and preparation why torment us with all this unnecessary sympathy?

As if the childish pleasure of getting his gilt robes and sceptre again could tempt him to act over again his misused station, as if at his years and with his experience, any thing was left but to die." [See an article, called Theatralia, in the second volume of the Reflector, by Charles Lamb.

Four things have struck us in reading LEAR:

That poetry is an interesting study, for this reason, that it relates to whatever is most interesting in human life. Whoever therefore has a contempt for poetry, has a contempt for himself and humanity. That the language of poetry is superior to the language of painting; because the strongest of our recollections relate to feelings, not to faces. That the greatest strength of genius is shewn in describing the strongest passions: for the power of the imagination, in works of invention, must be in proportion to the force of the natural impressions, which are the subject of them.

That the circumstance which balances the pleasure against the pain in tragedy is, that in proportion to the greatness of the evil, is our sense and desire of the opposite good excited; and that our sympathy with actual suffering is lost in the strong impulse given to our natural affections, and carried away with the swelling tide of passion, that gushes from and relieves the heart.

Chapter 8

Characters in Shakespeare Play

RICHARD II

Richard II. is a play little known compared with Richard III. which last is a play that every unfledged candidate for theatrical fame chuses to strut and fret his hour upon the stage in; yet we confess that we prefer the nature and feeling of the one to the noise and bustle of the other; at least, as we are so often forced to see it acted. In richard II. the weakness of the king leaves us leisure to take a greater interest in the misfortunes of the man.

After the first act, in which the arbitrariness of his behaviour only proves his want of resolution, we see him staggering under the unlooked-for blows of fortune, bewailing his loss of kingly power, not preventing it, sinking under the aspiring genius of Bolingbroke, his authority trampled on, his hopes failing him, and his pride crushed and broken down under insults and injuries, which his own misconduct had provoked, but which he has not courage or manliness to resent.

The change of tone and behaviour in the two competitors for the throne according to their change of fortune, from the capricious sentence of banishment passed by Richard upon Bolingbroke, the suppliant offers and modest pretensions of the latter on his return, to the high and haughty tone with which he accepts Richard's resignation of the crown after the loss of all his power, the use which he makes of the deposed king to grace his triumphal progress through the streets of

London, and the final intimation of his wish for his death, which immediately finds a servile executioner, is marked throughout with complete effect and without the slightest appearance of effort. The steps by which Bolingbroke mounts the throne are those by which Richard sinks into the grave. We feel neither respect nor love for the deposed monarch; for he is as wanting in energy as in principle: but we pity him, for he pities himself.

His heart is by no means hardened against himself, but bleeds afresh at every new stroke of mischance, and his sensibility, absorbed in his own person, and unused to misfortune, is not only tenderly alive to its own sufferings, but without the fortitude to bear them. He is, however, human in his distresses; for to feel pain, and sorrow weakness, disappointment, remorse and anguish is the lot of humanity, and we sympathize with him accordingly. The sufferings of the man make us forget that he ever was a king.

The right assumed by sovereign power to trifle at its will with the happiness of others as a matter of course, or to remit its exercise as a matter of favour, is strikingly strewn in the sentence of banishment so unjustly pronounced on Bolingbroke and Mowbray, and in what Bolingbroke says when four years of his banishment are taken off, with as little reason.

"How long a time lies in one little word!
Four lagging winters and four wanton springs
End in a word: such is the breath of kings."

A more affecting image of the loneliness of a state of exile can hardly be given than by what Bolingbroke afterwards observes of his having "sighed his English breath in foreign clouds;" or than that conveyed in Mowbray's complaint at being banished for life.

"The language I have learned these forty years,
My native English, now I must forego;
And now my tongue's use is to me no more
Than an unstringed viol or a harp,
Or like a cunning instrument cas'd up,
Or being open, put into his hands

That knows no touch to tune the harmony.
I am too old to fawn upon a nurse,
Too far in years to be a pupil now."—

How very beautiful is all this, and at the same time how very English too!

Richard II. may be considered as the first of that series of English historical plays, in which "is hung armour of the invincible knights of old," in which their hearts seem to strike against their coats of mail, where their blood tingles for the fight, and words are but the harbingers of blows. Of this state of accomplished barbarism the appeal of Bolingbroke and Mowbray is an admirable specimen. Another of these "keen encounters of their wits," which serve to whet the talkers' swords, is where Aumerle answers in the presence of Bolingbroke to the charge which Bagot brings against him of being an accessory in Gloster's death.

"Fitzwater: If that thy velour stand on sympathies,
There is my gage, Aumerle, in gage to thine;
By that fair sun that shows me where thou stand'st
I heard thee say, and vauntingly thou spak'st it,
That thou wert cause of noble Gloster's death.
If thou deny'st it twenty times thou liest,
And I will turn thy falsehood to thy heart
Where it was forged, with my rapier's point.
Aumerle: Thou dar'st not, coward, live to see the day.
Fitzwater: Now, by my soul, I would it were this hour.
Aumerle: Fitzwater, thou art damn'd to hell for this.
Percy: Aumerle, thou liest; his honour is as true,
In this appeal, as thou art all unjust;
And that thou art so, there I throw my gage
To prove it on thee, to th' extremest point
Of mortal breathing. Seize it, if thou dar'st.
Aumerle: And if I do not, may my hands rot off,
And never brandish more revengeful steel
Over the glittering helmet of my foe.
Who sets me else? By heav'n, I'll throw at all.
I have a thousand spirits in my breast,
To answer twenty thousand such as you.

Surry. My lord Fitzwater, I remember well
The very time Aumerle and you did talk.
Fitzwater: My lord, 'tis true: you were in presence then:
And you can witness with me, this is true.
Surry: As false, by heav'n, as heav'n itself is true.
Fitzwater: Surry, thou liest.
Surry: Dishonourable boy,
That lie shall lye so heavy on my sword,
That it shall render vengeance and revenge,
Till thou the lie-giver and that lie rest
In earth as quiet as thy father's skull.
In proof whereof, there is mine honour's pawn:
Engage it to the trial, if thou dar'st.
Fitzwater: How fondly dost thou spur a forward horse:
If I dare eat or drink or breathe or live,
I dare meet Surry in a wilderness,
And spit upon him, whilst I say he lies,
And lies, and lies: there is my bond of faith,
To tie thee to thy strong correction.
As I do hope to thrive in this new world,
Aumerle is guilty of my true appeal."

The truth is, that there is neither truth nor honour in all these noble persons: they answer words with words, as they do blows with blows, in mere self defence: nor have they any principle whatever but that of courage in maintaining any wrong they dare commit, or any falsehood which they find it useful to assert. How different were these noble knights and "barons bold" from their more refined descendants in the present day, who instead of deciding questions of right by brute force, refer every thing to convenience, fashion, and good breeding! In point of any abstract love of truth or justice, they are just the same now that they were then.

The characters of old John of Gaunt and of his brother York, uncles to the King, the one stern and foreboding, the other honest, good-natured, doing all for the best, and therefore doing nothing, are well kept up. The speech of the former, in praise of England, is one of the most eloquent that ever was penned. We should perhaps hardly be disposed to feed the pampered egotism of our countrymen by quoting this description, were it not that the conclusion of it (which looks prophetic) may qualify any improper degree of exultation.

"This royal throne of kings, this sceptered isle,
This earth of Majesty, this seat of Mars,
This other Eden, demi-Paradise,
This fortress built by nature for herself
Against infection and the hand of war;
This happy breed of men, this little world,
This precious stone set in the silver sea,
Which serves it in the office of a wall
(Or as a moat defensive to a house)
Against the envy of less happy lands:
This nurse, this teeming womb of royal kings,
Fear'd for their breed and famous for their birth,
Renown'd for their deeds, as far from home,
For Christian service and true chivalry,
As is the sepulchre in stubborn Jewry
Of the world's ransom, blessed Mary's son;
This land of such dear souls, this dear dear land,
Dear for her reputation through the world,
Is now leas'd out (I die pronouncing it)
Like to a tenement or pelting farm.
England bound in with the triumphant sea,
Whose rocky shore beats back the envious surge
Of wat'ry Neptune, is bound in with shame,
With inky-blots and rotten parchment bonds.
That England, that was wont to conquer others,
Hath made a shameful conquest of itself."

The character of Bolingbroke, afterwards Henry IV. is drawn with a masterly hand:—patient for occasion, and then steadily availing himself of it, seeing his advantage afar off, but only seizing on it when he has it within his reach, humble, crafty, bold, and aspiring, encroaching by regular but slow degrees, building power on opinion, and cementing opinion by power. His disposition is first unfolded by Richard himself, who however is too self-willed and secure to make a proper use of his knowledge.

"Ourself and Bushy, Bagot here and Green,
Observed his courtship of the common people:
How he did seem to dive into their hearts,
With humble and familiar courtesy,
What reverence he did throw away on slaves;
Wooing poor craftsmen with the craft of smiles,
And patient under-bearing of his fortune,
As 'twere to banish their affections with him.
Off goes his bonnet to an oyster-wench;
A brace of draymen bid God speed him well,
And had the tribute of his supple knee,
With thanks my countrymen, my loving friends;
As were our England in reversion his,
And he our subjects' next degree in hope."
Afterwards, he gives his own character to Percy, in these words:
"I thank thee, gentle Percy, and be sure
I count myself in nothing else so happy,
As in a soul rememb'ring my good friends;
And as my fortune ripens with thy love,
It shall be still thy true love's recompense."

We know how he afterwards kept his promise. His bold assertion of his own rights, his pretended submission to the king, and the ascendancy which he tacitly assumes over him without openly claiming it, as soon as he has him in his power, are characteristic traits of this ambitious and politic usurper. But the part of Richard himself gives the chief interest to the play. His folly, his vices, his misfortunes, his reluctance to part with the crown, his fear to keep it, his weak and womanish regrets, his starting tears, his fits of hectic passion, his smothered majesty, pass in succession before us, and make a picture as natural as it is affecting.

Among the most striking touches of pathos are his wish "O that I were a mockery king of snow to melt away before the sun of Bolingbroke," and the incident of the poor groom who comes to visit him in prison, and tells him how "it yearned his heart that Bolingbroke upon his coronation day rode on Roan Barbary." We shall have occasion to return hereafter to the character of Richard II. in speaking of Henry VI. There is only one passage more, the description of his entrance into London with Bolingbroke, which we should like to quote here, if it had not been so used and worn out, so thumbed and got by rote, so praised and painted; but its beauty surmounts all these considerations.

"Duchess. My lord, you told me you would tell the rest,
When weeping made you break the story off
Of our two cousins coming into London.
York. Where did I leave?
Duchess. At that sad stop, my lord,
Where rude misgovern'd hands, from window tops,
Threw dust and rubbish on king Richard's head.
York. Then, as I said, the duke, great Bolingbroke,
Mounted upon a hot and fiery steed,
Which his aspiring rider seem'd to know,
With slow, but stately pace, kept on his course,
While all tongues cried—God save thee, Bolingbroke!
You would have thought the very windows spake,
So many greedy looks of young and old
Through casements darted their desiring eyes
Upon his visage; and that all the walls,
With painted imag'ry, had said at once—
Jesu preserve thee! welcome, Bolingbroke!
Whilst he, from one side to the other turning,
Bare-headed, lower than his proud steed's neck,
Bespake them thus—I thank you, countrymen:
And thus still doing thus he pass'd along.
Duchess. Alas, poor Richard! where rides he the while?
York. As in a theatre, the eyes of men,
After a well-grac'd actor leaves the stage,
Are idly bent on him that enters next,
Thinking his prattle to be tedious:
Even so, or with much more contempt, men's eyes
Did scowl on Richard; no man cried God save him!
No joyful tongue gave him his welcome home:
But dust was thrown upon his sacred head!
Which with such gentle sorrow he shook off—
His face still combating with tears and smiles,

The badges of his grief and patience—
That had not God, for some strong purpose, steel'd
The hearts of men, they must perforce have melted,
And barbarism itself have pitied him."

HENRY IV. IN TWO PARTS

If Shakespeare's fondness for the ludicrous sometimes led to faults in his tragedies (which was not often the case) he has made us amends by the character of Falstaff. This is perhaps the most substantial comic character that ever was invented! Sir John carries a most portly presence in the mind's eye; and in him, not to speak it profanely, "we behold the fulness of the spirit of wit and humour bodily."

We are as well acquainted with his person as his mind, and his jokes come upon us with double force and relish from the quantity of flesh through which they make their way, as he shakes his fat sides with laughter, or "lards the lean earth as he walks along." Other comic characters seem, if we approach and handle them, to resolve themselves into air, "into thin air;" but this is embodied and palpable to the grossest apprehension: it lies "three fingers deep upon the ribs," it plays about the lungs and the diaphragm with all the force of animal enjoyment.

His body is like a good estate to his mind, from which he receives rents and revenues of profit and pleasure in kind, according to its extent, and the richness of the soil. Wit is often a meagre substitute for pleasurable sensation; an effusion of spleen and petty spite at the comforts of others, from feeling none in itself. Falstaff's wit is an emanation of a fine constitution; an exuberance of good-humour and good-nature; an overflowing of his love of laughter, and good-fellowship; a giving vent to his heart's ease and over-contentment with himself and others.

He would not be in character, if he were not so fat as he is; for there is the greatest keeping in the boundless luxury of his imagination and the pampered self-indulgence of his physical appetites. He manures and nourishes his mind with jests, as he does his body with sack and sugar. He carves out his jokes, as he would a capon, or a haunch of venison, where there is cut and come again; and pours out upon them the oil of gladness.

His tongue drops fatness, and in the chambers of his brain "it snows of meat and drink." He keeps up perpetual holiday and open house, and we live with him in a round of invitations to a rump and dozen.—Yet we are not to suppose that he was a mere sensualist. All this is as much in imagination as in reality. His sensuality does not engross and stupify his other faculties, but "ascends me into the brain, clears away all the dull, crude vapours that environ it, and makes it full of nimble, fiery, and delectable shapes."

His imagination keeps up the ball after his senses have done with it. He seems to have even a greater enjoyment of the freedom from restraint, of good cheer, of his ease, of his vanity, in the ideal exaggerated descriptions which he gives of them, than in fact. He never fails to enrich his discourse with allusions to eating and drinking, but we never see him at table. He carries his own larder about with him, and he is himself "a ton of man."

His pulling out the bottle in the field of battle is a joke to shew his contempt for glory accompanied with danger, his systematic adherence to his Epicurean philosophy in the most trying circumstances. Again, such is his deliberate exaggeration of his own vices, that it does not seem quite certain whether the account of his hostess's bill, found in his pocket, with such an out-of-the-way charge for capons and sack with only one halfpenny-worth of bread, was not put there by himself as a trick to humour the jest upon his favourite propensities, and as a conscious caricature of himself.

He is represented as a liar, a braggart, a coward, a glutton, &c. and yet we are not offended but delighted with him; for he is all these as much to amuse others as to gratify himself. He openly assumes all these characters to shew the humourous part of them. The unrestrained indulgence of his own ease, appetites, and convenience, has neither malice nor hypocrisy in it. In a word, he is an actor in himself almost as much as upon the stage, and we no more object to the character of

Falstaff in a moral point of view than we should think of bringing an excellent comedian, who should represent him to the life, before one of the police offices.

We only consider the number of pleasant lights in which he puts certain foibles (the more pleasant as they are opposed to the received rules and necessary restraints of society) and do not trouble ourselves about the consequences resulting from them, for no mischievous consequences do result; Sir John is old as well as fat, which gives a melancholy retrospective tinge to the character; and by the disparity between his inclinations and his capacity for enjoyment, makes it still more ludicrous and fantastical.

The secret of Falstaff's wit is for the most part a masterly presence of mind, an absolute self-possession, which nothing can disturb. His repartees arise involuntary suggestions of his self-love; instinctive evasions of every thing that threatens to interrupt the career of his triumphant jollity and self-complacency. His very size floats him out of all his difficulties in a sea of rich conceits; and he turns round on the pivot of his convenience, with every occasion and at a moment's warning.

His natural repugnance to every unpleasant thought or circumstance of itself makes light of objections, and provokes the most extravagant and licentious answers in his own justification. His indifference to truth puts no check upon his invention, and the more improbable and unexpected his contrivances are, the more happily does he seem to be delivered of them, the anticipation of their effect acting as a stimulus to the gaiety of his fancy.

The success of one adventurous sally gives him spirits to undertake another: he deals always in round numbers, and his exaggerations and excuses are "open, palpable, monstrous as the father that begets them." His dissolute carelessness of what he says discovers itself in the first dialogue with the Prince.

"*Falstaff*: By the lord, thou say'st true, lad; and is not mine hostess of the tavern a most sweet wench?

P. Henry: As the honey of Hibla, my old lad of the castle; and is not a buff-jerkin a most sweet robe of durance?

Falstaff: How now, how now, mad wag, what in thy quips and thy quiddities? what a plague have I to do with a buff-jerkin?

P. Henry: Why, what a pox have I to do with mine hostess of the tavern?" In the same scene he afterwards affects melancholy, from pure satisfaction of heart, and professes reform, because it is the farthest thing in the world from his thoughts. He has no qualms of conscience, and therefore would as soon talk of them as of any thing else when the humour takes him.

"*Falstaff*: But Hal, I pr'ythee trouble me no more with vanity. I would to God thou and I knew where a commodity of good names were to be bought: an old lord of council rated me the other day in the street about you, sir; but I marked him not, and yet he talked very wisely, and in the street too.

P. Henry: Thou didst well, for wisdom cries out in the street, and no man regards it.

Falstaff: O, thou hast damnable iteration, and art indeed able to corrupt a saint. Thou hast done much harm unto me, Hal; God forgive thee for it. Before I knew thee, Hal, I knew nothing, and now I am, if a man should speak truly, little better than one of the wicked. I must give over this life, and I will give it over, by the lord; an I do not, I am a villain. I'll be damn'd for never a king's son in Christendom.

P. Henry: Where shall we take a purse to-morrow, Jack?

Falstaff: Where thou wilt, lad, I'll make one; an I do not, call me villain, and baffle me.

P. Henry: I see good amendment of life in thee, from praying to purse-taking.

Falstaff: Why, Hal, 'tis my vocation, Hal. 'Tis no sin for a man to labour in his vocation."

Of the other prominent passages, his account of his pretended resistance to the robbers, "who grew from four men in buckram into eleven" as the imagination of his own velour increased with his relating it, his getting off when the truth is discovered by pretending he knew the Prince, the scene in which in the person of the old king he lectures the prince and gives himself a good character, the soliloquy on honour, and description of his new-raised recruits, his meeting with the chief justice, his abuse of the Prince and Poins, who overhear him, to Doll Tearsheet, his reconciliation with Mrs. Quickly who has arrested him for an old debt, and whom he persuades to pawn her plate to lend him ten pounds more, and the scenes with Shallow and Silence, are all inimitable. Of all of them, the scene in which Falstaff plays the part, first, of the King, and then of Prince Henry, is the one that has been the most often quoted. We must quote it once more in illustration of our remarks.

Falstaff: Harry, I do not only marvel where thou spendest thy time, but also how thou art accompanied: for though the camomile, the more it is trodden on, the faster it grows, yet youth, the more it is wasted, the sooner it wears. That thou art my son, I have partly thy mother's word, partly my own opinion; but chiefly, a villainous trick of thine eye, and a foolish hanging of thy nether lip, that doth warrant me. If then thou be son to me, here lies the point;– –Why, being son to me, art thou so pointed at? Shall the blessed sun of heaven prove a micher, and eat blackberries?

A question not to be asked. Shall the son of England prove a thief, and take purses? a question not to be ask'd. There is a thing, Harry, which thou hast often heard of, and it is known to many in our land by the name of pitch: this pitch, as ancient writers do report, doth defile; so doth the company thou keepest: for, Harry, now I do not speak to thee in drink, but in tears; not in pleasure, but in passion; not in words only, but in woes also:—and yet there is a virtuous man, whom I have often noted in thy company, but I know not his name.

P. Henry: What manner of man, an it like your majesty?

Falstaff: A goodly portly man, i' faith, and a corpulent; of a cheerful look, a pleasing eye, and a most noble carriage; and, as I think, his age some fifty, or, by'r-lady, inclining to threescore; and now I do remember me, his name is Falstaff: if that man should be lewdly given, he deceiveth me; for, Harry, I see virtue in his looks. If then the fruit may be known by the tree, as the tree by the fruit, then peremptorily I speak it, there is virtue in that Falstaff: him keep with, the rest banish.

And tell me now, thou naughty varlet, tell me, where hast thou been this month?

P. Henry: Dost thou speak like a king? Do thou stand for me, and I'll play my father.

Falstaff. Depose me? if thou dost it half so gravely, so majestically, both in word and matter, hang me up by the heels for a rabbit-sucker, or a poulterer's hare.

P. Henry: Well, here I am set.

Falstaff: And here I stand:—judge, my masters.

P. Henry: Now, Harry, whence come you?

Falstaff: My noble lord, from Eastcheap.

P. Henry: The complaints I hear of thee are grievous.

Falstaff: S'blood, my lord, they are false:—nay, I'll tickle ye for a young prince, i'faith.

P. Henry: Swearest thou, ungracious boy? henceforth ne'er look on me. Thou art violently carried away from grace: there is a devil haunts thee, in the likeness of a fat old man; a tun of man is thy companion.

Why dost thou converse with that trunk of humours, that bolting-hutch of beastliness, that sworn parcel of dropsies, that huge bombard of sack, that stuff cloak-bag of guts, that roasted Manning-tree ox with the pudding in his belly, that reverend vice, that grey iniquity, that father ruffian, that vanity in years? wherein is he good, but to taste sack and drink it? wherein neat and cleanly, but to carve a capon and eat it? wherein cunning, but in craft? wherein crafty, but in villainy? wherein villainous, but in all things? wherein worthy but in nothing?

Falstaff: I would, your grace would take me with you; whom means your grace?

P. Henry: That villainous, abominable mis-leader of youth; Falstaff, that old white-bearded Satan.

Falstaff: My lord, the man I know.

P. Henry: I know thou dost.

Falstaff: But to say, I know more harm in him than in myself, were to say more than I know. That he is old (the more the pity) his white hairs do witness it: but that he is (saving your reverence) a whore-master, that I utterly deny. If sack and sugar be a fault, God help the wicked! if to be old and merry be a sin, then many an old host that I know is damned: if to be fat be to be hated, then Pharoah's lean kine are to be loved. No, my good lord; banish Peto, banish Bardolph, banish Poins: but for sweet Jack Falstaff, kind Jack Falstaff, true Jack Falstaff, valiant Jack Falstaff, and therefore more valiant, being as he is, old Jack Falstaff, banish not him thy Harry's company; banish plump Jack, and banish all the world.

P. Henry: I do, I will.

Knocking; and Hostess and Bardolph go out.

Re-enter BARDOLPH, running.

Bardolph: O, my lord, my lord; the sheriff:, with a most monstrous watch, is at the door.

Falstaff: Out, you rogue! play out the play: I have much to say in the behalf of that Falstaff."

One of the most characteristic descriptions of Sir John is that which Mrs. Quickly gives of him when he asks her "What is the gross sum that I owe thee?"

"*Hostess*: Marry, if thou wert an honest man, thyself, and the money too. Thou didst swear to me upon a parcel-gilt goblet, sitting in my Dolphin-chamber, at the round table, by a sea-coal fire on Wednesday in Whitsun-week, when the prince broke thy head for likening his father to a singing man of Windsor; thou didst swear to me then, as I was washing thy wound, to marry me, and make me my lady thy wife. Canst thou deny it?

Did not goodwife Keech, the butcher's wife, come in then, and call me gossip Quickly? coming in to borrow a mess of vinegar; telling us, she had a good dish of prawns; whereby thou didst desire to eat some;j whereby I told thee, they were ill for a green wound? And didst thou not, when she was gone down stairs, desire me to be no more so familiarity with such poor people; saying, that ere long they should call me madam? And didst thou not kiss me, and bid me fetch thee thirty shillings?

I put thee now to thy book-oath; deny it, if thou canst." This scene is to us the most convincing proof of Falstaff's power of gaining over the good will of those he was familiar with, except indeed Bardolph's somewhat profane exclamation on hearing the account of his death, "Would I were with him, wheresoe'er he is, whether in heaven or hell."

One of the topics of exulting superiority over others most common in Sir John's mouth is his corpulence and the exterior marks of good living which he carries about him, thus "turning his vices into commodity." He accounts for the friendship between the Prince and Poins, from "their legs being both of a bigness;" and compares Justice Shallow to "a man made after supper of a cheese-paring." There cannot be a more striking gradation of character than that between Falstaff and Shallow, and Shallow and Silence. It seems difficult at first to fall lower than the squire; but this fool, great as he is, finds an admirer and humble foil in his cousin Silence.

Vain of his acquaintance with Sir John, who makes a butt of him, he exclaims, "Would, cousin Silence, that thou had'st seen that which this knight and I have seen!"—"Aye, Master Shallow, we have heard the chimes at midnight," says Sir John. To Falstaff's observation "I did not think Master Silence had been a man of this mettle," Silence answers, "Who, I? I have been merry twice and once ere now."

What an idea is here conveyed of a prodigality of living? What good husbandry and economical self-denial in his pleasures? What a stock of lively recollections? It is curious that Shakespear has ridiculed in Justice Shallow, who was "in some authority under the king," that disposition to unmeaning tautology which is the regal infirmity of later times, and which, it may be supposed, he acquired from talking to his cousin Silence, and receiving no answers.

"*Falstaff*: You have here a goodly dwelling, and a rich.

Shallow: Barren, barren, barren; beggars all, beggars all, sir John marry, good air. Spread Davy, spread Davy. Well said, Davy.

Falstaff: This Davy serves you for good uses.

Shallow: A good varlet, a good varlet, a very good varlet. By the mass, I have drank too much sack at supper. A good varlet. Now sit down, now sit down. come, cousin."

The true spirit of humanity, the thorough knowledge of the stuff we are made of, the practical wisdom with the seeming fooleries in the whole of the garden-scene at Shallow's country seat, and just before in the exquisite dialogue between him and Silence on the death of old Double, have no parallel any where else. In one point of view, they are laughable in the extreme; in another they are equally affecting, if it is affecting to shew what a little thing is human life, what a poor forked creature man is!

The heroic and serious part of these two plays founded on the story of Henry IV. is not inferior to the comic and farcical. The characters of Hotspur and Prince Henry are two of the most beautiful and dramatic, both in themselves and from contrast, that ever were drawn. They are the essence of chivalry.

We like Hotspur the best upon the whole, perhaps because he was unfortunate.—The characters of their fathers, Henry IV. and old Northumberland, are kept up equally well. Henry naturally succeeds by his prudence and caution in keeping what he has got; Northumberland fails in his enterprise from an excess of the same quality, and is caught in the web of his own cold, dilatory policy. Owen Glendower is a masterly character. It is as bold and original as it is ineligible and thoroughly natural. The disputes between him and Hotspur are managed with infinite address and insight into nature. We cannot help pointing out here some very beautiful lines, where Hotspur describes the fight between Glendower and Mortimer.

"When on the gentle Severn's sedgy bank,
In single opposition hand to hand,
He did confound the best part of an hour
In changing hardiment with great Glendower:
Three times they breath'd, and three times did they drink,
Upon agreement, of swift Severn's flood;
Who then affrighted with their bloody looks,
Ran fearfully among the trembling reeds,
And hid his crisp head in the hollow bank,
Blood-stained with these valiant combatants."

The peculiarity and the excellence of Shakespeare's poetry is, that it seems as if he made his imagination the hand-maid of nature, and nature the play-thing of his imagination. He appears to have been all the characters, and in all the situations he describes. It is as if either he had had all their feelings, or had lent them all his genius to express themselves.

There cannot be stronger instances of this than Hotspur's rage when Henry IV. forbids him to speak of Mortimer, his insensibility to all that his father and uncle urge to calm him, and his fine abstracted apostrophe to honour, "By heaven methinks it were an easy leap to pluck bright honour from the moon," &c. After all, notwithstanding the gallantry, generosity, good temper, and idle freaks of the mad-cap Prince of Wales, we should not have been sorry, if Northumberland's force had come up in time to decide the fate of the battle at Shrewsbury, at least, we always heartily sympathise with Lady Percy's grief, when she exclaims,

"Had my sweet Harry had but half their numbers,
To-day might I (hanging on Hotspur's neck)
Have talked of Monmouth's grave."

The truth is, that we never could forgive the Prince's treatment of Falstaff; though perhaps Shakespear knew what was best, according to the history, the nature of the times, and of the man. We speak only as dramatic critics. What ever terror the French in those days might have of Henry V. yet to the readers of poetry at present, Falstaff is the better man of the two. We think of him and quote him oftener.

HENRY V

Henry v. in a very favourite monarch with the English nation, and he appears to have been also a favourite with Shakespear, who labours hard to apologise for the actions of the king, by shewing us the character of the man, as "the king of good fellows." He scarcely deserves this honour. He was fond of war and low company: we know little else of him. He was careless, dissolute, and ambitious; idle, or doing mischief. In private, he seemed to have no idea of the common decencies of life, which he subjected to a kind of regal licence; in public affairs, he seemed to have no idea of any rule of right or wrong, but brute force, glossed over with a little religious hypocrisy and archiepiscopal advice.

His principles did not change with his situation and professions. His adventure on Gadshill was a prelude to the affair of Agincourt, only a bloodless one; Falstaff was a puny prompter of violence and outrage, compared with the pious and politic Archbishop of Canterbury, who gave the king carte blanche, in a genealogical tree of his family, to rob and murder in circles of latitude and longitude abroad—to save the possessions of the church at home.

This appears in the speeches in Shakespear, where the hidden motives that actuate princes and their advisers in war and policy are better laid open than in speeches from the throne or woolsack. Henry, because he did not know how to govern his own kingdom, determined to make war upon his neighbours.

Because his own title to the crown was doubtful, he laid claim to that of France. Because he did not know how to exercise the enormous power, which had just dropped into his hands, to any one good purpose, he immediately undertook (a cheap and obvious resource of sovereignty) to do all the mischief he could. Even if absolute monarchs had the wit to find out objects of laudable ambition, they could only "plume up their wills" in adhering to the more sacred formula of the royal prerogative, "the right divine of kings to govern wrong," because will is only then triumphant when it is opposed to the will of others, because the pride of power is only then strewn, not when it consults the rights and interests of others, but when it insults and tramples on all justice and all humanity.

Henry declares his resolution "when France is his, to bend it to his awe, or break it all to pieces"—a resolution worthy of a conqueror, to destroy all that he cannot enslave; and what adds to the joke, he lays all the blame of the consequences of his ambition on those who will not submit tamely to his tyranny.

Such is the history of kingly power, from the beginning to the end of the world;—with this difference, that the object of war formerly, when the people adhered to their allegiance, was to depose kings; the object latterly, since the people swerved from their allegiance, has been to restore kings, and to make common cause against mankind. The object of our late invasion and conquest of France was to restore the legitimate monarch, the descendant of Hugh Capet, to the throne: Henry V. in his time made war on and deposed the descendant of this very Hugh Capet, on the plea that he was a usurper and illegitimate.

What would the great modern catspaw of legitimacy and restorer of divine right have said to the claim of Henry and the title of the descendants of Hugh Capet? Henry V. it is true, was a hero, a king of England, and the conqueror of the king of France. Yet we feel little love or admiration for him. He was a hero, that is, he was ready to sacrifice his own life for the pleasure of destroying thousands of other lives: he was a king of England, but not a constitutional one, and we only like kings according to the law; lastly, he was a conqueror of the French king, and for this we dislike him less than if he had conquered the French people.

How then do we like him? We like him in the play. There he is a very amiable monster, a very splendid pageant. As we like to gaze at a panther or a young lion in their cages in the Tower, and catch a pleasing horror from their glistening eyes, their velvet paws, and dreadless roar, so we take a very romantic, heroic, patriotic, and poetical delight in the boasts and feats of our younger Harry, as they appear on the stage and are confined to lines of ten syllables; where no blood follows the stroke that wounds our ears, where no harvest bends beneath horses' hoofs, no city flames, no little child is butchered, no dead men's bodies are found piled on heaps and festering the next morning—in the orchestra!

So much for the politics of this play; now for the poetry. Perhaps one of the most striking images in all Shakespeare is that given of war in the first lines of the Prologue.

"O for a muse of fire, that would ascend
The brightest heaven of invention,
A kingdom for a stage, princes to act,
And monarchs to behold the swelling scene!
Then should the warlike Harry, like himself,

Assume the port of Mars, and at his heels
Leash'd in like hounds, should famine, sword, and fire
Crouch for employment."

Rubens, if he had painted it, would not have improved upon this simile.

The conversation between the Archbishop of Canterbury and the Bishop of Ely relating to the sudden change in the manners of Henry V. is among the well-known Beauties of Shakespear. It is indeed admirable both for strength and grace. It has sometimes occurred to us that Shakespear, in describing "the reformation" of the Prince, might have had an eye to himself:

"Which is a wonder how his grace should glean it,
Since his addiction was to courses vain,
His companies unletter'd, rude and shallow,
His hours filled up with riots, banquets, sports;
And never noted in him any study,
Any retirement, any sequestration
From open haunts and popularity.
Ely. The strawberry grows underneath the nettle,
And wholesome berries thrive and ripen best
Neighbour'd by fruit of baser quality:
And so the prince obscur'd his contemplation
Under the veil of wildness, which no doubt
Grew like the summer-grass, fastest by night,
Unseen, yet crescive in his faculty."

This at least is as probable an account of the progress of the poet's mind as we have met with in any of the Essays on the Learning of Shakespeare.

Nothing can be better managed than the caution which the king gives the meddling Archbishop, not to advise him rashly to engage in the war with France, his scrupulous dread of the consequences of that advice, and his eager desire to hear and follow it.

"And God forbid, my dear and faithful lord,
That you should fashion, wrest, or bow your reading,
Or nicely charge your understanding soul
With opening titles miscreate, whose right

Suits not in native colours with the truth.
For God doth know how many now in health
Shall drop their blood, in approbation
Of what your reverence shall incite us to.
Therefore take heed how you impawn your person,
How you awake our sleeping sword of war;
We charge you in the name of God, take heed.
For never two such kingdoms did contend
Without much fall of blood, whose guiltless drops
Are every one a woe, a sore complaint
'Gainst him, whose wrong gives edge unto the swords
That make such waste in brief mortality.
Under this conjuration, speak, my lord;
For we will hear, note, and believe in heart,
That what you speak, is in your conscience wash'd,
As pure as sin with baptism."

Another characteristic instance of the blindness of human nature to every thing but its own interests is the complaint made by the king of "the ill neighbourhood" of the Scot in attacking England when she was attacking France.

"For once the eagle England being in prey,
To her unguarded nest the weasel Scot
Comes sneaking, and so sucks her princely eggs."

It is worth observing that in all these plays, which give an admirable picture of the spirit of the good old times, the moral inference does not at all depend upon the nature of the actions, but on the dignity or meanness of the persons committing them. "The eagle England" has a right "to be in prey," but "the weasel Scot" has none "to come sneaking to her nest," which she has left to pounce upon others.

Might was right, without equivocation or disguise, in that heroic and chivalrous age. The substitution of right for might, even in theory, is among the refinements and abuses of modern philosophy. A more beautiful rhetorical delineation of the effects of subordination in a commonwealth can hardly be conceived than the following:—

"For government, though high and low and lower,
Put into parts, doth keep in one consent,

Congruing in a full and natural close,
Like music.
Therefore heaven doth divide
The state of man in divers functions,
Setting endeavour in continual motion;
To which is fixed, as an aim or butt,
Obedience: for so work the honey bees;
Creatures that by a rule in nature, teach
The art of order to a peopled kingdom.
They have a king, and officers of sorts
Where some, like magistrates, correct at home;
Others, like merchants, venture trade abroad;
Others, like soldiers, armed in their stings,
Make boot upon the summer's velvet buds;
Which pillage they with merry march bring home
To the tent-royal of their emperor;
Who, busied in his majesty, surveys
The singing mason building roofs of gold,
The civil citizens kneading up the honey,
The poor mechanic porters crowding in
Their heavy burthens at his narrow gate;
The sad-eyed justice, with his surly hum,
Delivering o'er to executors pale
The lazy yawning drone. I this infer,
That many things, having full reference
To one consent, may work contrariously:
As many arrows, loosed several ways,
Come to one mark; as many ways meet in one town;
As many fresh streams meet in one salt sea;
As many lines close in the dial's centre;
So may a thousand actions, once a-foot,
End in one purpose, and be all well borne
Without defeat."

Henry V. is but one of Shakespear's second-rate plays. Yet by quoting passages, like this, from his second-rate plays alone, we might make a volume "rich with his praise,"

"As is the oozy bottom of the sea
With sunken wrack and sumless treasuries."

Of this sort are the king's remonstrance to Scroop, Grey, and Cambridge, on the detection of their treason, his address to the soldiers at the siege of Harfleur, and the still finer one before the battle of Agincourt, the description of the night before the battle, and the reflections on ceremony put into the mouth of the king.

"O hard condition; twin-born with greatness,
Subjected to the breath of every fool,
Whose sense no more can feel but his own wringing!
What infinite heart's ease must kings neglect,
That private men enjoy? and what have kings,
That privates have not too, save ceremony?
Save general ceremony?
And what art thou, thou idol ceremony?
What kind of god art thou, that suffer'st more
Of mortal griefs, than do thy worshippers?
What are thy rents? what are thy comings-in?
O ceremony, shew me but thy worth!
What is thy soul, O adoration?
Art thou aught else but place, degree, and form,
Creating awe and fear in other men?
Wherein thou art less happy, being feared,
Than they in fearing.
What drink'st thou oft, instead of homage sweet,
But poison'd flattery? O, be sick, great greatness,
And bid thy ceremony give thee cure!
Think'st thou, the fiery fever will go out
With titles blown from adulation?
Will it give place to flexure and low bending?
Can'st thou, when thou command'st the beggar's knee,
Command the health of it? No, thou proud dream,
That play'st so subtly with a king's repose,
I am a king, that find thee: and I know,
'Tis not the balm, the sceptre, and the ball,
The sword, the mace, the crown imperial,
The enter-tissu'd robe of gold and pearl,
The farsed title running 'fore the king,
The throne he sits on, nor the tide of pomp

That beats upon the shore of the world,
No, not all these, thrice-gorgeous ceremony,
Not all these, laid in bed majestical,
Can sleep so soundly as the wretched slave;
Who, with a body filled, and vacant mind,
Gets him to rest, cramm'd with distressful bread,
Never sees horrid night, the child of hell:
But, like a lacquey, from the rise to set,
Sweats in the eye of Phoebus, and all night
Sleeps in Elysium; next day, after dawn,
Doth rise, and help Hyperion to his horse;
And follows so the ever-running year
With profitable labour, to his grave:
And, but for ceremony, such a wretch,
Winding up days with toil, and nights with sleep,
Has the forehand and vantage of a king.
The slave, a member of the country's peace,
Enjoys it; but in gross brain little wots,
What watch the king keeps to maintain the peace,
Whose hours the peasant best advantages."

Most of these passages are well known: there is one, which we do not remember to have seen noticed, and yet it is no whit inferior to the rest in heroic beauty. It is the account of the deaths of York and Suffolk.

"Exeter: The duke of York commends him to your majesty.
K. Henry: Lives he, good uncle? thrice within this hour,
I saw him down; thrice up again, and fighting;
From helmet to the spur all blood he was.
Exeter: In which array (brave soldier) doth he lie,
Larding the plain: and by his bloody side
(Yoke-fellow to his honour-owing wounds)
The noble earl of Suffolk also lies.
Suffolk first died: and York, all haggled o'er,
Comes to him, where in gore he lay insteep'd,
And takes him by the beard; kisses the gashes,
That bloodily did yawn upon his face;
And cries aloud—Tarry, dear cousin Sufolk!
My soul shall thine keep company to heaven:

Tarry, sweet soul, for mine, then fly a-breast;
As, in this glorious and well-foughten field,
We kept together in our chivalry!
Upon these words I came, and cheer'd him up:
He smil'd me in the face, raught me his hand,
And, with a feeble gripe, says—Dear my lord,
Commend my service to my sovereign.
So did he turn, and over Suffolk's neck
He threw his wounded arm, and kissed his lips;
And so, espous'd to death, with blood he seal'd
A testament of noble-ending love."

But we must have done with splendid quotations. The behaviour of the king, in the difficult and doubtful circumstances in which he is placed, is as patient and modest as it is spirited and lofty in his prosperous fortune.

The character of the French nobles is also very admirably depicted; and the Dauphin's praise of his horse shews the vanity of that class of persons in a very striking point of view. Shakespear always accompanies a foolish prince with a satirical courtier, as we see in this instance.

The comic parts of Henry V. are very inferior to those of Henry IV. Falstaff is dead, and without him, Pistol, Nym, and Bardolph, are satellites without a sun. Fluellen the Welchman is the most entertaining character in the piece. He is good-natured, brave, choleric, and pedantic. His parallel between Alexander and Harry of Monmouth, and his desire to have "some disputations" with Captain Macmorris on the discipline of the Roman wars, in the heat of the battle, are never to be forgotten.

His treatment of Pistol is as good as Pistol's treatment of his French prisoner. There are two other remarkable prose passages in this play: the conversation of Henry in disguise with the three centinels on the duties of a soldier, and his courtship of Katherine in broken French. We like them both exceedingly, though the first savours perhaps too much of the king, and the last too little of the lover.

HENRY VI. IN THREE PARTS.

During the time of the civil wars of York and Lancaster,

England was a perfect bear-garden, and Shakespear has given us a very lively picture of the scene. The three parts of HENRY VI. convey a picture of very little else; and are inferior to the other historical plays. They have brilliant passages; but the general ground-work is comparatively poor and meagre, the style "flat and unraised." There are few lines like the following:—

"Glory is like a circle in the water;
Which never ceaseth to enlarge itself,
Till by broad spreading it disperse to naught."

The first part relates to the wars in France after the death of Henry V. and the story of the Maid of Orleans. She is here almost as scurvily treated as in Voltaire's Pucelle. Talbot is a very magnificent sketch: there is something as formidable in this portrait of him, as there would be in a monumental figure of him or in the sight of the armour which he wore.

The scene in which he visits the Countess of Auvergne, who seeks to entrap him, is a very spirited one, and his description of his own treatment while a prisoner to the French not less remarkable.

"Salisbury: Yet tell'st thou not how thou wert entertain'd.
Talbot: With scoffs and scorns, and contumelious taunts,
In open market-place produced they me,
To be a public spectacle to all.
Here, said they, is the terror of the French,
The scarecrow that affrights our children so.
Then broke I from the officers that led me,
And with my nails digg'd stones out of the ground,
To hurl at the beholders of my shame.
My grisly countenance made others fly,
None durst come near for fear of sudden death.
In iron walls they deem'd me not secure:
So great a fear my name amongst them spread,
That they suppos'd I could rend bars of steel,
And spurn in pieces posts of adamant.
Wherefore a guard of chosen shot I had:
They walk'd about me every minute-while;
And if I did but stir out of my bed,
Ready they were to shoot me to the heart."

The second part relates chiefly to the contests between the nobles during the minority of Henry, and the death of Gloucester, the good Duke Humphrey. The character of Cardinal Beaufort is the most prominent in the group: the account of his death is one of our author's master-pieces. So is the speech of Gloucester to the nobles on the loss of the provinces of France by the king's marriage with Margaret of Anjou. The pretensions and growing ambition of the Duke of York, the father of Richard III. are also very ably developed. Among the episodes, the tragi-comedy of Jack Cade, and the detection of the impostor Simcox are truly edifying.

The third part describes Henry's loss of his crown: his death takes place in the last act, which is usually thrust into the common acting play of Richard III. The character of Gloucester, afterwards King Richard, is here very powerfully commenced, and his dangerous designs and long-reaching ambition are fully described in his soliloquy in the third act, beginning, "Aye, Edward will use women honourably." Henry VI. is drawn as distinctly as his high-spirited Queen, and notwithstanding the very mean figure which Henry makes as a king, we still feel more respect for him than for his wife.

We have already observed that Shakespear was scarcely more remarkable for the force and marked contrasts of his characters than for the truth and subtlety with which he has distinguished those which approached the nearest to each other. For instance, the soul of Othello is hardly more distinct from that of Iago than th at of Desdemona is shewn to be from Aemilia's; the ambition of Macbeth is as distinct from the ambition of Richard III. as it is from the meekness of Duncan; the real madness of Lear is as different from the feigned madness of Edgar There is another instance of the same distinction in Hamlet and Ophelia.

Hamlet's pretended madness would make a very good real madness in any other author.] as from the babbling of the fool; the contrast between wit and folly in Falstaff and Shallow is not more characteristic though more obvious than the gradations of folly, loquacious or reserved, in Shallow and Silence; and again, the gallantry of Prince Henry is as little confounded with that of Hotspur as with the cowardice of Falstaff, or as the sensual and philosophic cowardice of the Knight is with the pitiful and cringing cowardice of Parolles. All these several personages were as different in Shakespear as they would have been in themselves: his imagination borrowed from the life, and every circumstance, object, motive, passion, operated there as it would in reality, and produced a world of men and women as distinct, as true and as various as those that exist in nature.

The peculiar property of Shakespear's imagination was this truth, accompanied with the unconsciousness of nature: indeed, imagination to be perfect must be unconscious, at least in production; for nature is so.—We shall attempt one example more in the characters of Richard II. and Henry VI. 8 The characters and situations of both these persons were so nearly alike, that they would have been completely confounded by a common-place poet. Yet they are kept quite distinct in Shakespear. Both were kings, and both unfortunate.

Both lost their crowns owing to their mismanagement and imbecility; the one from a thoughtless, wilful abuse of power, the other from an indifference to it. The manner in which they bear their misfortunes corresponds exactly to the causes which led to them. The one is always lamenting the loss of his power which he has not the spirit to regain; the other seems only to regret that he had ever been king, and is glad to be rid of the power, with the trouble; the effeminacy of the one is that of a voluptuary, proud, revengeful, impatient of contradiction, and inconsolable in his misfortunes; the effeminacy of the other is that of an indolent, good-natured mind, naturally averse to the turmoils of ambition and the cares of greatness, and who wishes to pass his time in monkish indolence and contemplation. Richard bewails the loss of the kingly power only as it was the means of gratifying his pride and luxury; Henry regards it only as a means of doing right, and is less desirous of the advantages to be derived from possessing it than afraid of exercising it wrong. In knighting a young soldier, he gives him ghostly advice 9 "Edward Plantagenet, arise a knight,

And learn this lesson, draw thy sword in right." 10 Richard II. in the first speeches of the play betrays his real character. In the first alarm of his pride, on hearing of Bolingbroke's rebellion, before his presumption has met with any check, he exclaims 11 "Mock not my senseless conjuration, lords:

This earth shall have a feeling, and these stones
Prove armed soldiers, ere her native king
Shall faulter under proud rebellious arms.
Not all the water in the rough rude sea
Can wash the balm from an anointed king;
The breath of worldly man cannot depose
The Deputy elected by the Lord.
For every man that Bolingbroke hath prest,
To lift sharp steel against our golden crown,
Heaven for his Richard hath in heavenly pay
A glorious angel; then if angels fight,

Weak men must fall; for Heaven still guards the right." 12 Yet, notwithstanding this royal confession of faith, on the very first news of actual disaster, all his conceit of himself as the peculiar favourite of Providence vanishes into air. 13 "But now the blood of twenty thousand men

Did triumph in my face, and they are fled.
All souls that will be safe fly from my side;

For time hath set a blot upon my pride." 14 Immediately after, however, recollecting that "cheap defence" of the divinity of kings which is to be found in opinion, he is for arming his name against his enemies. 15 "Awake, thou coward Majesty, thou sleep'st;

Is not the King's name forty thousand names?
Arm, arm, my name: a puny subject strikes

At thy great glory." 16 King Henry does not make any such vapouring resistance to the loss of his crown, but lets it slip from off his head as a weight which he is neither able nor willing to bear; stands quietly by to see the issue of the contest for his kingdom, as if it were a game at push-pin, and is pleased when the odds prove against him. 17 When Richard first hears of the death of his favourites, Bushy, Bagot, and the rest, he indignantly rejects all idea of any further efforts, and only indulges in the extravagant impatience of his grief and his despair, in that fine speech which has been so often quoted:—

18 "Aumerle. Where is the duke my father, with his power?

K. Richard. No matter where: of comfort no man speak:
Let's talk of graves, of worms, and epitaphs,
Make dust our paper, and with rainy eyes
Write sorrow in the bosom of the earth!
Let's chuse executors, and talk of wills:
And yet not so for what can we bequeath,
Save our deposed bodies to the ground?
Our lands, our lives, and all are Bolingbroke's,
And nothing can we call our own but death,
And that small model of the barren earth,
Which serves as paste and cover to our bones.
For heaven's sake let us sit upon the ground,
And tell sad stories of the death of Kings:
How some have been depos'd, some slain in war;
Some haunted by the ghosts they dispossess'd;
Some poisoned by their wives, some sleeping kill'd;
All murder'd: for within the hollow crown,
That rounds the mortal temples of a king,
Keeps death his court: and there the antic sits,
Scoffing his state, and grinning at his pomp!
Avowing him a breath, a little scene
To monarchize, be fear'd, and kill with looks;
Infusing him with self and vain conceit
As if this flesh, which walls about our life,
Were brass impregnable; and, humour'd thus,
Comes at the last, and, with a little pin,
Bores through his castle wall, and farewell king!
Cover your heads, and mock not flesh and blood
With solemn reverence; throw away respect,
Tradition, form, and ceremonious duty,
For you have but mistook me all this while:
I live on bread like you, feel want, taste grief,
Need friends, like you; subjected thus,
How can you say to me I am a king?" 19 There is as little

sincerity afterwards in his affected resignation to his fate, as there is fortitude in this exaggerated picture of his misfortunes before they have happened. 20 When Northumberland comes back with the message from Bolingbroke, he exclaims, anticipating the result, 21 "What must the king do now? Must he submit?

The king shall do it: must he be depos'd?
The king shall be contented: must he lose
The name of king? O' God's name let it go.
I'll give my jewels for a set of beads;
My gorgeous palace for a hermitage;
My gay apparel for an alms-man's gown;
My figur'd goblets for a dish of wood;
My sceptre for a palmer's walking staff;
My subjects for a pair of carved saints,
And my large kingdom for a little grave

A little, little grave, an obscure grave." 22 How differently is all this expressed in King Henry's soliloquy during the battle with Edward's party: 23 "This battle fares like to the morning's war,

When dying clouds contend with growing light,
What time the shepherd blowing of his nails,
Can neither call it perfect day or night.
Here on this mole-hill will I sit me down;
To whom God will, there be the victory!
For Margaret my Queen and Clifford too
Have chid me from the battle, swearing both
They prosper best of all whence I am thence.
Would I were dead, if God's good will were so.
For what is in this world but grief and woe?
O God! methinks it were a happy life
To be no better than a homely swain,
To sit upon a hill as I do now,
To carve out dials quaintly, point by point,
Thereby to see the minutes how they run:
How many make the hour full complete,
How many hours bring about the day,
How many days will finish up the year,
How many years a mortal man may live.

When this is known, then to divide the times:
So many hours must I tend my flock,
So many hours must I take my rest,
So many hours must I contemplate,
So many hours must I sport myself;
So many days my ewes have been with young,
So many weeks ere the poor fools will yean,
So many months ere I shall shear the fleece:
So many minutes, hours, weeks, months, and years
Past over, to the end they were created,
Would bring white hairs unto a quiet grave.
Ah! what a life were this! how sweet, how lovely!
Gives not the hawthorn bush a sweeter shade
To shepherds looking on their silly sheep,
Than doth a rich embroidered canopy
To kings that fear their subjects' treachery?
O yes it doth, a thousand fold it doth.
And to conclude, the shepherds' homely curds,
His cold thin drink out of his leather bottle,
His wonted sleep under a fresh tree's shade,
All which secure and sweetly he enjoys,
Is far beyond a prince's delicates,
Hid viands sparkling in a golden cup,
His body couched in a curious bed,

When care, mistrust, and treasons wait on him." 24 This is a true and beautiful description of a naturally quiet and contented disposition, and not, like the former, the splenetic effusion of disappointed ambition. 25 In the last scene of Richard II. his despair lends him courage: he beats the keeper, slays two of his assassins, and dies with imprecations in his mouth against Sir Pierce Exton, who "had staggered his royal person." Henry, when he is seized by the deer-stealers, only reads them a moral lecture on the duty of allegiance and the sanctity of an oath; and when stabbed by Gloucester in the Tower, reproaches him with his crimes, but pardons him his own death.

RICHARD III.

Richard III. may be considered as properly a stage-play:

it belongs to the theatre, rather than to the closet. We shall therefore criticise it chiefly with a reference to the manner in which we have seen it performed. It is the character in which Garrick came out: it was the second character in which Mr. Kean appeared, and in which he acquired his fame. Shakespeare we have always with us: actors we have only for a few seasons; and therefore some account of them may be acceptable, if not to our cotemporaries, to those who come after us, if "that rich and idle personage, Posterity," should deign to look into our writings.

It is possible to form a higher conception of the character of Richard than that given by Mr. Kean: but we cannot imagine any character represented with greater distinctness and precision, more perfectly articulated in every part. Perhaps indeed there is too much of what is technically called execution. When we first saw this celebrated actor in the part, we thought he sometimes failed from an exuberance of manner, and dissipated the impression of the general character by the variety of his resources. To be complete, his delineation of it should have more solidity, depth, sustained and impassioned feeling, with somewhat less brilliancy, with fewer glancing lights, pointed transitions, and pantomimic evolutions.

The Richard of Shakespear is towering and lofty; equally impetuous and commanding; haughty, violent, and subtle; bold and treacherous; confident in his strength as well as in his cunning; raised high by his birth, and higher by his talents and his crimes; a royal usurper, a princely hypocrite, a tyrant and a murderer of the house of Plantagenet.

"But I was born so high:
Our aery buildeth in the cedar's top,
And dallies with the wind, and scorns the sun."

The idea conveyed in these lines (which are indeed omitted in the miserable medley acted for RICHARD III.) is never lost sight of by Shakespear, and should not be out of the actor's mind for a moment. The restless and sanguinary Richard is not a man striving to be great, but to be greater than he is; conscious of his strength of will, his power of intellect, his daring courage, his elevated station; and making use of these advantages to commit unheard-of crimes, and to shield himself from remorse and infamy.

If Mr. Kean does not entirely succeed in concentrating all the lines of the character, as drawn by Shakespear, he gives an animation, vigour, and relief to the part which we have not seen equalled. He is more refined than Cooke; more bold, varied, and original than Kemble in the same character. In some parts he is deficient in dignity, and particularly in the scenes of state business, he has by no means an air of artificial authority. There is at times an aspiring elevation, an enthusiastic rapture in his expectations of attaining the crown, and at others a gloating expression of sullen delight, as if he already clenched the bauble, and held it in his grasp.

The courtship scene with Lady Anne is an admirable exhibition of smooth and smiling villainy. The progress of wily adulation, of encroaching humility, is finely marked by his action, voice and eye. He seems, like the first Tempter, to approach his prey, secure of the event, and as if success had smoothed his way before him.

The late Mr. Cooke's manner of representing this scene was more vehement, hurried, and full of anxious uncertainty. This, though more natural in general, was less in character in this particular instance. Richard should woo less as a lover than as an actor—to shew his mental superiority, and power of making others the play-things of his purposes. Mr. Kean's attitude in leaning against the side of the stage before he comes forward to address Lady Anne, is one of the most graceful and striking ever witnessed on the stage. It would do for Titian to paint.

The frequent and rapid transition of his voice from the expression of the fiercest passion to the most familiar tones of conversation was that which gave a peculiar grace of novelty to his acting on his first appearance. This has been since imitated and caricatured by others, and he himself uses the artifice more sparingly than he did. His bye-play is excellent. His manner of bidding his friends "Good night," after pausing with the point of his sword, drawn slowly backward and forward on the ground, as if considering the plan of the battle next day, is a particularly happy and natural thought.

He gives to the two last acts of the play the greatest animation and effect. He fills every part of the stage; and makes up for the deficiency of his person by what has been sometimes objected to as an excess of action. The concluding scene in which he is killed by Richmond is the most brilliant of the whole. He fights at last like one drunk with wounds; and the attitude in which he stands with his hands stretched out, after his sword is wrested from him, has a preternatural and terrific grandeur, as if his will could not be disarmed, and the very phantoms of his despair had power to kill.—Mr. Kean has since in a great measure effaced the impression of his Richard III. by the superior efforts of his genius in Othello (his masterpiece), in the murder-scene in Macbeth, in Richard II.

But stronger Shakespear felt for man alone in Sir Giles Overreach, and lastly in Oroonoko; but we still like to look back to his first performance of this part, both because it first assured his admirers of his future success, and because we bore our feeble but, at that time, not useless testimony to the merits of this very original actor, on which the town was considerably divided for no other reason than because they were original.

The manner in which Shakespear's plays have been generally altered or rather mangled by modern mechanists, is a disgrace to the English stage. The patch-work RICHARD III. which is acted under the sanction of his name, and which was manufactured by Cibber, is a striking example of this remark.

The play itself is undoubtedly a very powerful effusion of Shakespear's genius. The ground-work of the character of Richard, that mixture of intellectual vigour with moral depravity, in which Shakespear delighted to shew his strength—gave full scope as well as temptation to the exercise of his imagination. The character of his hero is almost every where predominant, and marks its lurid track throughout. The original play is however too long for representation, and there are some few scenes which might be better spared than preserved, and by omitting which it would remain a complete whole.

The only rule, indeed, for altering Shakespear is to retrench certain passages which may be considered either as superfluous or obsolete, but not to add or transpose any thing. The arrangement and developement of the story, and the mutual contrast and combination of the dramatis personae, are in general as finely managed as the developement of the characters or the expression of the passions.

This rule has not been adhered to in the present instance. Some of the most important and striking passages in the principal character have been omitted, to make room for idle and misplaced extracts from other plays; the only intention of which seems to have been to make the character of Richard as odious and disgusting as possible. It is apparently for no other purpose than to make Gloucester stab King Henry on the stage, that the fine abrupt introduction of the character in the opening of the play is lost in the tedious whining morality of the uxorious king (taken from another play);—we say tedious, because it interrupts the business of the scene, and loses its beauty and effect by having no intelligible connection with the previous character of the mild, well-meaning monarch.

The passages which the unfortunate Henry has to recite are beautiful and pathetic in themselves, but they have nothing to do with the world that Richard has to "bustle in." In the same spirit of vulgar caricature is the scene between Richard and Lady Anne (when his wife) interpolated without any authority, merely to gratify this favourite propensity to disgust and loathing. With the same perverse consistency, Richard, after his last fatal struggle, is raised up by some Galvanic process, to utter the imprecation, without any motive but pure malignity, which Shakespear has so properly put into the mouth of Northumberland on hearing of Percy's death.

To make room for these worse than needless additions, many of the most striking passages in the real play have been omitted by the foppery and ignorance of the prompt-book critics. We do not mean to insist merely on passages which are fine as poetry and to the reader, such as Clarence's dream, &c. but on those which are important to the understanding of the character, and peculiarly adapted for stage-effect. We will give the following as instances among several others. The first is the scene where Richard enters abruptly to the queen and her friends to defend himself:—

"Gloucester. They do me wrong, and I will not endure it.
Who are they that complain unto the king,
That I forsooth am stern, and love them not?
By holy Paul, they love his grace but lightly,
That fill his ears with such dissentious rumours:
Because I cannot flatter and look fair;
Smile in men's faces, smooth, deceive, and cog,
Duck with French nods, and apish courtesy,
I must be held a rancourous enemy.
Cannot a plain man live, and think no harm,
But thus his simple truth must be abus'd
With silken, sly, insinuating Jacks?
Gray. To whom in all this presence speaks your grace?
Gloucester. To thee, that hast nor honesty nor grace;
When have I injur'd thee, when done thee wrong?
Or thee? or thee? or any of your faction?
A plague upon you all!"

Nothing can be more characteristic than the turbulent pretensions to meekness and simplicity in this address. Again, the versatility and adroitness of Richard is admirably described in the following ironical conversation with Brakenbury:—

"Brakenbury: I beseech your graces both to pardon me.
His majesty hath straitly given in charge,
That no man shall have private conference,
Of what degree soever, with your brother.
Gloucester: E'en so, and please your worship, Brakenbury,
You may partake of any thing we say:
We speak no treason, man—we say the king
Is wise and virtuous, and his nohle queen
Well strook in years, fair, and not jealous.
We say that Shore's wife hath a pretty foot,
A cherry lip, a passing pleasing tongue;
That the queen's kindred are made gentlefolks.
How say you, sir? Can you deny all this?

Brakenbury: With this, my lord, myself have nought to do.
Gloucester. What, fellow, naught to do with mistress Shore?
I tell you, sir, he that doth naught with her,
Excepting one, were best to do it secretly alone.
Brakenbury: What one, my lord?

Gloucester: Her husband, knave—would'st thou betray me?"

The feigned reconciliation of Gloucester with the queen's kinsmen is also a master-piece. One of the finest strokes in the play, and which serves to shew as much as any thing the deep, plausible manners of Richard, is the unsuspecting security of Hastings, at the very time when the former is plotting his death, and when that very appearance of cordiality and good-humour on which Hastings builds his confidence arises from Richard's consciousness of having betrayed him to his ruin. This, with the whole character of Hastings, is omitted.

Perhaps the two most beautiful passages in the original play are the farewel apostrophe of the queen to the Tower, where her children are shut up from her, and Tyrrel's description of their death. We will finish our quotations with them.

"Queen: Stay, yet look back with me unto the Tower;
Pity, you ancient stones, those tender babes,
Whom envy hath immured within your walls
Rough cradle for such little pretty ones,
Rude, rugged nurse, old sullen play-fellow,
For tender princes!"

The other passage is the account of their death by Tyrrel:—

"Dighton and Forrest, whom I did suborn
To do this piece of ruthless butchery,
Albeit they were flesh'd villains, bloody dogs,
Wept like to children in their death's sad story:
O thus! quoth Dighton, lay the gentle babes;
Thus, thus, quoth Forrest, girdling one another
Within their innocent alabaster arms;
Their lips were four red roses on a stalk,
And in that summer beauty kissed each other;
A book of prayers on their pillow lay,

Which once, quoth Forrest, almost changed my mind:
But oh the devil!—there the villain stopped;
When Dighton thus told on—we smothered
The most replenished sweet work of nature,
That from the prime creation ere she framed."

These are some of those wonderful bursts of feeling, done to the life, to the very height of fancy and nature, which our Shakespear alone could give. We do not insist on the repetition of these last passages as proper for the stage: we should indeed be loth to trust them in the mouth of almost any actor: but we should wish them to be retained in preference at least to the fantoccini exhibition of the young princes, Edward and York, bandying childish wit with their uncle.

HENRY VIII.

This play contains little action or violence of passion, yet it has considerable interest of a more mild and thoughtful cast, and some of the most striking passages in the author's works. The character of Queen Katherine is the most perfect delineation of matronly dignity, sweetness, and resignation, that can be conceived. Her appeals to the protection of the king, her remonstrances to the cardinals, her conversations with her women, shew a noble and generous spirit accompanied with the utmost gentleness of nature. What can be more affecting than her answer to Campeius and Wolsey, who come to visit her as pretended friends.

Nay, forsooth, my friends,
They that my trust must grow to, live not here;
They are, as all my comforts are, far hence,
In mine own country, lords."

Dr. Johnson observes of this play, that "the meek sorrows and virtuous distress of Katherine have furnished some scenes, which may be justly numbered among the greatest efforts of tragedy. But the genius of Shakespear comes in and goes out with Katherine. Every other part may be easily conceived and easily written." This is easily said; but with all due deference to so great a reputed authority as that of Johnson, it is not true. For instance, the scene of Buckingham led to execution is one of the most affecting and natural in Shakespear, and one to which there is hardly an approach in any other author.

Again, the character of Wolsey, the description of his pride and of his fall, are inimitable, and have, besides their gorgeousness of effect, a pathos, which only the genius of Shakespear could lend to the distresses of a proud, bad man, like Wolsey. There is a sort of child-like simplicity in the very helplessness of his situation, arising from the recollection of his past overbearing ambition. After the cutting sarcasms of his enemies on his disgrace, against which he bears up with a spirit conscious of his own superiority, he breaks out into that fine apostrophe—

"Farewel, a long farewel, to all my greatness!
This is the state of man; to-day he puts forth
The tender leaves of hope, to-morrow blossoms,
And bears his blushing honours thick upon him;
The third day, comes a frost, a killing frost;
And—when he thinks, good easy man, full surely
His greatness is a ripening—nips his root,
And then he falls, as I do. I have ventur'd,
Like little wanton boys that swim on bladders,
These many summers in a sea of glory;
But far beyond my depth: my high-blown pride
At length broke under me; and now has left me,
Weary and old with service, to the mercy
Of a rude stream, that must for ever hide me.
Vain pomp and glory of the world, I hate ye!
I feel my heart new open'd: O how wretched
Is that poor man, that hangs on princes' favours!
There is betwixt that smile we would aspire to,
That sweet aspect of princes, and our ruin,
More pangs and fears than war and women have;
And when he falls, he falls like Lucifer,
Never to hope again!"—

There is in this passage, as well as in the well-known dialogue with Cromwell which follows, something which stretches beyond common-place; nor is the account which Griffiths gives of Wolsey's death less Shakespearian; and the candour with which Queen Katherine listens to the praise of "him whom of all men while living she hated most" adds the last graceful finishing to her character.

Among other images of great individual beauty might be mentioned the description of the effect of Ann Boleyn's presenting herself to the crowd at her coronation.

"While her grace sat down
To rest awhile, some half an hour or so,
In a rich chair of state, opposing freely
The beauty of her person to the people.
Believe me, sir, she is the goodliest woman
That ever lay by man. Which when the people
Had the full view of, such a noise arose
As the shrouds make at sea in a stiff tempest,
As loud and to as many tunes."

The character of Henry VIII. is drawn with great truth and spirit. It is like a very disagreeable portrait, sketched by the hand of a master. His gross appearance, his blustering demeanour, his vulgarity, his arrogance, his sensuality, his cruelty, his hypocrisy, his want of common decency and common humanity, are marked in strong lines. His traditional peculiarities of expression complete the reality of the picture. The authoritative expletive, "Ha!" with which he intimates his indignation or surprise, has an effect like the first startling sound that breaks from a thunder-cloud.

He is of all the monarchs in our history the most disgusting: for he unites in himself all the vices of barbarism and refinement, without their virtues.

Other kings before him (such as Richard III.) were tyrants and murderers out of ambition or necessity: they gained or established unjust power by violent means: they destroyed their enemies, or those who barred their access to the throne or made its tenure insecure. But Henry VIII.'s power is most fatal to those whom he loves: he is cruel and remorseless to pamper his luxurious appetites: bloody and voluptuous; an amorous murderer; an uxorious debauchee. His hardened insensibility to the feelings of others is strengthened by the most profligate self-indulgence.

The religious hypocrisy, under which he masks his cruelty and his lust, is admirably displayed in the speech in which he describes the first misgivings of his conscience and its increasing throes and terrors, which have induced him to divorce his queen.

The only thing in his favour in this play is his treatment of Cranmer: there is also another circumstance in his favour, which is his patronage of Hans Holbein.—It has been said of Shakespear—"No maid could live near such a man." It might with as good reason be said—"No king could live near such a man." His eye would have penetrated through the pomp of circumstance and the veil of opinion. As it is, he has represented such persons to the life—his plays are in this respect the glass of history—he has done them the same justice as if he had been a privy counsellor all his life, and in each successive reign.

Kings ought never to be seen upon the stage. In the abstract, they are very disagreeable characters: it is only while living, that they are "the best of kings." It is their power, their splendour, it is the apprehension of the personal consequences of their favour or their hatred, that dazzles the imagination and suspends the judgment of their favourites or their vassals; but death cancels the bond of allegiance and of interest; and seen as they were, their power and their pretensions look monstrous and ridiculous.

The charge brought against modern philosophy as inimical to loyalty is unjust, because it might as well be brought against other things. No reader of history can be a lover of kings. We have often wondered that Henry VIII. as he is drawn by Shakespear, and as we have seen him represented in all the bloated deformity of mind and person, is not hooted from the English stage.

KING JOHN.

King John is the last of the historical plays we shall have to speak of; and we are not sorry that it is. If we are to indulge our imaginations, we had rather do it upon an imaginary theme; if we are to find subjects for the exercise of our pity and terror, we prefer seeking them in fictitious danger and fictitious distress.

It gives a soreness to our feelings of indignation or sympathy, when we know that in tracing the progress of sufferings and crimes, we are treading upon real ground, and recollect that the poet's "dream" denoted a foregone conclusion—irrevocable ills, not conjured up by fancy, but placed beyond the reach of poetical justice. That the treachery of King John, the death of Arthur, the grief of Constance, had a real truth in history, sharpens the sense of pain, while it hangs a leaden weight on the heart and the imagination.

Something whispers us that we have no right to make a mock of calamities like these, or to turn the truth of things into the puppet and play-thing of our fancies. "To consider thus" may be "to consider too curiously;" but still we think that the actual truth of the particular events, in proportion as we are conscious of it, is a drawback on the pleasure as well as the dignity of tragedy.

King Jonh has all the beauties of language and all the richness of the imagination to relieve the painfulness of the subject. The character of King John himself is kept pretty much in the back-ground; it is only marked in by comparatively slight indications. The crimes he is tempted to commit are such as are thrust upon him rather by circumstances and opportunity then of his own seeking: he is here represented as more cowardly than cruel, and as more contemptible than odious. The play embraces only a part of his history. There are however few characters on the stage that excite more disgust and loathing.

He has no intellectual grandeur or strength of character to shield him from the indignation which his immediate conduct provokes: he stands naked and defenseless, in that respect, to the worst we can think of him: and besides, we are impelled to put the very worst construction on his meanness and cruelty by the tender picture of the beauty and helplessness of the object of it, as well as by the frantic and heart-rending pleadings of maternal despair. We do not forgive him the death of Arthur because he had too late revoked his doom and tried to prevent it, and perhaps because he has himself repented of his black design, our moral sense gains courage to hate him the more for it. We take him at his word, and think his purposes must be odious indeed, when he himself shrinks back from them.

The scene in which King John suggests to Hubert the design of murdering his nephew is a master-piece of dramatic skill, but it is still inferior, very inferior to the scene between Hubert and Arthur, when the latter learns the orders to put out his eyes. If any thing ever was penned, heart-piercing, mixing the extremes of terror and pity, of that which shocks and that which soothes the mind, it is this scene. We will give it entire, though perhaps it is tasking the reader's sympathy too much.

"Enter Hubert and Executioner.

Hubert: Heat me these irons hot, and look you stand
Within the arras; when I strike my foot
Upon the bosom of the ground, rush forth
And bind the boy, which you shall find with me,
Fast to the chair: be heedful: hence, and watch.
Executioner: I hope your warrant will bear out the deed.
Hubert: Uncleanly scruples! fear not you; look to't.—
Young lad, come forth; I have to say with you.

Enter Arthur.

Arthur: Good morrow, Hubert.
Hubert: Morrow, little Prince.
Arthur: As little prince (having so great a title
To be more prince) as may be. You are sad.
Hubert: Indeed have been merrier.
Arthur: Mercy on me!
Methinks no body should be sad but I;
Yet I remember when I was in France,
Young gentlemen would be as sad as night,
Only for wantonness. By my Christendom,
So were I out of prison, and kept sheep,
I should be merry as the day is long.
And so I would be here, but that I doubt
My uncle practices more harm to me.

He is afraid of me, and I of him.
Is it my fault that I was Geoffery's son?
Indeed it is not, and I would to heav'n
I were your son, so you would love me, Hubert.
Hubert: If I talk to him, with his innocent prate
He will awake my mercy, which lies dead;
Therefore I will be sudden, and dispatch. [Aside.
Arthur: Are you sick, Hubert? you look pale to-day?
In sooth, I would you were a little sick,
That I might sit all night and watch with you.
Alas, I love you more than you do me.
Hubert: His words do take possession of my bosom.
Read here, young Arthur— [Shewing a paper.
How now, foolish rheum, [Aside.
Turning dis-piteous torture out of door!
I must be brief, lest resolution drop
Out at mine eyes in tender womanish tears.—
Can you not read it? Is it not fair writ?
Arthur: Too fairly, Hubert, for so foul effect.
Must you with irons burn out both mine eyes?
Hubert: Young boy, I must.
Arthur: And will you?
Hubert: And I will.
Hubert: Have you the heart? When your head did but ache,
I knit my handkerchief about your brows,
(The best I had, a princess wrought it me)
And I did never ask it you again;
And with my hand at midnight held your head;
And, like the watchful minutes to the hour,
Still and anon chear'd up the heavy time,
Saying, what lack you? and where lies your grief?
Or, what good love may I perform for you?
Many a poor man's son would have lain still,
And ne'er have spoke a loving word to you;
But you at your sick service had a prince.
Nay, you may think my love was crafty love,
And call it cunning. Do, and if you will:
If heav'n be pleas'd that you must use me ill,

Why then you must.—Will you put out mine eyes?
These eyes, that never did, and never shall,
So much as frown on you?
Hubert: I've sworn to do it;
And with hot irons must I burn them out.
Arthur: Oh if an angel should have come to me,
And told me Hubert should put out mine eyes,
I would not have believ'd a tongue but Hubert's.
Hubert: Come forth; do as I bid you.
[Stamps, and the men enter.
Arthur: O save me, Hubert, save me! my eyes are out
Even with the fierce looks of these bloody men.
Hubert: Give me the iron, I say, and bind him here.
Arthur: Alas, what need you be so boist'rous rough?
I will not struggle, I will stand stone-still.
For heav'n's sake, Hubert, let me not be bound.
Nay, hear me, Hubert, drive these men away,
And I will sit as quiet as a lamb.
I will not stir, nor wince, nor speak a word,
Nor look upon the iron angrily:
Thrust but these men away, and I'll forgive you,
Whatever torment you do put me to.
Hubert: Go, stand within; let me alone with him.
Executioner: I am best pleas'd to be from such a deed.
[Exit.
Arthur: Alas, I then have chid away my friend.
He hath a stern look, but a gentle heart;
Let him come back, that his compassion may
Give life to yours.
Hubert: Come, boy, prepare yourself.
Arthur: Is there no remedy?
Hubert: None, but to lose your eyes.
Arthur. O heav'n! that there were but a moth in yours,
A grain, a dust, a gnat, a wand'ring hair,
Any annoyance in that precious sense:
Then feeling what small things are boisterous there,
Your vile intent must needs seem horrible.
Hubert: Is this your promise? go to, hold your tongue.

Arthur: Let me not hold my tongue; let me not, Hubert;
Or, Hubert, if you will, cut out my tongue,
So I may keep mine eyes. O spare mine eyes!
Though to no use, but still to look on you.
Lo, by my troth, the instrument is cold,
And would not harm me.
Hubert: I can heat it, boy.
Arthur: No, in good sooth, the fire is dead with grief.
Being create for comfort, to be us'd
In undeserv'd extremes; see else yourself,
There is no malice in this burning coal;
The breath of heav'n hath blown its spirit out,
And strew'd repentant ashes on its head.
Hubert: But with my breath I can revive it, boy.
Arthur: All things that you should use to do me wrong,
Deny their office; only you do lack
That mercy which fierce fire and iron extend,
Creatures of note for mercy-lacking uses.
Hubert: Well, see to live; I will not touch thine eyes
For all the treasure that thine uncle owns:
Yet I am sworn, and I did purpose, boy,
With this same very iron to burn them out.
Arthur: O, now you look like Hubert. All this while
You were disguised.
Hubert: Peace no more. Adieu,
Your uncle must not know but you are dead.
I'll fill these dogged spies with false reports
And, pretty child, sleep doubtless and secure,
That Hubert, for the wealth of all the world,
Will not offend thee.
Arthur: O heav'n! I thank you, Hubert.
Hubert: Silence, no more; go closely in with me;
Much danger do I undergo for thee. [Exeunt."

His death afterwards, when he throws himself from his prison-walls, excites the utmost pity for his innocence and friendless situation, and well justifies the exaggerated denunciations of Falconbridge to Hubert whom he suspects wrongfully of the deed.

"There is not yet so ugly a fiend of hell
As thou shalt be, if thou did'st kill this child.
If thou did'st but consent
To this most cruel act, do but despair:
And if thou want'st a cord, the smallest thread
That ever spider twisted from her womb
Will strangle thee; a rush will be a beam
To hang thee on: or would'st thou drown thyself,
Put but a little water in a spoon,
And it shall be as all the ocean,
Enough to stifle such a villain up."

The excess of maternal tenderness, rendered desperate by the fickleness of friends and the injustice of fortune, and made stronger in will, in proportion to the want of all other power, was never more finely expressed than in Constance. The dignity of her answer to King Philip, when she refuses to accompany his messenger, "To me and to the state of my great grief, let kings assemble," her indignant reproach to Austria for deserting her cause, her invocation to death, "that love of misery," however fine and spirited, all yield to the beauty of the passage, where, her passion subsiding into tenderness, she addresses the Cardinal in these words:—

"Oh father Cardinal, I have heard you say
That we shall see and know our friends in heaven:
If that be, I shall see my boy again,
For since the birth of Cain, the first male child,
To him that did but yesterday suspire,
There was not such a gracious creature born.
But now will canker-sorrow eat my bud,
And chase the native beauty from his cheek,
And he will look as hollow as a ghost,
As dim and meagre as an ague's fit,
And so he'll die; and rising so again,
When I shall meet him in the court of heav'n,
I shall not know him; therefore never, never
Must I behold my pretty Arthur more.
K. Philip. You are as fond of grief as of your child.
Constance. Grief fills the room up of my absent child:

Lies in his bed, walks up and down with me;
Puts on his pretty looks, repeats his words,
Remembers me of all his gracious parts;
Stuffs out his vacant garments with his form.
Then have I reason to be fond of grief."

The contrast between the mild resignation of Queen Katherine to her own wrongs, and the wild, uncontroulable affliction of Constance for the wrongs which she sustains as a mother, is no less naturally conceived than it is ably sustained throughout these two wonderful characters.

The accompaniment of the comic character of the Bastard was well chosen to relieve the poignant agony of suffering, and the cold, cowardly policy of behaviour in the principal characters of this play. Its spirit, invention, volubility of tongue, and forwardness in action, are unbounded. Aliquando sufflaminandus erat, says Ben Jonson of Shakespeare. But we should be sorry if Ben Jonson had been his licenser. We prefer the heedless magnanimity of his wit infinitely to all Jonson's laborious caution. The character of the Bastard's comic humour is the same in essence as that of other comic characters in Shakespeare; they always run on with good things and are never exhausted; they are always daring and successful. They have words at will and a flow of wit, like a flow of animal spirits. The difference between Falconbridge and the others is that he is a soldier, and brings his wit to bear upon action, is courageous with his sword as well as tongue, and stimulates his gallantry by his jokes, his enemies feeling the sharpness of his blows and the sting of his sarcasms at the same time.

Among his happiest sallies are his descanting on the composition of his own person, his invective against "commodity, tickling commodity," and his expression of contempt for the Archduke of Austria, who had killed his father, which begins in jest but ends in serious earnest. His conduct at the siege of Angiers shews that his resources were not confined to verbal retorts. The same exposure of the policy of courts and camps, of kings, nobles, priests, and cardinals, takes place here as in the other plays we have gone through, and we shall not go into a disgusting repetition.

This, like the other plays taken from English history, is written in a remarkably smooth and flowing style, very different from some of the tragedies, Macbeth, for instance. The passages consist of a series of single lines, not running into one another.

This peculiarity in the versification, which is most common in the three parts of Henry VI. has been assigned as a reason why those plays were not written by Shakespear. But the same structure of verse occurs in his other undoubted plays, as in Richard II. and in King John. The following are instances:

"That daughter there of Spain, the lady Blanch,
Is near to England; look upon the years
Of Lewis the dauphin, and that lovely maid.
If lusty love should go in quest of beauty,
Where should he find it fairer than in Blanch?
If zealous love should go in search of virtue,
Where should he find it purer than in Blanch?
If love ambitious sought a match of birth,
Whose veins bound richer blood than lady Blanch?
Such as she is, in beauty, virtue, birth,
Is the young dauphin every way complete:
Is not complete of, say he is not she;
And she wants nothing, to name want,
If want it be not, that she is not he.
He is the half part of a blessed man,
Left to be finished by such as she;
And she a fair divided excellence,
Whose fulness of perfection lies in him.
O, two such silver currents, when they join,
Do glorify the banks that bound them in:
And two such shores to two such streams made one,
Two such controuling bounds, shall you be, kings,
To these two princes, if you marry them."

Another instance, which is certainly very happy as an example of the simple enumeration of a number of particulars, is Salisbury's remonstrance against the second crowning of the king.

"Therefore to be possessed with double pomp,
To guard a title that was rich before;
To gild refined gold, to paint the lily,
To throw a perfume on the violet,
To smooth the ice, to add another hue
Unto the rainbow, or with taper light
To seek the beauteous eye of heav'n to garnish;
Is wasteful and ridiculous excess."

Chapter 9

Twelfth Night; or, What You Will

This is justly considered as one of the most delightful of Shakespeare's comedies. It is full of sweetness and pleasantry. It is perhaps too good-natured for comedy. It has little satire, and no spleen. It aims at the ludicrous rather than the ridiculous. It makes us laugh at the follies of mankind, not despise them, and still less bear any ill-will towards them. Shakespeare's comic genius resembles the bee rather in its power of extracting sweets from weeds or poisons, than in leaving a sting behind it.

He gives the most amusing exaggeration of the prevailing foibles of his characters, but in a way that they themselves, instead of being offended at, would almost join in to humour; he rather contrives opportunities for them to shew themselves off in the happiest lights, than renders them contemptible in the perverse construction of the wit or malice of others. There is a certain stage of society in which people become conscious of their peculiarities and absurdities, affect to disguise what they are, and set up pretensions to what they are not.

This gives rise to a corresponding style of comedy, the object of which is to detect the disguises of self-love, and to make reprisals on these preposterous assumptions of vanity, by marking the contrast between the real and the affected character as severely as possible, and denying to those, who would impose on us for what they've not, even the merit which they have. This is the comedy of artificial life, of wit and satire, such as we see it in Congreve, Wycherley, Vanbrugh, &c. To this succeeds a state of society from which the same sort of affectation and presence are banished by a greater knowledge of the world or by their successful exposure on the stage; and which by neutralizing the materials of comic character, both natural and artificial, leaves no comedy at all but the sentimental. Such is our modern comedy.

There is a period in the progress of manners anterior to both these, in which the foibles and follies of individuals are of nature's planting, not the growth of art or study; in which they are therefore unconscious of them themselves, or care not who knows them, if they can but have their whim out, and in which, as there is no attempt at imposition, the spectators rather receive pleasure from humouring the inclinations of the persons they laugh at, than wish to give them pain by exposing their absurdity. This may be called the comedy of nature, and it is the comedy which we generally find in Shakespear.

Whether the analysis here given be just or not, the spirit of his comedies is evidently quite distinct from that of the authors above mentioned, as it is in its essence the same with that of Cervantes, and also very frequently of Moliere, though he was more systematic in his extravagance than Shakespear. Shakespear's comedy is of a pastoral and poetical cast. Folly is indigenous to the soil, and shoots out with native, happy, unchecked luxuriance. Absurdity has every encouragement afforded it; and nonsense has room to flourish in. Nothing is stunted by the churlish, icy hand of indifference or severity. The poet runs riot in a conceit, and idolises a quibble. His whole object is to turn the meanest or rudest objects to a pleasurable account.

The relish which he has of a pun, or of the quaint humour of a low character, does not interfere with the delight with which he describes a beautiful image, or the most refined love. The clown's forced jests do not spoil the sweetness of the character of Viola; the same house is big enough to hold Malvolio, the Countess, Maria, Sir Toby, and Sir Andrew Ague-cheek.

For instance, nothing can fall much lower than this last character in intellect or morals: yet how are his weaknesses nursed and candled by Sir Toby into something "high fantastical," when on Sir Andrew's commendation of himself for dancing and fencing, Sir Toby answers—"Wherefore are these things hid? Wherefore have these gifts a curtain before them?

Are they like to take dust like mistress Moll's picture? Why dost thou not go to church in a galliard, and come home in a coranto? My very walk should be a jig! I would not so much as make water but in a cinque-pace. What dost thou mean? Is this a world to hide virtues in?

I did think by the excellent constitution of thy leg, it was framed under the star of a galliard!" How Sir Toby, Sir Andrew, and the Clown afterwards chirp over their cups, how they "rouse the night-owl in a catch, able to draw three souls out of one weaver?" What can be better than Sir Toby's unanswerable answer to Malvolio, "Dost thou think, because thou art virtuous, there shall be no more cakes and ale?"—In a word, the best turn is given to every thing, instead of the worst.

There is a constant infusion of the romantic and enthusiastic, in proportion as the characters are natural and sincere: whereas, in the more artificial style of comedy, every thing gives way to ridicule and indifference, there being nothing left but affectation on one side, and incredulity on the other.—Much as we like Shakespear's comedies, we cannot agree with Dr. Johnson that they are better than his tragedies, nor do we like them half so well.

If his inclination to comedy sometimes led him to trifle with the seriousness of tragedy, the poetical and impassioned passages are the best parts of his comedies. The great and secret charm of twelfth night is the character of Viola. Much as we like catches and cakes and ale, there is something that we like better.

We have a friendship for Sir Toby, we patronise Sir Andrew; we have an understanding with the Clown, a sneaking kindness for Maria and her rogueries; we feel a regard for Malvolio, and sympathise with his gravity, his smiles, his cross garters, his yellow stockings, and imprisonment in the stocks. But there is something that excites in us a stronger feeling than all this—it is Viola's confession of her love.

"Duke. What's her history?
Viola. A blank, my lord, she never told her love:
She let concealment, like a worm i' th' bud,
Prey on her damask cheek, she pin'd in thought,
And with a green and yellow melancholy,
She sat like Patience on a monument,
Smiling at grief. Was not this love indeed?
We men may say more, swear more, but indeed,
Our shews are more than will; for still we prove
Much in our vows, but little in our love.
Duke: But died thy sister of her love, my boy?
Viola. I am all the daughters of my father's house,
And all the brothers too; and yet I know not."—
Shakespeare alone could describe the effect of his own poetry.
"Oh, it came o'er the ear like the sweet south
That breathes upon a bank of violets,
Stealing and giving odour."

What we so much admire here is not the image of Patience on a monument, which has been generally quoted, but the lines before and after it. "They give a very echo to the seat where love is throned." How long ago it is since we first learnt to repeat them; and still, still they vibrate on the heart, like the sounds which the passing wind draws from the trembling strings of a harp left on some desert shore! There are other passages of not less impassioned sweetness. Such is Olivia's address to Sebastian whom she supposes to have already deceived her in a promise of marriage.

"Blame not this haste of mine: if you mean well,
Now go with me and with this holy man
Into the chantry by: there before him,
And underneath that consecrated roof,
Plight me the full assurance of your faith,
That my most jealous and too doubtful soul
May live at peace."

We have already said something of Shakespear's songs. One of the most beautiful of them occurs in this play, with a preface of his own to it.

"Duke. O fellow, come; the song we had last night.
Mark it, Cesario, it is old and plain;
The spinsters and the knitters in the sun,
And the free maids that weave their thread with bones,
Do use to chaunt it: it is silly sooth,
And dallies with the innocence of love,
Like the old age.
Song.
Come away, come away, death,
And in sad cypress let me be laid;
Fly away, fly away, breath;
I am slain by a fair cruel maid.
My shroud of white, stuck all with yew,
O prepare it;
My part of death no one so true
Did share it.
Not a flower, not a flower sweet,
On my black coffin let there be strewn;
Not a friend, not a friend greet
Dry poor corpse, where my bones shall be thrown.
A thousand thousand sighs to save,
Lay me, O! where
Sad true-love never find my grave,
To weep there."

Who after this will say that Shakespear's genius was only fitted for comedy? Yet after reading other parts of this play, and particularly the garden-scene where Malvolio picks up the letter, if we were to say that his genius for comedy was less than his genius for tragedy, it would perhaps only prove that our own taste in such matters is more saturnine than mercurial.

"Enter Maria.

Sir Toby. Here comes the little villain:—How now, my nettle of India?

Maria Get ye all three into the box-tree: Malvolio's

coming down this walk: he has been yonder i' the sun, practicing behaviour to his own shadow this half hour: observe him, for the love of mockery; for I know this letter will make a contemplative idiot of him. Close, in the name of jesting! Lie thou there; for here come's the trout that must be caught with tickling.

They hide themselves. Maria throws down a letter, and Exit.

Enter Malvolio.

Malvolio: 'Tis but fortune; all is fortune. Maria once told me, she did affect me; and I have heard herself come thus near, that, should she fancy, it should be one of my complexion. Besides, she uses me with a more exalted respect than any one else that follows her. What should I think on't?

Sir Toby: Here's an over-weening rogue!

Fabian: O, peace! Contemplation makes a rare turkey-cock of him; how he jets under his advanced plumes!

Sir Andrew: 'Slight, I could so beat the rogue:—

Sir Toby: Peace, I say.

Malvolio: To be count Malvolio;—

Sir Toby: Ah, rogue!

Sir Andrew: Pistol him, pistol him.

Sir Toby: Peace, peace!

Malvolio: There is example for't; the lady of the Strachy married the yeoman of the wardrobe.

Sir Andrew: Fie on him, Jezebel!

Fabian: O, peace! now he's deeply in; look, how imagination blows him.

Malvolio: Having been three months married to her, sitting in my chair of state,——

Sir Toby: O for a stone bow, to hit him in the eye!

Malvolio: Calling my officers about me, in my branch'd velvet gown; having come from a day-bed, where I have left Olivia sleeping.

Sir Toby: Fire and brimstone!

Fabian: O peace, peace!

Malvolio: And then to have the humour of state: and after

a demure travel of regard, telling them, I know my place, as I would they should do theirs, to ask for my kinsman Toby.

Sir Toby: Bolts and shackles!

Fabian: O, peace, peace, peace! now, now.

Malvolio: Seven of my people, with an obedient start, make out for him. I frown the while; and, perchance, wind up my watch, or play with some rich jewel. Toby approaches; curtsies there to me:

Sir Toby: Shall this fellow live?

Fabian: Though our silence be drawn from us with cares, yet peace.

Malvolio: I extend my hand to him thus, quenching my familiar smile with an austere regard of controul:

Sir Toby: And does not Toby take you a blow o'the lips then?

Malvolio: Saying—Cousin Toby, my fortunes having cast me on your niece, give me this prerogative of speech;—

Sir Toby: What, what?

Malvolio: You must amend your drunkenness.

Fabian: Nay, patience, or we break the sinews of our plot.

Malvolio: Besides, you waste the treasure of your time with a foolish knight—

Sir Andrew: That's me, I warrant you.

Malvolio: One Sir Andrew——

Sir Andrew: I knew, 'twas I; for many do call me fool.

Malvolio: What employment have we here? [Taking up the letter."

The letter and his comments on it are equally good. If poor Malvolio's treatment afterwards is a little hard, poetical justice is done in the uneasiness which Olivia suffers on account of her mistaken attachment to Cesario, as her insensibility to the violence of the Duke's passion is atoned for by the discovery of Viola's concealed love of him.

Chapter 10

The Two Gentlemen of Verona

This is little more than the first outlines of a comedy loosely sketched in. It is the story of a novel dramatised with very little labour or pretension; yet there are passages of high poetical spirit, and of inimitable quaintness of humour, which are undoubtedly Shakespeare's, and there is throughout the conduct of the fable, a careless grace and felicity which marks it for his. One of the editors (we believe, Mr. Pope) remarks in a marginal note to the two gentlemen of verona "It is observable (I know not for what cause) that the style of this comedy is less figurative, and more natural and unaffected than the greater part of this author's, though supposed to be one of the first he wrote."

Yet so little does the editor appear to have made up his mind upon this subject, that we find the following note to the very next (the second) scene. "This whole scene, like many in these plays (some of which I believe were written by Shakespeare, and others interpolated by the players) is composed of the lowest and most trifling conceits, to be accounted for only by the gross taste of the age he lived in: Populo ut placerent. I wish I had authority to leave them out, but I have done all I could, set a mark of reprobation upon them, throughout this edition."

It is strange that our fastidious critic should fall so soon from praising to reprobating. The style of the familiar parts of this comedy is indeed made up of conceits—low they may be for what we know, but then they are not poor, but rich ones.

The scene of Launce with his dog (not that in the second, but that in the fourth act) is a perfect treat in the way of farcical drollery and invention; nor do we think Speed's manner of proving his master to be in love deficient in wit or sense, though the style may be criticised as not simple enough for the modern taste.

"*Valentine:* Why, how know you that I am in love?

Speed: Marry, by these special marks first, you have learned, like Sir Protheus, to wreathe your arms like a malcontent, to relish a love-song like a robin-red-breast, to walk alone like one that had the pestilence, to sigh like a schoolboy that had lost his A B C, to weep like a young wench that had lost her grandam, to fast like one that takes diet, to watch like one that fears robbing, to speak puling like a beggar at Hallowmas. You were wont, when you laughed, to crow like a cock; when you walked, to walk like one of the lions; when you fasted, it was presently after dinner; when you looked sadly, it was for want of money; and now you are metamorphosed with a mistress, that when I look on you, I can hardly think you my master."

The tender scenes in this play, though not so highly wrought as in some others, have often much sweetness of sentiment and expression. There is something pretty and playful in the conversation of Julia with her maid, when she shews such a disposition to coquetry about receiving the letter from Protheus; and her behaviour afterwards and her disappointment, when she finds him faithless to his vows, remind us at a distance of Imogen's tender constancy. Her answer to Lucetta, who advises her against following her lover in disguise, is a beautiful piece of poetry.

"Lucetta: I do not seek to quench your love's hot fire,
But qualify the fire's extremest rage,
Lest it should burn above the bounds of reason.
Julia: The more thou damm'st it up, the more it burns;
The current that with gentle murmur glides,
Thou know'st, being stopp'd, impatiently doth rage;
But when his fair course is not hindered,
He makes sweet music with th' enamell'd stones,

Giving a gentle kiss to every sedge
He overtaketh in his pilgrimage:
And so by many winding nooks he strays,
With willing sport, to the wild ocean.
Then let me go, and hinder not my course;
I'll be as patient as a gentle stream,
And make a pastime of each weary step,
Till the last step have brought me to my love;
And there I'll rest, as after much turmoil,
A blessed soul doth in Elysium."

If Shakespear indeed had written only this and other passages in the two gentlemen of verona, he would almost have deserved Milton's praise of him:

"And sweetest Shakespear, Fancy's child,
Warbles his native wood-notes wild."

But as it is, he deserves rather more praise than this.

Chapter 11

The Merchant of Venice

This is a play that in spite of the change of manners and of prejudices still holds undisputed possession of the stage. Shakespeare's malignant has outlived Mr. Cumberland's benevolent Jew. In proportion as Shylock has ceased to be a popular bugbear, "baited with the rabble's curse," he becomes a half-favourite with the philosophical part of the audience, who are disposed to think that Jewish revenge is at least as good as Christian injuries. Shylock is a good hater; "a man no less sinned against than sinning."

If he carries his revenge too far, yet he has strong grounds for "the lodged hate he bears Anthonio," which he explains with equal force of eloquence and reason. He seems the depositary of the vengeance of his race; and though the long habit of brooding over daily insults and injuries has crusted over his temper with inveterate misanthropy, and hardened him against the contempt of mankind, this adds but little to the triumphant pretensions of his enemies. There is a strong, quick, and deep sense of justice mixed up with the gall and bitterness of his resentment.

The constant apprehension of being burnt alive, plundered, banished, reviled, and trampled on, might be supposed to sour the most forbearing nature, and to take something from that "milk of human kindness," with which his persecutors contemplated his indignities. The desire of revenge is almost inseparable from the sense of wrong; and we can hardly help sympathising with the proud spirit, hid beneath his "Jewish gabardine," stung to madness by repeated undeserved provocations, and labouring to throw off the load of obloquy and oppression heaped upon him and all his tribe by one desperate act of "lawful" revenge, till the ferociousness of the means by which he is to execute his purpose, and the pertinacity with which he adheres to it, turn us against him, but even at last, when disappointed of the sanguinary revenge with which he had glutted his hopes, and exposed to beggary and contempt by the letter of the law on which he had insisted with so little remorse, we pity him, and think him hardly dealt with by his judges. In all his answers and retorts upon his adversaries, he has the best not only of the argument but of the question, reasoning on their own principles and practice.

They are so far from allowing of any measure of equal dealing, of common justice or humanity between themselves and the Jew, that even when they come to ask a favour of him, and Shylock reminds them that "on such a day they spit upon him, another spurned him, another called him dog, and for these curtesies request he'll lend them so much monies"—Anthonio, his old enemy, instead of any acknowledgment of the shrewdness and justice of his remonstrance, which would have been preposterous in a respectable Catholic merchant in those times, threatens him with a repetition of the same treatment—

"I am as like to call thee so again,
To spit on thee again, to spurn thee too."

After this, the appeal to the Jew's mercy, as if there were any common principle of right and wrong between them, is the rankest hypocrisy, or the blindest prejudice; and the Jew's answer to one of Anthonio's friends, who asks him what his pound of forfeit flesh is good for, is irresistible—

"To bait fish withal; if it will feed nothing else, it will feed my revenge. He hath disgraced me, and hinder'd me of half a million, laugh'd at my losses, mock'd at my gains, scorn'd my nation, thwarted my bargains, cooled my friends, heated mine enemies; and what's his reason? I am a Jew. Hath not a Jew eyes; hath not a Jew hands, organs, dimensions, senses, affections, passions; fed with the same food, hurt with the same weapons, subject to the same diseases, healed by the same means, warmed and cooled by the same winter and summer that a Christian is? If you prick us, do we not bleed? If you tickle us, do we not laugh? If you poison us, do we not die? and if you wrong us, shall we not revenge?

If we are like you in the rest, we will resemble you in that. If a Jew wrong a Christian, what is his humility? revenge. If a Christian wrong a Jew, what should his sufferance be by Christian example? why revenge. The villainy you teach me I will execute, and it shall go hard but I will better the instruction."

The whole of the trial-scene, both before and after the entrance of Portia, is a master-piece of dramatic skill. The legal acuteness, the passionate declamations, the sound maxims of jurisprudence, the wit and irony interspersed in it, the fluctuations of hope and fear in the different persons, and the completeness and suddenness of the catastrophe, cannot be surpassed. Shylock, who is his own counsel, defends himself well, and is triumphant on all the general topics that are urged against him, and only fails through a legal flaw. Take the following as an instance:—

"Shylock. What judgment shall I dread, doing no wrong?
You have among you many a purchas'd slave,
Which, like your asses, and your dogs, and mules,
You use in abject and in slavish part,
Because you bought them:—shall I say to you,
Let them be free, marry them to your heirs?
Why sweat they under burdens? let their beds
Be made as soft as yours, and let their palates
Be season'd with such viands? you will answer,
The slaves are ours:—so do I answer you:
The pound of flesh, which I demand of him,
Is dearly bought, is mine, and I will have it:
If you deny me, fie upon your law!
There is no force in the decrees of Venice:
I stand for judgement: answer; shall I have it?"

The keenness of his revenge awakes all his faculties, and he beats back all opposition to his purpose, whether grave or gay, whether of wit or argument, with an equal degree of earnestness and self-possession. His character is displayed as distinctly in other less prominent parts of the play, and we may collect from a few sentences the history of his life—his descent and origin, his thrift and domestic economy, his affection for his daughter, whom he loves next to his wealth, his courtship and his first present to Leah, his wife! "I would not have parted with it" (the ring which he first gave her) "for a wilderness of monkies!" What a fine Hebraism is implied in this expression!

Portia is not a very great favourite with us, neither are we in love with her maid, Nerissa. Portia has a certain degree of affectation and pedantry about her, which is very unusual in Shakespear's women, but which perhaps was a proper qualification for the office of a "civil doctor," which she undertakes and executes so successfully. The speech about Mercy is very well; but there are a thousand finer ones in Shakespear. We do not admire the scene of the caskets; and object entirely to the Black Prince Morocchius.

We should like Jessica better if she had not deceived and robbed her father, and Lorenzo, if he had not married a Jewess, though he thinks he has a right to wrong a Jew. The dialogue between this newly-married couple by moonlight, beginning "On such a night," &c. is a collection of classical elegancies. Launcelot, the Jew's man, is an honest fellow. The dilemma in which he describes himself placed between his "conscience and the fiend," the one of which advises him to run away from his master's service and the other to stay in it, is exquisitely humourous.

Gratiano is a very admirable subordinate character. He is the jester of the piece: yet one speech of his, in his own defence, contains a whole volume of wisdom.

"Anthonio: I hold the world but as the world, Gratiano,
A stage, where every one must play his part;
And mine a sad one.
Gratiano: Let me play the fool:
With mirth and laughter let old wrinkles come.
And let my liver rather heat with wine,
Than my heart cool with mortifying groans.
Why should a man, whose blood is warm within,

Sit like his grandsire cut in alabaster?
Sleep when he wakes? and creep into the jaundice
By being peevish? I tell thee what, Anthonio—
I love thee, and it is my love that speaks;—
There are a sort of men, whose visages
Do cream and mantle like a standing pond:
And do a wilful stillness entertain,
With purpose to be drest in an opinion
Of wisdom, gravity, profound conceit;
As who should say, I am Sir Oracle,
And when I ope my lips, let no dog bark!
O, my Anthonio, I do know of these,
That therefore only are reputed wise,
For saying nothing; who, I am very sure,
If they should speak, would almost damn those ears,
Which hearing them, would call their brothers, fools.
I'll tell thee more of this another time:
But fish not, with this melancholy bait,
For this fool's gudgeon, this opinion."

Gratiano's speech on the philosophy of love, and the effect of habit in taking off the force of passion, is as full of spirit and good sense. The graceful winding up of this play in the fifth act, after the tragic business is despatched, is one of the happiest instances of Shakespear's knowledge of the principles of the drama. We do not mean the pretended quarrel between Portia and Nerissa and their husbands about the rings, which is amusing enough, but the conversation just before and after the return of Portia to her own house, beginning "How sweet the moonlight sleeps upon this bank," and ending "Peace! how the moon sleeps with Endymion, and would not be awaked." There is a number of beautiful thoughts crowded into that short space, and linked together by the most natural transitions.

When we first went to see Mr. Kean in Shylock, we expected to see, what we had been used to see, a decrepid old man, bent with age and ugly with mental deformity, grinning with deadly malice, with the venom of his heart congealed in the expression of his countenance, sullen, morose, gloomy, inflexible, brooding over one idea, that of his hatred, and fixed on one unalterable purpose, that of his revenge. We were disappointed, because we had taken our idea from other actors, not from the play. There is no proof there that Shylock is old, but a single line, "Bassanio and old Shylock, both stand forth,"—which does not imply that he is infirm with age—and the circumstance that he has a daughter marriageable, which does not imply that he is old at all.

It would be too much to say that his body should be made crooked and deformed to answer to his mind, which is bowed down and warped with prejudices and passion. That he has but one idea, is not true; he has more ideas than any other person in the piece: and if he is intense and inveterate in the pursuit of his purpose, he shews the utmost elasticity, vigour, and presence of mind, in the means of attaining it.

But so rooted was our habitual impression of the part from seeing it caricatured in the representation, that it was only from a careful perusal of the play itself that we saw our error. The stage is not in general the best place to study our author's characters in. It is too often filled with traditional commonplace conceptions of the part, handed down from sire to son, and suited to the taste of the great vulgar and the small.—"'Tis an unweeded garden: things rank and gross do merely gender in it!" If a man of genius comes once in an age to clear away the rubbish, to make it fruitful and wholesome, they cry, "'Tis a bad school: it may be like nature, it may be like Shakespeare, but it is not like us." Admirable critics!—

Chapter 12

The Winter's Tale

We wonder that Mr. Pope should have entertained doubts of the genuineness of this play. He was, we suppose, shocked (as a certain critic suggests) at the Chorus, Time, leaping over sixteen years with his crutch between the third and fourth act, and at Antigonus's landing with the infant Perdita on the sea-coast of Bohemia. These slips or blemishes however do not prove it not to be Shakespear's; for he was as likely to fall into them as any body; but we do not know any body but himself who could produce the beauties.

The stuff of which the tragic passion is composed, the romantic sweetness, the comic humour, are evidently his. Even the crabbed and tortuous style of the speeches of Leontes, reasoning on his own jealousy, beset with doubts and fears, and entangled more and more in the thorny labyrinth, bears every mark of Shakespear's peculiar manner of conveying the painful struggle of different thoughts and feelings, labouring for utterance, and almost strangled in the birth. For instance:—

"Ha' not you seen, Camillo?
(But that's past doubt; you have, or your eye-glass
Is thicker than a cuckolds horn) or heard?
(For to a vision so apparent, rumour
Cannot be mute) or thought (for cogitation
Resides not within man that does not think,)
My wife is slippery; if thou wilt, confess,
Or else be impudently negative,
To have nor eyes, nor ears, nor thought."

Here Leontes is confounded with his passion, and does not know which way to turn himself, to give words to the anguish, rage, and apprehension, which tug at his breast. It is only as he is worked up into a clearer conviction of his wrongs by insisting on the grounds of his unjust suspicions to Camillo, who irritates him by his opposition, that he bursts out into the following vehement strain of bitter indignation: yet even here his passion staggers, and is as it were oppressed with its own intensity.

"Is whispering nothing?
Is leaning cheek to cheek? is meeting noses?
Kissing with inside lip? stopping the career
Of laughter with a sigh? (a note infallible
Of breaking honesty!) horsing foot on foot?
Skulking in corners? wishing clocks more swift?
Hours, minutes? the noon, midnight? and all eyes
Blind with the pin and web, but theirs; theirs only,
That would, unseen, be wicked? is this nothing?
Why then the world, and all that's in't, is nothing,
The covering sky is nothing, Bohemia's nothing,
My wife is nothing!"

The character of Hermione is as much distinguished by its saint-like resignation and patient forbearance, as that of Paulina is by her zealous and spirited remonstrances against the injustice done to the queen, and by her devoted attachment to her misfortunes, Hermione's restoration to her husband and her child, after her long separation from them, is as affecting in itself as it is striking in the representation. Camillo, and the old shepherd and his son, are subordinate but not uninteresting instruments in the developement of the plot, and though last, not least, comes Autolycus, a very pleasant, thriving rogue; and (what is the best feather in the cap of all knavery) he escapes with impunity in the end.

THE WINTER'S TALE is one of the best-acting of our author's plays. We remember seeing it with great pleasure many years ago. It was on the night that King took leave of the stage, when he and Mrs. Jordan played together in the after-piece of the Wedding-day. Nothing could go off with more eclat, with more spirit, and grandeur of effect. Mrs. Siddons played Hermione, and in the last scene acted the painted statue to the life—with true monumental dignity and noble passion; Mr. Kemble, in Leontes, worked himself up into a very fine classical phrensy; and Bannister, as Autolycus, roared as loud for pity as a sturdy beggar could do who felt none of the pain he counterfeited, and was sound of wind and limb.

We shall never see these parts so acted again; or if we did, it would be in vain. Actors grow old, or no longer surprise us by their novelty. But true poetry, like nature, is always young; and we still read the courtship of Florizel and Perdita, as we welcome the return of spring, with the same feelings as ever.

"Florizel. Thou dearest Perdita,
With these forc'd thoughts, I pr'ythee, darken not
The mirth o'the feast: or, I'll be thine, my fair,
Or not my father's: for I cannot be
Mine own, nor any thing to any, if
I be not thine. To this I am most constant,
Tho' destiny say, No. Be merry, gentle;
Strangle such thoughts as these, with any thing
That you behold the while. Your guests are coming:
Lift up your countenance; as it were the day
Of celebration of that nuptial, which
We two have sworn shall come.
Perdita. O lady fortune,
Stand you auspicious!

Enter Shepherd, Clown, Mopsa, Dorcas, Servants; with Polixenes, and Camillo, disguised.

Florizel. See, your guests approach.
Address yourself to entertain them sprightly,
And let's be red with mirth.
Shepherd. Fie, daughter! when my old wife liv'd, upon
This day, she was both pantler, butler, cook;
Both dame and servant: welcom'd all, serv'd all:
Would sing her song, and dance her turn: now here
At upper end o' the table, now i' the middle:
On his shoulder, and his: her face o' fire
With labour; and the thing she took to quench it
She would to each one sip. You are retir'd,
As if you were a feasted one, and not

The hostess of the meeting. Pray you, bid
These unknown friends to us welcome; for it is
A way to make us better friends, more known.
Come, quench your blushes; and present yourself
That which you are, mistress o' the feast. Come on,
And bid us welcome to your sheep-shearing,
As your good flock shall prosper.
Perdita. Sir, welcome! [To Polixenes and Camillo.
It is my father's will I should take on me
The hostess-ship o' the day: you're welcome, sir!
Give me those flowers there, Dorcas.--Reverend sirs,
For you there's rosemary and rue; these keep
Seeming, and savour, all the winter long:
Grace and remembrance be unto you both,
And welcome to our shearing!
Polixenes: Shepherdess,
(A fair one are you) well you fit our ages
With flowers of winter.
Perdita: Sir, the year growing ancient,
Not yet on summer's death, nor on the birth
Of trembling winter, the fairest flowers o' the season
Are our carnations, and streak'd gilly-flowers,
Which some call nature's bastards: of that kind
Our rustic garden's barren; and I care not
To get slips of them.
Polixenes: Wherefore, gentle maiden,
Do you neglect them?
Perdita: For I have heard it said
There is an art, which, in their piedness, shares
With great creating nature.
Polixenes: Say, there be:
Yet nature is made better by no mean,
But nature makes that mean: so, o'er that art
Which, you say, adds to nature, is an art
That nature makes. You see, sweet maid, we marry
A gentler scyon to the wildest stock;
And make conceive a bark of baser kind
By bud of nobler race. This is an art

Which does mend nature, change it rather: but
The art itself is nature.
Perdita: So it is.
Polixenes: Then make your garden rich in gilly-flowers,
And do not call them bastards.
Perdita: I'll not put
The dibble in earth, to set one slip of them;
No more than, were I painted, I would wish
This youth should say, 'twere well; and only therefore
Desire to breèd by me. Here's flowers for you;
Hot lavender, mints, savoury, marjoram;
The marigold, that goes to bed with the sun,
And with him rises, weeping: these are flowers
Of middle summer, and, I think, they are given
To men of middle age. You are very welcome.
Camillo. I should leave grazing, were I of your flock,
And only live by gazing.
Perdita. Out, alas!
You'd be so lean, that blasts of January
Would blow you through and through. Now my fairest friends,
I would I had some flowers o' the spring, that might
Become your time of day; and your's, and your's,
That wear upon your virgin branches yet
Your maiden-heads growing: O Proserpina,
For the flowers now, that, frighted, thou let'st fall
From Dis's waggon! daffodils,
That come before the swallow dares, and take
The winds of March with beauty: violets dim,
But sweeter than the lids of Juno's eyes,
Or Cytherea's breath; pale primroses,
That die unmarried, ere they can behold
Bright Phoebus in his strength (a malady
Most incident to maids); bold oxlips, and
The crown-imperial; lilies of all kinds,
The fleur-de-lis being one! O, these I lack
To make you garlands of; and, my sweet friend
To strong him o'er and o'er.
Florizel: What, like a corse?

Perdita: No, like a bank, for love to lie and play on;
Not like a corse; or if not to be buried,
But quick, and in mine arms. Come, take your flowers;
Methinks, I play as I have seen them do
In Whitsun pastorals: sure this robe of mine
Does change my disposition.
Florizel: What you do,
Still betters what is done. When you speak, sweet,
I'd have you do it ever: when you sing,
I'd have you buy and sell so; so, give alms;
Pray, so; and for the ordering your affairs,
To sing them too: When you do dance, I wish you
A wave o' the sea, that you might ever do
Nothing but that: move still, still so,
And own no other function. Each your doing,
So singular in each particular,
Crowns what you're doing in the present deeds,
That all your acts are queens.
Perdita. O Doricles,
Your praises are too large; but that your youth
And the true blood, which peeps forth fairly through it,
Do plainly give you out an unstained shepherd;
With wisdom I might fear, my Doricles,
You woo'd me the false way.
Florizel. I think you have
As little skill to fear, as I have purpose
To put you to't. But come, our dance, I pray:
Your hand, my Perdita: so turtles pair,
That never mean to part.
Perdita. I'll swear for 'em.
Polixenes. This is the prettiest low-born lass that ever
Ran on the green-sward; nothing she does, or seems,
But smacks of something greater than herself,
Too noble for this place.
Camillo. He tells her something
That makes her blood look out: good sooth she is
The queen of curds and cream."

This delicious scene is interrupted by the father of the

prince discovering himself to Florizel, and haughtily breaking of the intended match between his son and Perdita. When Polixenes goes out, Perdita says,

"Even here undone:
I was not much afraid; for once or twice
I was about to speak; and tell him plainly,
The self-same sun that shines upon his court,
Hides not his visage from our cottage, but
Looks on't alike. Wilt please you, sir, be gone? [To Florizel.
I told you what would come of this. Beseech you,
Of your own state take care: this dream of mine,
Being now awake, I'll queen it no inch farther,
But milk my ewes and weep."

As Perdita, the supposed shepherdess, turns out to be the daughter of Hermione, and a princess in disguise, both feelings of the pride of birth and the claims of nature are satisfied by the fortunate event of the story, and the fine romance of poetry is reconciled to the strictest court-etiquette.

Chapter 13

All's Well that Ends Well

All's well that ends well is one of the most pleasing of our author's comedies. The interest is however more of a serious than of a comic nature. The character of Helen is one of great sweetness and delicacy. She is placed in circumstances of the most critical kind, and has to court her husband both as a virgin and a wife: yet the most scrupulous nicety of female modesty is not once violated.

There is not one thought or action that ought to bring a blush into her cheeks, or that for a moment lessens her in our esteem. Perhaps the romantic attachment of a beautiful and virtuous girl to one placed above her hopes by the circumstances of birth and fortune, was never so exquisitely expressed as in the reflections which she utters when young Roussillon leaves his mother's house, under whose protection she has been brought up with him, to repair to the French king's court.

"Helena: Oh, were that all—I think not on my father,
And these great tears grace his remembrance more
Than those I shed for him. What was he like?
I have forgot him. My imagination
Carries no favour in it, but my Bertram's.
I am undone, there is no living, none,
If Bertram be away. It were all one
That I should love a bright particular star,
And think to wed it; he is so above me:
In his bright radiance and collateral light

Must I be comforted, not in his sphere.
Th' ambition in my love thus plagues itself
The hind that would be mated by the lion,
Must die for love. 'Twas pretty, tho' a plague,
To see him every hour, to sit and draw
His arched brows, his hawking eye, his curls
In our hears's table: heart too capable
Of every line and trick of his sweet favour.
But now he's gone, and my idolatrous fancy
Must sanctify his relics."

The interest excited by this beautiful picture of a fond and innocent heart is kept up afterwards by her resolution to follow him to France, the success of her experiment in restoring the king's health, her demanding Bertram in marriage as a recompense, his leaving her in disdain, her interview with him afterwards disguised as Diana, a young lady whom he importunes with his secret addresses, and their final reconciliation when the consequences of her stratagem and the proofs of her love are fully made known.

The persevering gratitude of the French king to his benefactress, who cures him of a languishing distemper by a prescription hereditary in her family, the indulgent kindness of the Countess, whose pride of birth yields, almost without a struggle, to her affection for Helen, the honesty and uprightness of the good old lord Lafeu, make very interesting parts of the picture. The wilful stubbornness and youthful petulance of Bertram are also very admirably described.

The comic part of the play turns on the folly, boasting, and cowardice of Parolles, a parasite and hanger-on of Bertram's, the detection of whose false pretensions to bravery and honour forms a very amusing episode. He is first found out by the old lord Lafeu, who says, "The soul of this man is in his clothes," and it is proved afterwards that his heart is in his tongue, and that both are false and hollow.

The adventure of "the bringing off of his drum" has become proverbial as a satire on all ridiculous and blustering undertakings which the person never means to perform: nor can any thing be more severe than what one of the bye-standers remarks upon what Parolles says of himself, "Is it possible he should know what he is, and be that he is?"

Yet Parolles himself gives the best solution of the difficulty afterwards when he is thankful to escape with his life and the loss of character; for, so that he can live on, he is by no means squeamish about the loss of pretensions, to which he had sense enough to know he had no real claim, and which he had assumed only as a means to live.

"Parolles: Yet I am thankful: if my heart were great,
'Twould burst at this. Captain, I'll be no more,
But I will eat and drink, ant sleep as soft
As captain shall. Simply the thing I am
Shall make me live: who knows himself a braggart,
Let him fear this; for it shall come to pass,
That every braggart shall be found an ass.
Bust sword, cool blushes, and Parolles live
Safest in shame; being fooled, by fool'ry thrive;
There's place and means for every man alive.
I'll after them."

The story of all's well that ends, and of several others of Shakespear's plays, is taken from Boccacio. The poet has dramatised the original novel with great skill and comic spirit, and has preserved all the beauty of character and sentiment without improving upon it, which was impossible. There is indeed in Boccacio's serious pieces a truth, a pathos, and an exquisite refinement of sentiment, which is hardly to be met with in any other prose writer whatever. Justice has not been done him by the world. He has in general passed for a mere narrator of lascivious tales or idle jests.

This character probably originated in his obnoxious attacks on he monks, and has been kept up by the grossness of mankind, who revenged their own want of refinement on Boccacio, and only saw in his writings what suited the coarseness of their own tastes.

But the truth is, that he has carried sentiment of every kind to its very highest purity and perfection. By sentiment we would here understand the habitual workings of some one powerful feeling, where the heart reposes almost entirely upon itself, without the violent excitement of opposing duties or untoward circumstances.

In this way, nothing ever came up to the story of Frederigo Alberigi and his Falcon. The perseverance in attachment, the spirit of gallantry and generosity displayed in it, has no parallel in the history of heroical sacrifices. The feeling is so unconscious too, and involuntary, is brought out in such small, unlooked-for, and unostentatious circumstances, as to show it to have been woven into the very nature and soul of the author. The story of Isabella is scarcely less fine, and is more affecting in the circumstances and in the catastrophe.

Dryden has done justice to the impassioned eloquence of the Tancred and Sigismunda; but has not given an adequate idea of the wild preternatural interest of the story of Honoria. Cimon and Iphigene is by no means one of the best, notwithstanding the popularity of the subject. The proof of unalterable affection given in the story of Jeronymo, and the simple touches of nature and picturesque beauty in the story of the two holiday lovers, who were poisoned by tasting of a leaf in the garden at Florence, are perfect master-pieces.

The epithet of Divine was well bestowed on this great painter of the human heart. The invention implied in his different tales is immense: but we are not to infer that it is all his own. He probably availed himself of all the common traditions which were floating in his time, and which he was the first to appropriate.

Homer appears the most original of all authors probably for no other reason than that we can trace the plagiarism no farther. Boccacio has furnished subjects to numberless writers since his time, both dramatic and narrative. The story of Griselda is borrowed from his Decameron by Chaucer; as is the Knight's Tale (Palamon and Arcite) from his poem of the Theseid.

Chapter 14

Attacking the Cult-Historicists

In a sequence of recent writing, Richard Levin and Tom McAlindon have attacked what they see as the slipshod criticism and political dogmatism of New Historicism and Cultural Materialism. There is, of course, nothing new about such attacks. As Richard Dutton points out in the postscript to his volume on New Historicism and Renaissance drama, such iconoclastic approaches 'could hardly fail to stir up controversy' (Wilson and Dutton 1992, 219), and he goes on to detail some of the objections raised to New Historicism both by other theorists and traditional scholars.

Most telling perhaps are the objections of Carol Thomas Neely (the ambivalent term 'cult-historicists' is hers) that the 'new approaches are not new enough' (Wilson and Dutton 1992, 221), and those of Alan Liu that New Historicism is 'in fact a version of neo-formalism, applying the methodologies of New Criticism' to what might best be termed cultural history (Wilson and Dutton 1992, 225). Levin and McAlindon echo some of these accusations, but they do so from a position of hostility rather than sympathy, focusing on questions of methodology, and in particular on the relationship between theory and practice in the readings produced by the leading figures associated with the movements, Stephen Greenblatt and Jonathan Dollimore.

A similar stance underlies Levin's earlier attack on feminist readings of Shakespeare which produced a vigorous reply by leading feminist critics (Levin 1998; Forum 1989).

Undeterred, Levin, in what seems to be a personal crusade, has continued to snipe away at the new theorists and their apparent disregard for sound scholarship and intellectual rigour. Something more is at stake, however, than academic infighting.

One of Levin's most recent pieces appears in the same volume of *Studies in Philology* as an essay by McAlindon berating New Historicism, so that between them they dominate much of one edition of a major journal. In this sense Levin and McAlindon, along with *Studies in Philology,* seem to be claiming that what they have to say is both of significance and importance; that it needs to be considered and weighed not merely as part of a debate but as a set of serious charges which New Historicists and Cultural Materialists need to defend themselves against. The rest of this article will be taken up with looking at what Levin and McAlindon write and with trying to sift through their essays to see if they really are as provocative and contentious as they appear to claim.

I start with the essay produced by Levin in 1992 called 'The Cultural Materialist Attack on Artistic Unity, and the Problem of Ideological Criticism'. This is the most approachable of the group of essays, perhaps because it was part of a conference.

Levin's paper, though caustic, has that conference air about it - witty, direct, and intended to generate cheers of support from the audience. Not that Levin is a lightweight opponent. He has obviously read widely in theory and handles all the big names with barely a show of respect. Indeed, central to Levin's (sometimes knockabout) method is a deliberate strategy of running critical names and points together in a sort of pastiche. Levin's quarry in the essay are 'the new Marxists or cultural materialists and feminists associated with them' (Levin 1992, 39). The slightly insensitive phrasing here is typical of Levin's style and the way he conducts his case.

This, in essence, is to defend the idea of artistic unity together with the New-Critical formalist approach to texts that is associated with it, a defence he mounts through ridicule, lumping together various statements from Eagleton, Barker,

Hulme, Stallybrass and others which apparently demonstrate an attack on the idea of organic unity as merely a strategy to smooth out contradictions, a fraud perpetrated either by formalist criticism or 'the literary text itself' (Levin 1992, 41). Levin goes on:

Although these two explanations differ in their location of the blame, they yield the same result: a literary work that appears to be unified ... but that actually turns out to be disunified when interpreted correctly

Levin argues (not without insight or cleverness) that by taking this model of surface and deep meaning for its analytic base, Cultural Materialism is in fact acting like New Criticism, and that, ironically, the Cultural Materialists have merely changed the critical terms of what they do, not the basic mechanism of interpretation (Levin 1992, 43). With further irony Levin then notes how difficult it is to detect the grounds for the Cultural Materialists' distinction between the surface and the real meaning since they deny that texts can have meaning not produced by the criticism that reads it. Yet, Levin continues, the critics themselves seem to suggest that the disunity is actually there; it is 'within', 'innate'; it 'is always affirmed in the language of real presence' (Levin 1992, 44). Surely, however, Levin continues, what they should be saying is that this 'disunity is no more real than ... unity' and 'must be "produced" by their own approach' (Levin 1992, 44).

Teasing out such apparent inconsistencies and contradictions is the keynote of Levin's analysis, though whether he also realises that his irony also works to undermine his own position so that we start to see that the opposite case must also be true - that unity is produced by the criticism that reads texts as well as disunity - is unclear. Perhaps he does, because at this point Levin turns back to the old New Criticism and how it searched for unity but did not always find it except in 'superior works' (Levin 1992, 45), whereas Cultural Materialists 'never fail to find' disunity (Levin 1992, 45). Once on this tack Levin lets himself score a number of easy goals against a criticism that always seems to read texts in a certain way. Levin is not, of course, interested in what these readings produce or whether they add to our sense of the texts or of criticism as an activity, only in mocking the apparently rigid determinism of the Cultural Materialists in their quest to find disunity at the expense of the notion of artistic unity.

At this stage Levin turns towards the concept of unity itself. He suggests that the term has several meanings, including 'thematic unity' whereby a work has a central theme or meaning as well as the Aristotelian unity of plot (Levin 1992, 46). A third kind favoured by Levin has to do with 'unity as something that is intended by the author' so that it can be 'employed both as a working hypothesis for interpreting works ... and as one of the criteria for judging them' (Levin 1992, 46). However, Levin is keen to point out that unity is something of an ideal, ''a target to aim at', not 'an all-or-nothing proposition' (Levin 1992, 47). Whether this means by definition that authors never achieve unity is not raised by Levin who instead seeks to argue that 'artistic unity as the intended goal of authors ... seems to be confirmed by actual experience' (Levin 1992, 47). Thus Hamlet's instructions to the clowns '"to speak no more than is set down for them"' (Levin 1992, 48) are read as confirmatory evidence that Renaissance dramatists thought of their plays as unified wholes. And, Levin continues, 'if audiences then were anything like us, they assumed that the play they were witnessing was meant to provide a complete, unified experience' (Levin 1992, 48).

Having made this somewhat simple-minded appeal to common experience, Levin switches direction once again by noting that Cultural Materialists are not interested in this kind of artistic unity but rather in the ideology of texts, their political unconscious. He therefore starts another attack on the Cultural Materialists as really rather old-fashioned, like those critics who saw literature in terms of a conflict between classicism and romanticism. As throughout the essay, Levin's tactic is to identify Cultural Materialism with its opposite and to make it look ridiculous by showing, for example, the way Cultural Materialists always seem to deny the idea of the universal and of essences and then constantly talk about literature in terms such as '"always already"' (Levin 1992, 50). Again, Levin notes how Cultural Materialists always discover disunity as if it were a constant feature of all texts, so espousing the idea of eternal verities. Here Levin is clearly astute as he is also when he sees how the Marxist system of base and superstructure always-already leads to this kind of epistemological trap.

In place of this dispute about whether a work is 'really unified' (Levin 1992, 51) Levin offers another proposition. He suggests we insert the term *qua* into criticism so that this allows for different perspectives: we could 'adopt the formalist perspective and look at a literary work *qua* artistic product' (Levin 1992, 51) or read texts *qua* other approaches. Levin, however, well knows that this is barmy and that neither Cultural Materialists nor anyone else could or would accept such a proposition. Indeed, as he admits at the end of his essay, 'it is difficult to see how non-Marxists could ever be persuaded by a Marxist interpretation' (Levin 1992, 54) or a non-feminist by a feminist given the lack of 'any neutral or agreed-upon evidence' (Levin 1992, 54). Yet even as he reaches this conclusion Levin wants to back away from it and plead for the rejection of the 'cultural materialists' rejection of objectivism and pluralism' (Levin 1992, 55). What thus becomes evident as Levin draws his argument to a close is a sense of a deep gulf between the two sides, of all critical approaches 'hermeneutically sealed off' (Levin 1992, 55) from one another by their interpreters' ideologies.

The rather gloomy ending to Levin's article may reflect the state of things in 1992 when the rival camps were much more intense in their mutual contempt than perhaps now. One of the things about theory, however, is that it shifts all the time. Levin constructs a battle scenario with old adversaries who may well have moved on and become something else, discovered new texts and topics for their energies. This is a problem with any attack on theory: it is not a fixed entity and is much more protean than Levin's pluralist yet strangely rigid criticism allows for. But there are, too, other problems with Levin's attack which it shares with the more recent articles.

Levin sees Cultural Materialism as producing the text's disunity, but does not acknowledge the extent to which New

Criticism's search for unity was predicated upon certain political values and ideas. Might there not have been something seriously wrong with the New Criticism model? Why should authors strive to produce so much unity and harmony, searching only for order? Have authors no political commitment to change or to challenge? These are simple questions that won't go away by quoting Hamlet's directions to the clowns; at that moment Hamlet is engaged on the most dangerous project in the Renaissance, of trying to prove the king is a murderer; small wonder he doesn't want the clowns messing with the text.

Levin takes up the case of traditional criticism again in his article on 'The new and old Historicizing of Shakespeare'. In many ways this a follow-on piece with the same quarry of New Historicists, Cultural Materialism and feminists, though oddly Levin ends by saying he supports the feminist agenda for political action. His particular argument in the essay is about historical criticism of Shakespeare and how far theory accords with practice. As in the first essay, Levin's method consists of comparing the old and the new, but also of teasing out the implications of Montrose's famous 'chiasmus':

The new orientation to history in Renaissance literary studies ... may be succinctly characterized, on the one hand, by its acknowledgement of the *historicity of texts* ... On the other hand, this new orientation is characterized by its acknowledgement of the *textuality of history*

Here is plenty for Levin to get his knife into, and he wastes no time in emphasising what he sees as a central contradiction in New Historicism: for all their talk of the reciprocal interaction between texts and history, the New Historicists often begin their essays with the same historical facts as traditional scholars and then apply these to the texts 'just like the old historicists' (Levin 1995a, 426). As Levin also notes, New Historicists do tend to treat historical fact as facts, and, secondly, they do tend to start with history and then go to texts. (The exception here is the very brilliant Richard Wilson who gets no mention in Levin.) Levin rightly criticises what he sees as the sloganising of everything as textual as if were the end rather than the beginning of an epistemology (Levin 1995a, 429), a point he demonstrates by looking at the different textual status of the Stationers' Register entry and *King Lear* and how we interpret them differently.

Levin presses on with this analysis of history, politics and *King Lear* in a comparison of various conflicting readings by New Historicists of the play and its sexual politics. As usual, Levin capitalises on the differences among the New Historicists about the play, though he doesn't go as far as suggesting that *Lear* may be simultaneously, for example, criticising and supporting patriarchy. Instead what Levin proposes is that the new historical criticism is thesis-driven (Levin 1995a, 431), caught in its own imperatives, and determined by the critics' politics. Paradoxically, however, Levin also contends that the methodology of the new historicizing replicates the three basic approaches that underpin the old historicizing. First, suggests Levin, is occasionalism, 'where the critic argues that a play was designed ... for a special group assembled at special occasion' (Levin 1995a, 432).

Levin as usual is more than a little astute at spotting how old and new criticisms follow the same pattern of linking texts to specific moments or time. He is, however, less than keen to admit that this might be a strength, that what the new historicizing does is reread the old context, that there is nothing wrong with the notion of occasionalism per se. The same holds good for the idea of topicalism where the implications of the new reading might be very different as, say, in Marion Wynne-Davies' partial identification of Tamora with Elizabeth. What Levin seems unwilling to accept or cannot see is that the new historical critics may recognise that the older history may still be useful.

The third area of overlap in methodology is that of 'the ideas-of-the-time approach' (Levin 1995a, 435). Even Levin is forced to admit that the New Historicism has routed the old Tillyard world of peace and harmony (although this was already under severe attack in the 1950s) and that we should be grateful we can now see there were 'different and even contradictory "Elizabethan ideas" on most subjects' (Levin

1995a, 435). However, characteristically here Levin side-steps once again and takes up the New Historicists' claim that texts had a real effect on the audience and shaped their view as opposed to the passive view attributed to texts by traditional criticism. Levin is right to say this misrepresents the position though in general it is the case that older critics tended to present texts as non-interrogative and offering rather boring and obvious moral lessons.

Levin's conclusions from this stage of his analysis are that there is an 'irreconcilable contradiction' (Levin 1995a, 437) in the New Historicists' treatment of history and texts and that it is impossible to put into practice Montrose's chiasmus. But there is, contends Levin, a further set of problems entangled in the new historical approaches, and that is the apparent split between radicalism and accuracy. Political readings of texts, Levin argues citing various critics, do not pretend to be more accurate but only more radical. Levin rejects this position and suggests that persuasion is more likely by an accurate than just a political reading and that radicalism itself depends on accuracy.

And here Levin's real project becomes much more obvious - to depoliticise criticism, even though he admits that '"Everything is political"' (Levin 1995a, 440). This, however, he regards as another useless slogan, one he interrogates by exploring the idea of how plays are still politically relevant. The trick as usual with Levin is to push together several quotations from his enemies and then change register by slipping into some journalistic writing about how these critics derive 'Marxist or feminist messages' (Levin 1995a, 440) from past texts. Cleverly Levin sees this kind of politically relevant reading as dehistoricizing Shakespeare since it makes no recognition of change over time. And he goes to argue, again with the appearance of great logic, that what is going on here is an essentializing of the force of history and of capitalism outside of history (Levin 1995a, 442).

Not perhaps surprisingly, the conclusion that Levin reaches is that the political commitment of the new historicizers inevitably undermines their commitment to the textuality of history, for time after time what they show is that events are real and really existed. In that sense old and new historicizers end up carrying out the same process and doing the same thing, that is 'creating a history of the Renaissance that fits their own preconceptions' (Levin 1995a, 444). But more, Levin sees the new theory as simply replacing the old one of a society in harmony with a society torn apart in real material conditions as in Kathleen McLuskie's reading of the socio-sexual relations in *Lear*.

Levin's attack on McLuskie, though, itself raises a number of problems about the way he uses evidence for his case. He omits, for example, her larger reading of the play and its dynamic of the conflict between emotive and contractual obligations and the way older critics simply stressed the emotive.

The effect of this, ironically, is to reduce Levin's own position to one where he seems just to focus on slogans or headlines from his opponents, and this throws doubt on his argument and his methodology. Can you really lump all Cultural Materialist critics together in this way and take odd one-liners from here and there? The article is a defence of artistic unity - what of critical unity, of the details of the case made? When it comes to generalising to make a point, Levin is just as guilty as his rivals, and not a bit ashamed of doing so.

Levin's third attack is titled 'Negative Evidence'. He starts with the double premise that we 'cannot hope to prove any proposition unless we look for negative evidence that might contradict it', and that we tend 'to look only for positive evidence that confirms a proposition we want to prove' (Levin 1995b, 384). He illustrates his thesis by applying it to a series of critical positions, beginning with the way older critics cite parallels between texts and how such parallels cannot prove anything. Of course, it might be objected that nobody ever really thought that such parallels proved anything definite but had more to do with ideas and possibilities than hard evidence. The same objection might be levelled at Levin's analysis of the failure of old historicism and its attempts to relate texts to topical circumstances or to connect dramatic characters to real figures.

At this point Levin introduces a further condition into his argument, that not only must we examine negative evidence but 'also that we cannot hope to prove any proposition unless this negative evidence could exist' (Levin 1995b, 389). Put another way, this seems to mean that a proposition cannot be tested unless it invites 'disconfirmation': 'If it is not disprovable, it is not provable' (Levin 1995b, 389). This is an apparently sound scientific principle, though its logic seems to be that something which is provable is also disprovable. In which case both sides presumably cancel each other out. Not those problems bother Levin who sets about demolishing various studies, including such occasionalist critics as Josephine Bennett on *Measure for Measure* (Levin 1995b, 391).

He then goes on to the New Critics to prove that the themes they found in texts were already there, that they have 'a serious methodological flaw' (Levin 1995b, 392) and no way of proving what they want to prove. Having attacked the old historicists and the New Critics, Levin turns, not without some predictability, to the New Historicists who are seen to repeat the mistakes of the old historicizers of occasionalism and topicalism (though Levin offers no negative evidence that this is so, and so presumably proves nothing by his attack). More narrowly, Levin focuses on Marxism and Freudianism both of which he sees as totalising schemes that won't admit of negative evidence; they are 'self- confirming rather than self-correcting' (Levin 1995b, 399), predetermined by theorists who attack 'the motivation of objectors' (Levin 1995b, 400). We might notice that this once more is a universalising statement made by Levin - all Marxists, all Freudians - without any real consideration of other evidence.

Here and there Levin seems to make a fair point in his attacks, so that, for example, we might have some sympathy with the case he puts about neo-Freudian readings of Othello which claim 'Othello treats Desdemona as a mother figure' (Levin 1995b, 403). 'The most important negative evidence, of course', writes Levin, 'is that Othello never expresses this attitude toward her' (Levin 1995b, 404), which seems correct until we remember that Othello gives her a handkerchief made by his mother and we start to think about its implications. A similar pause for reflection follows Levin's ridiculing of Kiernan Ryan's reading of *Lear* as a play about class division: 'He does not confront the obvious negative evidence that all the tragic actions in both plots involve relations between members of the same ruling class and so cannot be caused by class divisions' (Levin 1995b, 407). This is not an argument likely to convince many.

Levin ends by saying that evidence is under attack in the academy, that it has been associated with naive right wingers. He claims evidence is not like that even though he clearly has a political agenda throughout his work. He denies this and cites other humanists who support his view that the new theorists are intolerant of all opposition. But where in 'Negative Evidence' does Levin offer any positive examples of modern theorists working with evidence? Where does he make his concessions? Is there any point in evidence if all criticism is so deeply flawed as Levin's article makes out? The obvious riposte to Levin is that you must cite the positive as well as well the negative view, that the appeal simply to what is not there doesn't work in literary studies.

As I noted above, Levin's essay is followed by a complementary piece by Tom McAlindon in *Studies in Philology* called 'Testing the New Historicism: "Invisible Bullets" Reconsidered'. Where Levin generalises his attack, McAlindon examines specific examples of the new theoretical criticism, in this case Stephen Greenblatt's famous essay on *Henry IV* and *Henry V* reprinted and revised in his *Shakespearean Negotiations*. McAlindon sees the essay as having 'cult status' (McAlindon 1995a, 411), and suggests that because of its importance his investigation of the coherence, evidence and methodology of Greenblatt's argument should be seen as 'in effect a localized inquiry into standards of excellence in the professional study of literature today' (McAlindon 1995a, 411).

McAlindon starts by outlining Greenblatt's influential thesis about power, that 'Shakespeare's subversive conservatism is the product of an unjust social order which sustains itself by means of deceit and illusion.... and so subversion is both produced and contained' (McAlindon 1995a, 412). McAlindon's analysis, however, initially focuses on Greenblatt's discussion of the discourse of power in Machiavelli, Harriot's *Brief and true report of the new found land of Virginia*, and Harman's cony-catching pamphlet on vagabonds and the resulting interpretive model that is applied to Shakespeare. Greenblatt argues that Machiavelli sees Old Testament religion originating '"in a series of clever tricks, fraudulent illusions perpetrated by Moses"' (McAlindon 1995a, 413), but, as McAlindon notes, even Greenblatt admits that his argument is '"not actually found in Machiavelli"' (McAlindon 1995a, 413).

Equally revealing is McAlindon's demonstration of how Greenblatt sometimes runs texts or ideas into one another, or fails to make clear where his evidence exactly comes from. Indeed, McAlindon argues that Greenblatt is 'circuitous and entirely incorrect' in his reading of Machiavelli, Moses and religion. We need here, of course, to judge several kinds of evidence - Greenblatt, Machiavelli and also McAlindon. My view of the evidence sides more with McAlindon than Greenblatt, though a difficulty arises here. In a literal sense McAlindon seems right, but there is always something more in a text than the literal sense and how we read it does matter.

There can, for example, surely be no denying Greenblatt's seizing on the Virginia narrative is brilliantly done. The original title of Greenblatt's essay, of course, relates to the attempts by the Indians to explain why so many of them died of diseases introduced by the English. Some thought that:

it was God punishing them for their hostility to the English ... some thought they were being shot at by invisible English bullets.

It is this last explanation, 'the invisible-bullets theory', notes McAlindon, which Greenblatt sees as 'the subversive voice' (McAlindon 1995a, 418):

it is the materialist explanation - viral infection - which science will discover centuries later, and which invalidates the moral 'Christian' explanation: 'In the very moment that the moral conception is busily authorizing itself, it registers the possibility (indeed from our advantage point, the inevitability) of its own destruction.'

McAlindon's objection - that both explanations are moral and that the invisible bullets theory is in no sense subversive - is, on one level, fairly put. Again, the point that Greenblatt changes his mind about whether Harriot was or was not aware of testing out the idea of religion as a means of control and so simply ends up with 'impressively phrased' paradoxes is not without weight. But, of course, what Greenblatt up to is not so much a totalising reading as exploring the relationship between subversion and containment.

This is not an easy relationship to figure, as McAlindon's own essay suggests in its careful examination of Greenblatt's discussion of Harman. Thus, while McAlindon shows how Greenblatt's claim that subversion occurs again and again in rogue literature but only offers one example as evidence, McAlindon himself supplies evidence that Greenblatt's interpretation of how writing and printing are caught up in deceit and treachery is correct, even though in McAlindon's example 'it is not the upper but the lower classes who excel in the arts and crafts of deceit'. In turn, as McAlindon notes, this raises some interesting problems about culture and power that Greenblatt cannot go into since for him power is always contained and is always directed downwards. It also, however, raises a number of political problems that disturb McAlindon's counter-reading of Greenblatt's analysis of *Henry IV* and *Henry V*.

Greenblatt's reading of Shakespeare's plays, McAlindon notes, appears to be systematic and consistent with his analysis of Harriot's text and its practices of testing, recording and explaining. What is less consistent is McAlindon's unexpected interpretation of Greenblatt's view of Hal as the embodiment of self-subverting power:

If Greenblatt, as seems likely, sees the modern state very much in terms of the government which sacrificed a generation of young Americans to the killing fields of Vietnam, we may have a clue to the extraordinary picture of Hal offered in these pages.

This is precisely the sort of double guessing that McAlindon accuses Greenblatt of. But what McAlindon also does at this point is characterize his opponent as a sort of leftish draft-dodger sympathiser who cannot get his head round the Shakespeare text.

Having slipped this in McAlindon goes on to examine some of the key moments in the play where Greenblatt's thesis about the production and containment of disorder comes into focus, starting with Hal's soliloquy at the end of the second scene. Greenblatt argues that here Hal is deceiving men's hopes, but for McAlindon the only one who is deceived is Falstaff. McAlindon may be factually right, but does not Hal also mislead his father, Hotspur and others who see him as a wastrel? McAlindon also contends that Greenblatt is wrong to see Falstaff's conscripts as subversive voices and denies that Falstaff is their apotheosis since they are rather his victims. Again, McAlindon has to be correct as far as he goes, but isn't it also the case that Falstaff no less than Hal functions on a number of different levels and that the problem of subversion and authority is bound up in the dramatisation of the two figures, not separated out into individual character?

A third moment involves Francis the drawer and again McAlindon takes issue with Greenblatt's view about how we are to make sense of the curious incident where Hal brings Francis to a standstill. For McAlindon this is a moment of 'exuberant humour', for Greenblatt it is sinister cruelty. We might ask why Hal needs to demonstrate such linguistic power, turning Francis into a sort of human parrot. 'Only a determinedly humorless response could produce the interpretation of the scene offered by "Invisible Bullets", McAlindon contends, but perhaps humour, cruelty, authority and subversion are not exclusive categories. McAlindon is so eager, however, to maintain that Hal is a figure of good that slowly the discussion of power and subversion is lost sight of as the argument becomes more and more about character and essences.

Indeed, there is an almost stubborn resistance by McAlindon to the idea of any sort of real political issues in Shakespeare's history plays. Greenblatt may be wrong to miss the difference between John and Hal in *2 Henry IV*, but that does not invalidate his point that Hal looks good at court because John tidies up the rebels through treachery. But McAlindon can't see this; indeed, for McAlindon '[i]n this world of lies and broken promises Hal is in fact the exception' (McAlindon 1995a, 429); he is 'a prince who from the start invites us to match his words against his deeds, actively repudiating the Machiavellian ethic'.

More interesting is McAlindon's discussion of Greenblatt's reading of *Henry V*. Greenblatt sees the play as combining '"every nuance of royal hypocrisy, ruthlessness, and bad faith"' with a '"a celebration, a collective panegyric" to a "charismatic leader". McAlindon accuses Greenblatt of using paradox to 'gloss over the contradictoriness and implausibility' of his reading, but there is more than paradox to Greenblatt's argument about how subversive doubts about royal power might serve to strengthen rather than lessen its grip. There is, to begin with, the problem over the question of national unity in the play and whether, as Greenblatt proposes, the Irish, Welsh, and Scottish are symbolically in an analogous position to the American natives.

McAlindon rejects this, arguing that 'unity in diversity is a conspicuous political ideal in the play'. It might well be argued, however, that unity in diversity, both in the sixteenth and twentieth century, invariably means English unity (and language) overriding others' diversity, and that this holds good as much for pluralism in criticism as in politics. No less problematic is the question of Bardolph's being hanged for stealing the pax (no one seems to have noticed the considerable irony of that word in a play about war, but no matter). Henry's action in approving of the sentence is upheld by McAlindon and one can see why: given his favourable view of Hal he's not likely to be convinced by Greenblatt's reference to 'Henry's "responsibility for the execution of his erstwhile boon companion"'. On Greenblatt's side is Pistol, on McAlindon's

Fluellen's, but the issue might be more correctly put in terms of the evasion of responsibility by Henry.

Perhaps the key area of contention in *Henry V* is the debate in Act IV between Henry, Bates, Court and Williams. While McAlindon is correct to state that Bates endorses part of Henry's reply about who is responsible for men dying badly in war, he, like Henry, evades the major question raised by the speech of the king's overall responsibility; nor does he note that Henry never admits to the other three that he is the king. The debate is fought with one side in the dark. McAlindon, though, believes Greenblatt is determined 'to damn Henry' and therefore 'simply dismisses' or ignores any evidence that might weaken his case. The trouble is that McAlindon is all too willing to defend Henry, including, for example, his stratagem of persuading Harfleur to surrender under threat of violence and rape:

We cannot disprove that Henry would have expected *his* men to commit such crimes, or condoned them if committed, had his oration failed; but it would have been entirely out of character if he had done so. This looks like pretty flimsy criticism by any standard, but especially in an 'inquiry into standards of excellence in the professional study of literature'.

McAlindon's concludes his examination of Greenblatt by suggesting that the 'novelty of his argument lies mainly in pushing the New-Critical position to an extreme point where ambivalence becomes a schizoid condition...represented as profound paradox' (McAlindon 1995a, 437). He describes him as 'audacious' but maintains that he disregards 'the principles of scholarly inquiry and sound reasoning' (McAlindon 1995a, 437) - he is inconsistent, he inflates his evidence or wraps it in 'ambiguous phrasing, and insinuating collocation'. And McAlindon ends by suggesting how the American academy is losing respect for 'certain values which should endure through changing fashions' of criticism and 'without which it is impossible to lay claim to disciplinary vigor' (McAlindon 1995a, 438) High moral stuff, indeed, but there is little point in clinging to such values if it involves reading Shakespeare, as McAlindon evidently wishes us to, through the lens of character. Such a reading, it needs to be said, offers the modern reader nothing. At least Greenblatt tries to suggest that Shakespeare may have been caught up in something more serious than the depiction of Prince Hal: in McAlindon's essay Shakespeare has stopped speaking to us.

Clearly McAlindon has little time for Greenblatt, but he saves his real wrath for his assault on the Cultural Materialists in an essay which has the rather long title of 'Cultural Materialism and the Ethics of Reading; or, the Radicalizing of Jacobean Tragedy' and which is aimed specifically at Jonathan Dollimore's *Radical Tragedy*. McAlindon admits this is the most 'engaging and substantial example' (McAlindon 1995b, 830) of Cultural Materialism, 'a key work in the history of postmodernist Shakespearean criticism' (McAlindon 1995b, 830). As in the previous essay, what McAlindon does is to test 'Dollimore's use of evidence and the reliability of his claims and conclusions' (McAlindon 1995b, 830), though first of all he gives Dollimore a chance to put his case. In sum this is that the more important tragedies of the period demystified and subverted two beliefs which were fundamental to the dominant ideology of the time: God's providential ordering of human affairs, and the existence of an essential human nature which is fundamentally the same throughout history.

In turn these twin beliefs, McAlindon contends, reflect the twin assumptions in Dollimore's position, that 'a radical transformation in society' (McAlindon 1995b, 831) is only possible once we recognise that human nature is constructed and that 'belief in an essential human nature' (McAlindon 1995b, 831) functions to maintain the political status quo. In addition, McAlindon notes how Dollimore's thesis involves the idea that the drama along with other important texts of the period 'severely interrogated "the essentialist view of man" inherited "from sixteenth-century Christianity and its stoic and humanists derivatives"' (McAlindon 1995b, 832).

From this point McAlindon goes on to subject to careful questioning the contextual evidence provided by Dollimore to support his contention that many of the major thinkers shared this anti-essentialist outlook - More, Castiglione,

Machiavelli, Bacon, Montaigne, and Hobbes. McAlindon takes each of these by turn and seeks to refute Dollimore's assertions. In the case of More McAlindon simply cites a brief piece of evidence that More wrote about a hellhound called Pride 'deeply rooted in men's breasts' (McAlindon 1995b, 832) and so clearly held an essentialist conception of human nature. This piece of allegory hardly seems a substantial or impressive refutation of Dollimore; nor is the similarly short analysis of Castiglione and the passing attempt to refute Greenblatt's *Renaissance Self-Fashioning*.

More successful is McAlindon's analysis of Machiavelli's position on human nature, for it is generally agreed that Machiavelli's premises depend much on men as unchanging, and that a good number of Renaissance historians were indeed of the same belief. By contrast, where Dollimore at least acknowledges that Montaigne 'contradicts himself in his restless search for self-knowledge' (McAlindon 1995b, 835), McAlindon seems unwilling to acknowledge that even the 'Apologie of *Raymond Sebond*' is a serious questioning of human nature as fixed.

After this examination of Dollimore's contextual evidence McAlindon analyses Dollimore's 'centre-piece' (McAlindon 1995b, 836) chapter on *King Lear* as the key example of cultural materialism. Dollimore's position is that the humanist interpretation of the play is misguided 'because it mystifies suffering and invests man with a quasi-transcendent identity' (McAlindon 1995b, 836) instead of showing how the text makes visible '"social process and its forms of ideological misrecognition" ' (McAlindon 1995b, 836). Also involved is Dollimore's rejection or contestation that the play repudiates 'all claims for the value and importance of pity, fortitude, and knowledge, together with the concomitant belief in an essential human nature' (McAlindon 1995b, 836).

It is each of these that McAlindon takes in turn as he attacks Dollimore's reading. Dollimore, says McAlindon, argues that Gloucester's response to Poor Tom 'might seem "callous" to us but is in fact no more than the type of casual "unkindness that is built into the social consciousness" in such a society' (McAlindon 1995b, 837). 'A look at the context', says McAlindon, makes this suggestion 'seem preposterous' (McAlindon 1995b, 837). And it does seem as if Dollimore has missed the significance of Gloucester's action and of Lear's concern for the poor. Dollimore does not, however, deny that Lear feels pity but only that such pity is ineffectual: 'it cannot generate justice' (McAlindon 1995b, 837). McAlindon, though, is in no doubt that pity - 'the notion of sym-pathy/compassion/ feeling with' (McAlindon 1995b, 838) - has 'political value' (McAlindon 1995b, 838); he cites the action of the servant who kills Cornwall at the cost of his own life. Characteristically McAlindon turns this into an example of a figure redeeming 'human nature from the depths to which it has sunk' (McAlindon 1995b, 838) rather than seeing what mixed signs we get here of a peasant standing up against injustice but also acting out of loyalty to protect a corrupt feudal system.

The play, it has to be recognised, won't easily settle down in the way that either McAlindon or Dollimore wants. Where McAlindon scores over Dollimore is, for example, in the latter's reading of the killing of the soldier hanging Cordelia which Dollimore somehow sees as displacing '"his transitory pity"' (McAlindon 1995b, 837) for the poor. On the surface this seems a slightly bizarre view; the play clearly wants us to approve of Lear's act given that Cordelia is being hanged. Indeed, McAlindon goes on to propose that a central idea of the play is that 'people commit and tolerate injustice precisely because ... they will not "feel"' (McAlindon 1995b, 839).

Conversely, Dollimore's argument about stoic fortitude - that it is 'a mystification of suffering which simply supports the notion that the human condition cannot be alleviated' (McAlindon 1995b, 839); that 'both Lear's madness and Gloucester's near-madness' (McAlindon 1995b, 839) subvert such implicit essentialism; and that the play '"is, above all, a play about power, property and inheritance"' (McAlindon 1995b, 840) and that '"the cherished values of kindness and fortitude, as well as human relations and "even identity itself"' (McAlindon 1995b, 840) are all informed by this - has much to be said for it. The play manifestly begins with issues of inheritance and power; the great mad speeches do expose the real bonds that exist between injustice and wealth. None of this, however, need necessarily vitiate fortitude which, as McAlindon notes, seems central to the tragic mode: indeed, there seems every reason to see the play as simultaneously endorsing stoic fortitude while recognizing its political ineffectualness, as being caught between opposites that it cannot reconcile.

McAlindon perhaps too often gives the impression that Dollimore sees Lear as a thesis play with everything clear cut. McAlindon himself argues rather strangely that 'at least half the inhabitants of the *Lear* world are not subjects of the dominant ideology' (McAlindon 1995b, 842) of power, property and inheritance'. But this is to misunderstand what the play represents as the dominant material conditions governing life: the fact that some of the characters resist its most obvious excesses does not free them from it: Kent, after all, wishes Lear to maintain the kingdom and his power; his loyalty is not in a vacuum. Again, McAlindon's reading of how the text 'forces upon our attention *from the outset* the often startling autonomy of the self; its baffling individuality; its resistance to environmental "subjection" and formulaic explanation' (McAlindon 1995b, 842) may not be without its attractions, but it omits any account of the political thrust of the play, of what happens or of the relationships between the state and human actions.

That McAlindon wishes to defend the traditional reading of the play as one of growth in knowledge for the hero is self-evident. But more than that he also wants to return Shakespeare to humanist criticism, and this may explain the way he rather oddly shifts his focus at the end on to Alan Sinfield and attacks him for using the 'methods and materials of historical research to give authority' (McAlindon 1995b, 845) to his reading of *Macbeth* while also allowing himself 'complete liberty of interpretation as and when he chooses' (McAlindon 1995b, 845). McAlindon sees such 'insidious confusion' (McAlindon 1995b, 845) as the very heart of Cultural Materialism and its 'propagandist mode' (McAlindon 1995b,

845), and he ends with a tirade that 'justice is not divisible' (McAlindon 1995b, 846), that it is due 'not only to the oppressed and the marginalised but also to the dead authors' (McAlindon 1995b, 846) whose texts critics feed off:

> It is due also to those educable young readers who will lead better and richer lives if their minds are opened to the full variety and complexity of great literature, instead of being told that texts, if they mean anything at all, mean *only* subjection, oppression, and deception.

Such a conclusion has, of course, little to do with the problem of history, theory and texts which lies at the core of the modern debate about literature. Self-evidently it has everything to do with McAlindon and Levin wanting to take us back to where we were, with self-perpetuating readings advocating tired ideas. But educable young readers surely want to know what critics today are saying, about how theory has shaken up the old eternal verities and given criticism a new significance. Greenblatt and Dollimore may have got it wrong, their evidence may be shaky, they may be no more than passing fads, 'cult-historicists' of the moment, but that doesn't mean that their questions are wrong, that there isn't a problem about our understanding of the early modern period. What Dollimore and Greenblatt offer us is another way of reading that past which might enable us to move forward towards new ideas and even towards a clearer sense of justice. This is not to advocate that we should abandon rigour, scholarship, discipline, but it is to maintain that we should not abandon the possibility of change, of rethinking, of making a difference. That is the real challenge of the new theorists, as both Levin and McAlindon well know.

Chapter 15

Shakespeare Consciously Use Archaic English

Determining whether Shakespeare uses archaisms consciously requires a close examination of his language word by word. Such scrutiny should presuppose that the concept and identification of archaisms for Shakespeare's contemporaries is not necessarily identical to our own. Fortunately, the *Early Modern English Dictionary Database* provides a means for determining the status of potentially archaic words based on the early modern lexicographer's sense of the frequency and tone of such words. While some lexicographers indicate explicitly that a word is "old," more often the archaic tone of a word is suggested only tacitly by how the term appears in dictionary entries. I will discuss how such citations and other sources such as Chaucerian glossaries can provide a starting point for examining if and how Shakespeare used archaic words. This examination will provide, in turn, a means for discussing the nature of archaic terms which circumvents problematic classifications.

This difficulty of classifying and identifying archaic terms during Shakespeare's time is unavoidable, perhaps, when one considers the linguistic self-consciousness and instability of the sixteenth and early seventeenth centuries. Generally, definitions seem to slip between the ideas of a potentially archaic term as (a) old, (b) regional or rustic, and (c) poetic. In his *The Arte of English Poesie* (1589), George Puttenham's recommendation to poets marks this overlap in the definition of such terms. He advises:

> Do not follow Piers Plowman nor Gower nor Lydgate nor yet Chaucer, for their language is now out of use with us: neither shall he take the terms of the North-men. (qtd. Görlach 237)

The distinctions of old, poetic, and regional seem inclusive and blurred here but, perhaps, all of these are inter-related aspects in the diachronic development of an archaism. As Manfred Görlach points out, regionalism contributes to the obsolescence of a word when it is associated increasingly with a non-standard variety, is stigmatized and falls out of use (139). Such diachronic specification, however, does not provide a tidy taxonomy for archaic terms when one recalls that archaisms were not associated only with lower registers or regionalism. Indeed, by the end of the sixteenth century, "old words" were associated increasingly with poetic diction, especially in bible translations, or classified as Chaucerisms.

What exists are two quite different senses of archaic terms–a lower register and a higher register. Apparently, the poet ought to avoid some old words but exploit others. When they are used, however, it is clear that such terms would have possessed a potentially archaic tone in order to be manipulated for the desired poetic effect–the term would be recognized as "different" from the standard idiom but retrievable from within that idiom. This sense of archaic terms as potentially exploitable items is discussed by B.R. McElderry Jr. in his examination of the language of Spenser. He asserts that poetic terms are extracted from standard language rather than created or lifted from other sources:

> no one person can "create" a poetic diction. The most he can do is to embellish incidentally a relatively standard idiom. The main poetic effect is latent in the standard idiom, and it is the poet's business to bring it out. (McElderry 168)

Following McElderry, I suggest that Shakespeare also extracts archaic diction in just this manner. Our linguistic distance from the idiom of Shakespeare's time, however, does not allow us to identify intuitively which words are archaic, especially if they are as "latent" as McElderry contends in Spenser's case. Early modern lexicographers and, to a lesser degree, Chaucerian glossaries such as those by Paul Greaves in 1594 and Thomas Speght in 1602 have helped me determine the archaic tone of such words based on their contextual frequency, that is, in what syntactic situations or with what other words they most frequently appear. Such resources also indirectly reveal how Shakespeare may have changed the typical co-occurrence of words in collocates or idioms in order to exploit the latent archaic tone of such words.

My examination of several methodologies for identifying and describing archaic terms divides into two approaches: direct and indirect. By a direct approach I mean the examination of explicit references to "old words" by early modern lexicographers or those marked by John Bullokar with an asterisk. In the instructions to the reader in his *English Expositor* (1616), Bullokar explains that a word marked in this way is "an olde worde, onely used of some ancient writers and now growne out of use." Few of the words marked by Bullokar, however, are used by Shakespeare. When such terms marked by Bullokar are used by Shakespeare, these words often appear in the Chaucerian glossaries of Greaves and Speght. A sample of such words would include "bale," "cleape," "teene," "to weene," and "to wende."

If such words are generally held to be archaic and/or Chaucerian, it appears they have a literary application. In this process such old words are increasingly isolated to a poetic register. This suggests that the choice of such words is conscious, to a certain degree, but also that the words chosen are recognized as an aspect of the standard idiom in a sort of poetic sub-category–a kind of a roster of terms considered infrequent and of a specific tone. They are of such infrequent use that they warrant inclusion in Chaucerian glossaries and mark up in hard-word dictionaries such as Bullokar's *Expositor*.

Based on my research thus far, I have found very concrete instances supporting McElderry's comment that for poetic ends archaic words are extracted from everyday language. With reference to Shakespeare's language, I argue that he lifts words which, embedded in particular collocates and idiomatic phrases, rarely appear outside of their most frequent contexts.

This brings me to the second and, I believe, more interesting methodological possibility for identifying archaic words. This is not by simply looking them up in reference works but by indirectly determining their tone based on their contextual occurrences or grammatical uses. It is this method which provides a more solid means for suggesting that Shakespeare used archaic words consciously.

This indirect method requires an understanding of the nature of fossilized phrases. In these phrases, a given lexical item is frozen in a set of words. One item often predicts the other members of the phrase. A single item can predict what other terms follow it (which is called right-predictive) or what terms it follows (left-predictive; Kjellmer 112). For example the word "nonce" occurs in very limited collocations in Present Day English. These are "for the nonce" and as an attributive in the hyphenated compound "nonce-word." Thus "nonce" is left-predictive and right-predictive in Present Day English but in different phrases. A phrase such as "for the nonce" should be considered more correctly as what Göran Kjellmar calls a variable phrase. He defines such phrases as consisting "of two or more lexical words, some of them incorporating function words" (Kjellmer 114). The fixity of the phrase suggests that it functions as a single lexical item because it appears most frequently in an isolated context or functions so, as Kjellmer puts it, "simply by virtue of being more common" (Kjellmer 114). In Shakespeare's corpus, an example of a lexical item frozen in such a phrase is "nonce" which appears only in the collocation "for the nonce."

This instance of the phrasal fossilization of "nonce" can be contrasted with a word like "fay." Spenser uses "fay" as a non-fixed collocate; Shakespeare, only in the phrase "by my fay." Clearly the term has gained lexemic status as an asservative as it appears in Shakespeare. The EMEDD supports this view, for "fay" appears only in this phrase and is not an unbound lexeme:

Florio (1598) – no by my fay;

Cockeram (1623) – by my fay.

What I undertook to determine was whether Shakespeare

might extract a potentially archaic word which had been frozen in a given collocate just as Spenser ostensibly had with "fay." A reading of Shakespeare's *Titus Andronicus* revealed two terms that the EMEDD entries suggest are found more frequently in set phrases or consistently predict other items. These are "maugre" and "belike." The *Oxford English Dictionary* defines "maugre" as archaic in its prepositional function. The EMEDD citations dramatize this point. The most consistent re-occurrence of "maugre" is in a set phrase of a function and content words (usually a part of the body). These phrases provide definitions for such words as "violenter," "invitus," "aldispetto" or "malgrado":

Elyot (1538) – maugre his hedde;
Thomas (1587) – maugre thy/his head (four times);
Minsheu (1599) – maugre his beard.

The archaic tone of "maugre" seems to be exploited to translate a proverb in Cotgrave (1611) while Cockeram (1623) includes it in his dictionary of "hard English words." The archaic sense suggested by Cotgrave and Cockeram is dramatized by the citations, since "maugre" appears most frequently in a semi-variable phrase of long standing (i.e., from 1538-1599). None of the citations provides a purely prepositional function for the word. This function is revealed only in those set phrases which reflect a sense of the word's productivity. Thus the citations implicitly suggest that "maugre" is most common in such phrases rather than as a productive preposition. Shakespeare, however, does not use the term as it is cited by lexicographers but as a preposition which is not restricted to governing particular content words of a given semantic field (which had been parts of the body):

I love thee so, that, maugre all thy pride (*TN* 3.01.151);
this maugre all the world will I keep safe (*TIT* 4.02.110);
maugre thy strength, place, youth, and eminence (*LR* 5.03.132).

A word considered a component of a set phrase in the dictionaries of Shakespeare's time appears here as a poetic or archaic or hard word. Based on a comparison of these collocations in the EMEDD and in Shakespeare's works, I believe that "maugre" in Shakespeare's time is on its way to becoming fully fossilized in a phrase which functions phrasally as an adverb. This distinction provided his audience with the sense of this word as old. By way of analogy, one might consider how many set phrases in Present Day English contain terms which do not function outside of such phrases or could not be correctly used by speakers outside those particular phrases. In the expression "to boot"–a lexemic adverbial tag–for instance, "boot" is not known to many speakers of English as something other than footwear or a computer operation.

"Belike" functions somewhat like "maugre." Unlike maugre, however, it is not identified by the *Oxford English Dictionary* as archaic. Interestingly, "belike" underwent a functional shift from a verb to an adverb from Middle English to Early Modern English. Citations of the EMEDD suggest that "belike" quickly underwent a collocational freeze which was accompanied by the loss of the verb. Of thirty-one matches in the EMEDD, only three are verbs and the remainder are adverbs. The distribution of these functions is reflected in their lexicographers. Florio (1598) provides "belike" as a translation of the Italian verb of obligation ("dovere") while Cotgrave (1611) uses it as an adverb in a right-predictive function word phrase–"belike because." Cotgrave uses this phrase when he is about to provide a definition of which he is not certain:

. . . called so, belike, because many things . . .
. . . belike, because tis usually covered . . .
. . . belike because it alters so quickly . . .
. . . belike because he hanged himself . . .

These instances do not represent an idiom as much as the idiolect of this lexicographer. What this co-occurrence does illustrate, however, is the non-productivity of the term. For example, "belike" is not the first term to come to the lexicographers' minds when they are defining the Italian "forse" ("perhaps"). Matches for "forse" are:

Palsgrave, John (1530) – forse force s fe. vehemence se fe;
Thomas, William (1550) – perchaunce, or peradventure;
Florio, John (1598) – perhaps, by chance, by hap, per adventure.

These instances illustrate that "perhaps" is the term which most lexicographers first consider when they define foreign terms of the same meaning. Though "belike" had established an adverbial function to the peril of its verbal function, it never appears as a synonym for "perhaps" in any citation. Cotgrave's use of "belike" appears to reflect considerable certainty in the ability of "belike" to convey clearly an adverbial function. He illustrates this in his mannerist alliterative grouping of "belike" and "because." I believe this suggests that the term has some affective or literary potential because of this alliterative context but since the earliest citation of "belike" is 1533, can I argue that it had already become archaic in Shakespeare's language? Shakespeare uses "belike" more often than he uses "perhaps" in a ratio of 43:28. I think he is doing just what McElderry suggests is part of the manipulation of poetic diction–opting for the lesser used word, marking the difference between a frequent word and an infrequent one. This word was perhaps a "hard word": a possibility reinforced by the fact that its adverbial function was sufficiently questionable to warrant the addition–though short-lived–of the adverbial affix "-ly" (*OED* a 1552).

The examples of "maugre" and, to a lesser degree, "belike" illustrate that context is an essential consideration when determining the potentially archaic status of a word. This holds true for the contexts constructed for archaic words. The importance of syntactic context is illustrated by the word "welkin" which Shakespeare shares with E.K.'s glosses of Spenser and Greaves's *Chauceriana* glossary. This Old English word for "cloud" was pushed into the archaic/poetic register when the Old Norse loan "sky" functioned as the spoken register term. The ways in which Shakespeare uses these two words of roughly synonymous meaning and inter-related development may shed light on how he utilizes archaic terms generally. While Shakespeare had used "welkin" 19 times, he uses "sky" 48 times.

"Sky" is productive in compounds and affixes ("sky-aspiring," "skyey," "skyish," "sky-planted"). "Welkin," however, does not share in this formational productivity. This suggests, therefore, that its lexical status is fixed and does not fall under the rubric of day-to-day terms which are productive. In fact, the use of "welkin" in such a way may have been too mannered, if it is already considered a poetic or archaic term. One might conclude that poetic or archaic items could not be over-determined by attributive or phrasal contexts when used for poetic ends. Just as "maugre" was de-contextualized or extracted from its more frequent phrasal occurrences with the result of a foregrounding of its prepositional function and archaic tone, so "welkin" functions generally freed from phrasal and affixed contexts.

The words I have discussed are only a few of the many words–both content and function–that I have examined. What this study has illustrated so far is that archaism–and implicitly poetic diction–exists within the standard idiom. Archaisms, then, could be considered terms which are latently embedded within the standard idiom rather than within a poetic register set apart.

In some instances archaic tonality may just be a matter of recognizing that the status of old words is based on their relation to the standard idiom by the way they survive in that idiom as fossilized phrases. Such generalizations suggest that archaisms could have been readily available for use not only in the reference texts of Shakespeare's time but phrasally frozen in his day-to-day language.

Finally, I must answer the question this paper asks: Does Shakespeare use archaisms consciously? I must say both "yes" and "no." "Yes" when he extracts archaisms from variable phrases such as "maugre his head" but "no" when he uses a highly unbound lexeme which the dictionaries cite as archaic such as "teen" or "ween." A "yes" is my reply, however, when he manipulates two words of the same meaning such as "sky" and "welkin" quite differently.

The extraction of words from fossilized contexts–as in the case of "maugre"–and the non-determined contexts of others–as "welkin" demonstrates–suggests an intentionality on the bard's part. An analysis of the context in which these words appear most frequently in the EMEDD and of how

Shakespeare employs them provides a starting point for determining the level of his consciousness in the manipulation of such old words.

Jean E. Howard's Postmodern Marxist Feminism and the Economic Last Instance

For over a decade, the Marxist-feminist critic Jean Howard has been a keen observer of the shifting trends in Shakespeare studies. Her insightful commentary on the work of some of the newer, 'political' critics in this field — including the new historicists, cultural materialists, and feminists — has helped to clarify many of the theoretical and practical problems with which these writers have struggled in their efforts to counter the ahistorical formalism of an earlier era. More than a metacritic, however, Howard has also offered her own innovative analyses of the work of Shakespeare and his contemporaries and, in the process, has enlarged our understanding of the significance of a wide range of early modern 'theatrical practices'.

These well-deserved compliments paid, I now want to note a serious reservation that I have about Howard's work. Like many critics in recent years, Howard has become receptive to a number of 'postmodern' positions and ideas, so much so, in fact, that she has argued the need for a 'postmodern Marxist feminism' (Howard 1991). As a classical Marxist, I am convinced that the discourses of postmodernism and Marxism are largely incompatible, and in the following essay, I will attempt to illustrate how that incompatibility becomes all too evident in certain contradictions that arise between Howard's theory and practice.

I will begin by looking at an essay published by Howard in 1986 (written in 1984), entitled 'Scholarship, Theory, and More New Readings: Shakespeare for the 1990s'. In this work, she argues that [i]t is simply not possible to talk about Shakespeare and his culture without holding some sort of theory about their relationship; there is no escape into a realm of unmediated truth. The question, therefore, is whether the critic is going to be self-conscious about his or her theoretical position and examine it in the light of competing theories.

Without such self-consciousness, the critic inevitably conceals what is polemical or problematic in his or her critical practice and falls back on the defense of common sense: i.e., the position that a particular critical practice depends on assumptions so self-evident that their truth is not in question. (Howard 1986a, 135)

Howard is speaking in general terms here and is not arguing for or defending a particular critical approach. Nevertheless, her implication that there are no disinterested readings enables one to understand why, in this essay, she is so receptive to 'radical sorts of critical work' in the fields of 'historiography, ideology critique, and culture studies'.

The purpose of 'Scholarship, Theory, and More New Readings' is, ostensibly, to convince an exhausted, though still hegemonic, generation of humanists to think twice before condemning the new critical discourses as merely 'faddish'. According to Howard, 'Shakespeareans as a group need to look upon contemporary criticism and theory with less of a jaundiced and a dropping eye than has often been the case in the past', and with this admonishment, she proceeds to argue just how rich and productive a new cycle of 'readings' might be if propelled by Marxism, new historicism, response theory, feminism, and several other theories. This new work, however, would obviously differ in a number of ways from 'traditionalist' criticism.

Perhaps most crucially, it would avoid an error common to much thematic criticism of the past, which, Howard states (after citing an argument by Richard Levin), offered up readings that 'proclaimed to reveal the truth of the text, a truth which for centuries ha[d] lain undiscovered and which, having now been unearthed by the alert critic, [was] meant to displace all the other "true readings" previously proposed'. Howard agrees with Levin that this critical genre is 'played out'; however, she believes this not because 'the real, unchanging, commonsense meaning of Shakespeare's plays was discovered long ago, as Levin assumes', but because of 'an unwillingness [on the part of many thematic critics] to acknowledge that there can be no such freestanding meaning in the text, a meaning not in some way produced by the historical situation of the reader/interpreter'.

In much of the essay, then, Howard focuses on how the new critical discourses address both the problem of the reader's historical situation and the historicity of the Shakespearean text. Although she states that her goal is not to judge the 'competing claims' of various critics that she includes in her survey, there are several important precepts that Howard appears to embrace or at least find worthy of serious consideration: 1) critical self-consciousness is desirable; 2) critics do not have access to 'unmediated truth' 3) the literary is a social construction ('what a culture decides it will be at any given moment') rather than an essential thing; 4) literary texts perform a variety of functions: i.e., they may subvert or confirm 'the cultural materials by which they are traversed'; and 5) literature helps to construct 'what a culture takes reality to be', rather than simply reflecting some self-evident reality.

Many of these notions had become commonplaces of leftist or left-leaning criticism by the time Howard's essay was published; however, it is clear from this early theoretical piece that she is drawn to various poststructuralist and Marxist ideas that had gained currency in the 1970s and early 1980s, and that, in the hands of some critics, would eventually turn into 'post-Marxism'. Howard has not yet taken that path, though in later essays she has attempted to reconcile conflicting tendencies within Marxism, feminism, and poststructuralism (as we shall see below). Now, though, I want to turn to her next foray into theory: her 1986 critique of the new historicism.

In 'The New Historicism in Renaissance Studies', Howard continues to think about some of the problems touched on in 'Scholarship, Theory and More New Readings', including the epistemological status of the critic, the function of 'the literary', and the relationship between a text and 'history', Her discussion of these issues, though, is now provoked by the work of a group of scholars who write what is 'loosely called the "new history"' (Howard 1986b, 13). Howard has several objectives in writing this piece. One is to explain what the new historicism is; another is to point out the strengths and weaknesses of various new historical positions and ideas; and a third is to critique the work of two leading new historicists, Louis Montrose and Stephen Greenblatt. For the purposes of this essay, I am less concerned with what Howard thinks the new historicism is than with what she finds valuable and useful in this body of criticism.

In her view, the new historicists have clearly got certain things right. One is 'the notion that man is a construct, not an essence', an axiom that is commonly accepted these days by materialist critics. She also applauds the new historicists for their view that 'the historical investigator is likewise a product of his history and never able to recognize otherness in its pure form, but always in part through the framework of the present'. She then notes that '[t]his last point leads one to what is perhaps the crux of any "new" historical criticism, and that is to the issue of what one conceives history to be: a realm of retrievable fact or a *construct* made up of textualized traces assembled in various configurations by the historian/ interpreter'. It is clear from the discussion that follows that she believes the latter:

It increasingly seems that . . . a new historical criticism has to accept, first, that 'history' is not objective, transparent, unified, or easily knowable and consequently is extremely problematic as a concept for grounding the meaning of a literary text; second, that the very binarism we casually reinforce every time we speak of literature and history, text and context, is unproductive and misleading. Literature is *part* of history, the literary text as much a context for other aspects of cultural and material life as they are for it. Rather than erasing the problem of textuality, one must enlarge it in order to see that *both* social and literary texts are opaque, self-divided, and porous, that is, open to the mutual intertextual influences of one another. This move means according literature real power. Rather than passively reflecting external reality, literature is an agent in constructing a culture's sense of reality.

There are a number of influences at work here, including Derrida (there is no 'outside of the text'), Foucault (history is not 'objective'), and Raymond Williams via the new historicists (literature does not passively reflect 'external reality'). Although Howard is offering these observations in order to critique an outmoded, positivist historicism, she makes clear in this essay that traditional Marxists, as well as humanists, have been guilty of producing such work. I will interject here that if some Marxists have treated history as though it were always and everywhere a self-evident thing or a reified force, they did so not only erroneously but *undialectically*. Yet, as Fredric Jameson reminds us in *The Political Unconscious*, history finally is not just another text, 'simply one more code among others, with no particularly privileged status' (Jameson 1981, 100). It is rather the 'experience of Necessity, and it is this alone which can forestall its thematization or reification as a mere object of representation or as one master code among many others' (Jameson 1981, 102).

Jameson, of course, is making a case for a *particular* reading of history—one with which Howard is presumably in agreement to a greater or lesser extent, given her praise of Marxism in the new historicism essay (on which more in a moment). But he is also taking a clear stand on an issue that becomes blurred in Howard's treatment of the interplay between literary and social 'texts'. In her attack on a naïve historicism 'in which literature figures as the parasitic reflector of historical fact', Howard 'imagines a complex textualized universe in which literature participates in historical processes and in the political management of reality' (Howard 1986b, 25). In such a universe, the old hierarchy between history and literature would collapse so that, as Don Wayne, whom Howard paraphrases, has written, 'it becomes nearly impossible to pinpoint an origin or single cause for social change'. To this she adds, 'Many aspects of the social formation, including literary texts, work in a variety of ways and at a variety of speeds to produce the variegated entity we call history'.

Let us assume that all of this is true. Why, then, does Howard—or, for that matter, Stephen Greenblatt—pay so much attention to questions of political power? I suspect that there very well may not be a 'single cause for social change'; however, Howard's preoccupation with power and differential class and gender relations seems to attest to the fact that some aspects of 'the social formation' are more important than others. In an essay criticizing Raymond Williams' attack on the traditional base/superstructure concept, Terry Eagleton (1989) has argued that an egalitarian view of social determinants is not quite the same thing as Engels' belief that base and superstructure have a dialectical relationship. Like Williams, Howard and the new historicists seem obliged to do away with a determining base, thereby raising the question: If *everything* is 'determinant', can the word logically retain any force?

It is important to note, though, that Howard draws support for her views on the problem of cause and effect from Althusser, whose concept of the 'relative autonomy of the superstructure from the material base' (Howard 1986b, 27) is seen as providing a more sophisticated theoretical model of social change than 'traditional' Marxism. Although Althusser's notion of structural causality has been the source of considerable debate, one could argue that his comments on Engels' statement that the mode of production is determinant 'in the last instance' endorse the idea that the economic 'level' enjoys a certain privilege 'in the long run, the run of History', even though 'History "asserts itself" through the multiform world of the superstructures' (Althusser 1977, 112).

Howard's 'rethinking of the place of literature *in* history' (Howard 1986b, 27; Howard's emphasis) is also influenced by other Marxist concepts, most particularly the concept of ideology. Like cultural materialist Jonathan Dollimore, she defines ideology in two principal ways: 'first, as the false consciousness foisted on the working classes by a dominant class; second, as any practices by which one imagines one's relations to the actual conditions of one's existence'. Also like Dollimore, Howard states that 'it may be useful to retain both understandings of ideology: to retain the option of seeing some literature as the conscious and direct product of one power group or class's attempts to control another group or class by the misrepresentation of their historical condition; and at the same time to recognize that in most instances power groups or classes are both less self-conscious and less monolithic than such a formulation implies . . .'.

Again I will note Howard's concern here with 'power' (this time displayed by 'groups and classes'). One, of course, *need not* speak of power when discussing ideology; however, the fact that Howard does underscores my point that while one may theorise about a 'textualized universe' where origins of social change are 'impossible to pinpoint', in practice critics who align themselves with Marxism—as Howard arguably does in this essay—unfailingly pay homage to the determining power of the 'base' (one of whose components is, of course, 'class'). Howard's main reason for discussing what she calls 'recent developments in Marxist thought', in an essay on the new historicism, is to suggest ways in which the former will benefit the latter. She also correctly notes, though, that work by Greenblatt, Montrose, *et al.* already draws on a number of Marxist ideas. So what, then, is the problem with the new historicism? Howard's 'main reservation about much of this work', she writes, 'is its failure to reflect on itself':

Taking the form of the reading, a good deal of this criticism suppresses any discussion of its own methodology and assumptions. It assumes answers to the very questions that should be open to debate: questions such as why a particular context should have privilege over another in discussing a text, whether a work of art merely reflects or in some fundamental sense reworks, remakes, or even produces the ideologies and social texts it supposedly represents, and whether the social contexts used to approach literary texts have themselves more than the status of fictions.

The questions that Howard raises here are good ones; however, I am not sure that the new historicists can provide very satisfying answers to them, in view of some of the assumptions that she attributes to these writers. For example, given a 'theory' which lacks a strong concept of determination, can one *ever* make a persuasive argument as to 'why a particular context should have privilege over another in discussing a text'? But, then, if social and literary texts really are mutually constitutive (in a non-hierarchical fashion), one should not *have* to make such an argument. Why *not* talk about Indians from Virginia—or any number of other subjects—in the same breath as *Henry IV*? Of course, as Alan Liu (1989) has pointed out, *in practice* the new historicists always make a 'metaphorical' connection between the texts that they juxtapose—i.e., the texts are shown to be alike in some way, and it is inevitably in what they say about the functioning of 'power'.

Thus, if we take for an example the Greenblatt essay, 'Invisible Bullets', to which I just alluded, the *real* context being 'privileged' there is not that produced by Harriot's *Brief and True Report*, but the one that 'powers' both Shakespeare's *and* Harriot's work. That context—which a Marxist such as Jameson would call the absent cause of History (i.e., the history of class struggles)—is never fully theorised in new historicist work, because, of course, these writers *do not have* a theory of history as such. Greenblatt has in fact stated (in a book published subsequent to Howard's essay) that the new historicism is 'a practice' and not a theory of history or anything else (Greenblatt 1990, 146).

Howard's question about the (epistemological) 'status' of 'the social contexts used [by new historicists] to approach literary texts' is also a difficult one for these writers in light of their assumptions. If the new historicism is as (philosophically) conventionalist as Howard makes it out (or would like it) to be, its adherents can hardly make any strong claims about the truth of their histories. Although Althusser's ideology/science binary has been attacked by an army of erstwhile Althusserians, the realist position underwriting that binary—a position made possible by the objective fact of the extraction of surplus value within class societies—provides a ground from which one may speak. Where is that ground in new historicist work? The Foucauldian notion of the 'truth function'? The idea that all writing is political? As Hamlet said, 'I'll have grounds more relative than this' (though by 'relative' he meant 'cogent').

My objection to the new historicism (at least in its classic Greenblattian mode), then, is not so much that its practioners have been 'unreflective' about their assumptions, as that they have bought into poststructuralist and conventionalist attacks on the 'master-narrative' of Marxism and, as a result, have offered up a patchwork 'practice'—albeit a politicised one (but *what* politics?)—that oscillates 'somewhere between "totalization" [Greenblatt's code word for traditional Marxism] and "difference" (deconstruction at its ahistorical worst)'. I raise this objection because Howard seems determined in this essay and elsewhere to use new historicist assumptions to 'improve' Marxism, as much as she claims to want to do the converse. A classical Marxist might quote Lear at this point: 'That way madness lies'. But before jumping to conclusions, I want to examine one other theoretical essay by Howard, in which she attempts to define her current position as a 'postmodern' Marxist feminist.

In a 1991 paper originally given at a University of Essex symposium on 'Postmodernism, Marxism, History, and the Renaissance', Howard articulates several other questions that, in the view of a number of Marxists, have been raised and left dangling by certain new historicist/postmodernist work:

If one has no unmediated access to the real, including past reality, what is to keep the past from being other than a fiction woven from the language games of the present? If subjects have no access to true knowledge, why should one ideologically motivated narrative have priority over others? And if subjects cannot stand outside discourse and ideology in the place of scientific reason and objectivity, what is to ground a politics, understood as any attempt to act upon the world to make it 'better'? Is there any unmediated, 'enlightened' position from which to specify that 'better'? (Howard 1991, 106)

In attempting to answer these and other questions, Howard argues that, by 'enlist[ing] the resources of postmodernity', feminism can strengthen 'a politically committed historical practice'. In Part 1 of the essay, she discusses postmodernism's 'threat to humanist politics and positivist history'. For Howard, postmodernism 'specifies a constellation of discourses and practices, unique to the contemporary moment but not defining it totally, which stand in a relation of difference to discourses and practices which may be chronologically deployed alongside them, but which entail different assumptions about epistemology, rationality, the self-subject, and the relationship of popular to elite culture, etc.' Of all its assumptions, though, she writes, perhaps most crucial is postmodernity's challenge to the idea of the rational self, fully present to itself and able to make absolute truth claims on the basis of empirical knowledge of the real or to employ master-narratives about the real which aspire to the status of science.

Recognising no outside to ideology, no discourse of science which would, for example, allow something like false consciousness to be revealed to the subject from a position of truth, postmodernity admits no means of disentangling knowledge from power or a stable and unified self from the network of contradictory discourses which constitute subjectivity in historical time. Howard implies that this position is one that she finds congenial, though in Part 2 of the paper she notes that 'first-generation' feminists were frequently 'committed to a humanist conception of the unified self' and their own versions of the 'idea of "true" histories'. Yet, '[f]rom its early moments, feminist cultural analysis interrupted the dominant conventions of historical inquiry by calling attention to the fact that most accounts of culture were histories of one gender'. Thus, many earlier feminists understood that '[w]hat can be recognized as true depends, crucially, on the politically determined horizons of legitimacy prevalent at any historical conjuncture'.

Howard then argues that 'a second moment of feminist historical work has turned away from ahistorical theory building (the quest, above all, for a single, transhistorical explanation for patriarchy) and away from the valorisation of essential female difference and has devoted itself to elaborating the variety of ways in which gender difference has been culturally and historically transmitted'. This new work has acknowledged that 'even within a single historical period, women are not quite all sisters in any simple sense, but bear the plural marks of difference in their various inscriptions within systems of race, class, ethnicity and sexuality'.

This acknowledgment is of course crucial for any feminism that would ally itself with Marxism or represent itself as 'materialist', and yet Howard is less concerned in this section with elaborating on what it means to write Marxist-feminist history than she is with creating a rapprochement between feminists and new historicists, who, she argues, are 'linked by their opposition to the "universal, above-ideology" version of Shakespeare and other texts of Elizabethan "golden age" culture'. To her credit, Howard takes a tougher stance in this essay on the apolitical quality of much new historicist 'political' criticism (it lacks 'a declared political telos'); however, she largely remains an apologist for this work, which she views as being innovative and intellectually challenging (an evaluation that echoes her 1986 analysis of the new historicism).

In Part 3, Howard argues the main point of the paper: 'that while postmodern thought undermines some understandings of politics and history it opens new possibilities as well, possibilities for overcoming the dead ends of essentialist identity politics and scientism, for example, and opens space for a more mobile political practice justified less in terms of absolute truth claims and more in terms of its historically determined efficacy in attaining specific ends'. It seems reasonable to ask at this point just what are the 'specific ends' that Howard has in mind. Her answer is clear enough: 'freedom and equality for all'. Classical Marxism, of course, contained this same 'emancipatory . . . telos', so how does a "postmodern historical practice" hope to achieve what old-style Marxism (according to Howard) could not? At this point, of course, all of the questions that Howard (playing devil's advocate) earlier claimed were elicited by certain postmodern assumptions now demand answers.

The answers that she offers are 'provisional' and inspired in part by Donna Haraway's 'idea of "situated knowledges"'.

As Howard notes, 'a situated project of knowing means eschewing claims to see everything as if one were located outside of history, as if one were an omniscient, disembodied god. Feminists make feminist knowledge, not all knowledge; and they do so within the determinate ideological parameters of a specific time and place'. Yet Howard insists that 'acknowledgement of the many different positions from which knowledge can be made does not lead to pluralist indifference'. There are certain 'preferred knowledges and practices': 'those which lead to the alleviation of oppression and exploitation'.

A second point that Howard borrows from Haraway is that '[a] situated project of knowing and acting articulates neither the truth of a self nor the truth of everyone; it articulates a discursively generated and historically specific position which cannot be guaranteed by recourse to any transcendental or absolute grounds and which must constantly be refashioned under the pressures of historical contingencies'.

As described so far, the Howard-Haraway programme for 'the alleviation of oppression and exploitation' sounds very much like a Foucauldian 'micropolitics', which similarly rejects 'transcendental guarantees of truth' while advocating 'local' political action. And yet ultimately—and, one could argue, self-contradictorily—Howard appears to realise the limitations of micropolitical positions. Those limitations are made highly visible by Jennifer Wicke, whose analysis of the exploitation of Asian women working in low-paying, health-impairing jobs in electronics plants overseas is praised by Howard for (dare I say it?) the truths it reveals about the functioning of global capitalism. Agreeing with Wicke, Howard states that 'it is . . . important to realise that old modes of oppression and domination still continue, in tandem with the new, in both the first world and the third, though the economic exploitation of a "third world" woman in a Singapore electronics factory may be invisible to Western eyes, feminist though those eyes may be'. Precisely. And this is why Wicke (paraphrased here by Howard) 'implies' the following course of action:

. . . an urgent task for feminism is to forge a new logic of interconnections in a world in which the global reach of late capitalism is accompanied by, in fact depends upon, fragmentation: of subjectivities, knowledges, polities. To the extent that an emphasis in postmodern discourse on micropolitics and local knowledges blocks analysis of macrostructure of exploitation and domination on a global scale, to that extent it becomes complicit with techniques of domination prevalent in late capitalism. An alternative logic of interconnections will provide, by contrast, a knowledge of the links between various modalities of oppression with a culture and between cultures in the global village. That means being attentive to international divisions of labour and to the different positions of masculine and feminine subjects with those divisions at different points in a world economic system. It means being attentive, however, not only to how surplus labour is differentially extracted from subjects stratified by race and gender as well as by class, but also to the role of ideology in constructing exploitative and oppressive social relations in the supposedly 'private' domains of sexuality, domestic life and biological reproduction as well as in the supposedly 'public' domains of work and social reproduction.

I find nothing here with which a classical Marxist might disagree. These words could have been uttered by any number of writers who still cling to the Marxist 'master-narrative' of an ultimately determining economic base. Such a narrative, of course, does not deny the importance of 'local knowledges' and 'local struggle': And yet that narrative argues that one can hardly expect to change the world (guarantee freedom and equality for *all*) through local interventions alone. Howard acknowledges here that there are things called 'late capitalism' and the 'world economic system'. She also apparently believes that feminists 'need to employ "large narratives"' (a 'master-narrative' by any other word . . .) in order to understand how these large structures operate. Thus, while insisting that the knowledge one produces about these structures and the ideologies that authorise them is 'situated', Howard seems to realise after all that, whatever its utility on local terrain, a late-model postmodernism is perhaps not the best vehicle from which to view oppression in 'the global village'.

With the publication in 1994 of *The Stage and Social Struggle in Early Modern England,* Howard attempts to put into practice many of the ideas with which she had been concerned during the previous decade. In the book's Introduction, subtitled 'A Brief for Political Criticism', she re-emphasizes Harraway's argument that 'we all make knowledge from situated positions', thereby criticizing those who make their 'partial perspectives synonymous with objectivity and truth' (Howard 1994, 20-1).

On the same page, however, she implies that critics must strive to produce knowledge that is 'adequa[te] to their object of investigation'. The question that arises here, of course, is: What would constitute 'adequacy' if one assumes that objectivity and truth are myths? Like other postmodernists, Howard has no answer to this question, except to offer that '[t]here is no way to get the analysis right "for all time"'. And yet she also apparently believes that by employing Marxist-feminist theory one may at least *come close* to getting the analysis right today, since otherwise there would not be much point to saying anything.

Thus, Howard pays her respects to certain philosophically conventionalist ideas while subscribing to an all-important Marxist-realist assumption: namely, that changes in early modern England's material base altered the country's ideological superstructure. Evidence of this assumption is contained in the following passage, in which Howard, summarizing some thoughts by Louis Montrose (perhaps the most Marxist of the new historicists), attempts to account for the 'self-reflexivity' of many early modern plays:

... [T]he drama's incessant preoccupation with dramatic practices did not so much indicate theatrical narcissism as the widespread emergence of a 'dramatistic sense of life' resulting both from the secularization of Renaissance culture and from the social changes, including heightened social mobility, attendant upon the prolonged and uneven transition from feudalism to capitalism. . . . These changes unsettled identities and social positions, encouraging for better or worse, the sense that in some fundamental way men and women was actors in a self-scripted theater and must forge the identities once taken for granted.

No postmodern waffling here; this is Marxist 'epochal' analysis. The base changes, and, sooner or later, in 'uneven' fashion, so does *everything* else. Howard is making a grounding argument about a determining economic last instance upon which all subsequent discussion in this book is predicated. Yet epochal analysis can take one only so far. Every text considered by the Marxist critic 'has to be examined in its specificity'. One of Howard's main strengths as an historian of early modern social and literary texts, it seems to me, is her acute awareness of the contradictory quality of reality and, therefore, of the need to be as rigorous as possible when analyzing the local ramifications of the large-scale transformations described in the above passage.

In her Introduction, Howard states that she has three objectives. The first is to 'define the ideological work performed by a [discourse of theatricality] in early modern England'. This discourse, she writes, has a 'complex and sometimes contradictory role in producing and underwriting various modes of social and moral stratification'. Her second objective is 'to comment on the unique role of the public theater in ideological production in Renaissance England'. She wishes 'to investigate which social groups had their interests served through the public theater: to what extent it confirmed traditional distributions of power and to what extent it made space for emergent or marginalized groups'.

Finally, she hopes to show 'how particular, historically specific institutions, of which the Renaissance public theater is but one instance, effect social change in ways that may or may not be consistent across the range of their practices and may or may not be perceptible to those within such institutions or to contemporaneous observers of them'. She also notes that '[i]n regard to [the first two] questions, nearly all sweeping generalizations are likely to be vulnerable; nonetheless, I will venture some, while trying to remain alert to the contradictions and complexities that make this topic interesting and important, rather than merely an occasion for a mechanical application of a thesis about the rise of the bourgeoisie or the power of patriarchy'.

Before embarking on a series of fascinating discussions on a wide range of authors and texts, Howard first carves out some positions that she will attempt to support in the body of the book. Some of the most important ones are: 1) that 'the axes of domination and subordination in [Elizabethan/ Jacobean] culture were multiple and not necessarily homologous'; 2) that 'the drama enacted ideological contestation as much as it mirrored or reproduced anything that one could call the dominant ideology of single class, class faction, or sex'; and 3) that 'the material practices attendant upon stage production and theatergoing had ideological consequences for the audience that were in some instances at odds with the ideological import of the dramatic fables which that theater disseminated'. Overarchingly, though, Howard states that she is 'going to argue the materialist case that in order to understand the ideological function of Renaissance theater one must attend—not just to the ideological import of dramatic narratives considered as if they were the equivalent of a printed prose tale—but also to the whole ensemble of practices attendant upon theatrical production at the public theater'.

In the page of acknowledgments that prefaces her Introduction, Howard writes that '[l]ife makes finishing books hard' . . . (viii). Obviously, the tremendous intellectual challenge of producing the sort of materialist history that Howard has just described could not have made finishing *The Stage and Social Struggle* any easier. Evaluating the success of this project—which, as I mentioned, covers quite a bit of ground—would require a much fuller treatment of it than I can offer here; nevertheless, Howard's discussion of one of Shakespeare's comedies provides a good example of her current postmodern Marxist-feminist practice.

Howard's reading of *Much Ado About Nothing* is contained in a chapter entitled 'Antitheatricality Staged'. This title alludes to writings by a number of antitheatrical pamphleteers whose work was examined by Howard in a previous chapter. In her view, these writers generally believed the theater to be 'a powerful and potentially dangerous force', and 'while there are many variations within antitheatrical polemic, the tracts as a whole show the enormous pressure placed on certain ideological positions by changing social conditions and practices, of which the theater becomes a convenient symbol':

With varying degrees of passion, these treatises pay homage to a static conception of the social order and an essentialist view of human identity as God-given rather than as forged through participation in social processes. Such views are useful to any social group who feels its privileges (whether old or very newly acquired) threatened by the movements of others. In fact, what seems most troubling about the overt shapeshifting of actors and the elaborate and changing dress of women is that both expose the hollowness of essentialist rhetoric, its antihistorical refusal to acknowledge how changing material conditions in urban London make it possible, and in some cases inevitable, for men and women to assume new social positions and engage in new social practices which make talk of an unchanging social order or a 'true' unchanging identity seem either absurd or willfully repressive.

In focusing on various antitheatrical treatises and relating them to larger (macroeconomic and social) changes in Elizabethan England, Howard has established a 'context' for her subsequent discussion of a number of 'Renaissance plays that involve the representation of dramatic practices'; however, in the beginning of 'Antitheatricality Staged', she is quick to note that she did not choose this context because it provides the ultimate explanation of work by Dekker and Shakespeare, the playwrights discussed in this chapter. Rather, the choice appears to be a thematic one in that the plays that she wishes to examine participate in antitheatrical discourse—albeit in complex and, at times, contradictory ways. As was the case in her theoretical writings, Howard is careful to avoid claiming too much determining power for her given 'context', and yet that context is itself quite clearly determined, she suggests in the chapter on the antitheatrical pamphleteers, by changes in the social order. Thus, while Howard continues to promise (in theory) a 'postmodern' reading of determination, she delivers (in practice) an arguably classical Marxist view of the matter.

Such is the case, I would argue, in her critique of *Much Ado*, a play which, in Howard's view, 'seems irreproachably conservative in its insistence that the power of theatrical illusion-mongering belongs in the hands of the better sort and that their fictions simply reproduce the truths of nature'. The question raised here is: For *whom* are these ideas 'conservative'? Howard states that the play's 'representations of theatrical practice function with the Elizabethan context to produce and reproduce class and gender difference within a social order dependent on these differences to justify inequalities of power and privilege'.

She is careful to say that the play both 'produce[d] and reproduce[d] class and gender difference'; however, these differences were *already* a part of the 'Elizabethan context' before *Much Ado* came along to do its ideological work. In other words, I am simply making the classical Marxist point—and Howard is too, though evidently in spite of herself—that the 'social text' *is* prior to and determinant of the literary text, regardless of the ideological permutations engendered within or by the latter. This position in no way bars 'literature' from doing 'work', i.e., acting upon the other superstructures and the base, and there are of course no easy formulas for deciding what exactly that work is or what it accomplishes. As Howard correctly argues, 'the theater's role in culture was more complex than simply affirming masculine and aristocratic power. Neither *essentially* subversive nor recuperative [as many cultural materialists and new historicists would respectively argue], the institution could and did serve a variety of competing class and gender interests' (12; Howard's emphasis). This statement is true to some degree of *Much Ado*; however, as I just noted, Howard views the work as being largely 'recuperative.'

For Howard, ideology is the crucial concept in her analysis of the politics of Shakespeare's plays. In the instance of *Much Ado*, she writes, 'the ideological work performed by the discourse of theatricality in the play has to be unearthed through the work of ideology critique, through a strategy of reading aimed at speaking the unspoken of the text and of pressuring its contradictions to reveal its mediations of social struggle'. Here again is acknowledgment of the determining power of the base. The play is not so much producing social struggle as *mediating* a struggle that *already* exists. Also to be noted is the Machereyan strategy of discussing that struggle as 'the unspoken of the text'.

Of course, many materialist critics have produced readings of Shakespeare that attempt to construct various 'unspoken' ideologies. Howard's efforts in this direction, though, seem closest to Dollimore's in his essays on *Measure for Measure* and *Henry V*, since, like him, she posits a clear break between what I would call the 'ideology of the text' and Marxist-feminist knowledge of that ideology. In *Much Ado*, the ideology of the text seems to be more or less synonymous with the position articulated by a number of 'traditional' humanist critics. These critics have 'typically made two moves: one involves drawing clear moral distinctions between "good" and "bad" theatrical practices; the other involves reassuring readers that the play offers ways to cope with—to see through—omnipresent theatrical deception'.

The humanists, we learn, 'insist on Shakespeare's insistence that beneath the world of unstable appearances there is a world of essences to which man has access if he has, paradoxically, either faith or careful noting skills'. Howard is dubious about inferring authorial intentions from a dramatic script, yet it seems clear enough from her discussion of the 'dominant critical position' that the ideology encoded by Shakespeare's work—to borrow a manner of phrasing to which Howard might not object—and the meaning of the play as it is derived by a critic like John Henze, a 'traditional' humanist, have much in common.

Like Henze and other humanists, Howard extrapolates a theme for the play. 'At its center', she writes, '*Much Ado* seems to dramatize the social consequence of staging lies':

Don John precipitates the play's crisis by having a servant, Margaret, impersonate her mistress, Hero, in a love encounter observed by Hero's husband-to-be and Don John's brother. These theatrics make Hero appear a whore and lead directly to her denunciation in the church. This deception is clearly coded as evil: it is engineered by a bastard, involves the transgressive act of a servant wearing the clothes of one of higher rank, and leads to the threat of death for several of the play's characters.

Yet Don John is not the only 'dramatist' in the play, Howard notes: his brother, Don Pedro, also directs several productions in *Much Ado*; however, the latter's efforts, which also employ deception, are moralized by traditional critics as 'good' since Don Pedro's match-making goals are laudable. Howard writes that in her reading of the play, she will substitute 'a political and social for a moral analysis of [*Much Ado*'s] theatrical practices', In the process, she will examine 'the role of authority and authoritative discourse in delimiting what can be recognized as true'.

According to Howard, the deceptions of both brothers have 'ideological consequences':

> [Don John's] trick involves a transgression against hierarchy in which, as on the public stage itself, an inferior assumes the borrowed robes of a social superior. This action is not dramatized. Consigned to the realm of the 'unseen', its consequences disappear utterly—like a bad dream—at play's end. By contrast, Don Pedro's two most elaborate deceptions, the playlets put on for Benedick and Beatrice, are dramatized and are presented as part of the prerogatives of Messina's highest-ranking visitor. Ironically, these presentational choices naturalize Don Pedro's practice so that, as in all ideological effects, the arbitrary passes as the inevitable. . . . What results is the production of differences between similar activities in ways that obscure the social differences justified and held in place by moral categories. As in the theatrical tracts, a key question turns out to be: whose fiction-making activities are to be construed as legitimate?

Thus, Howard argues, the moral categories established by the play function to reproduce 'existing power relations and social arrangements', a point seldom noted by much 'moral criticism' of *Much Ado*. In demonstrating this thesis, Howard offers a compelling interpretation of the social implications of Don Pedro's matchmaking. In her view, he does not so much discover 'Benedick's and Beatrice's pre-existent love' as create it. In doing so, he 'control[s] threats to the social order' by making 'social renegades conform.' At the same time, though, Don Pedro's 'playlets . . . produce gender difference': 'To be a "normal" male is not the same as being a "normal" female', Howard writes. 'In discussing Beatrice before Benedick, Leonato and his friends construct her as a vulnerable pitiful victim. . . . The role mapped for Bendick is to be her rescuer, to become more "manly" by accepting his duty to succor women as well as to fight wars'. Howard also points out that Benedick's position as a lover eventually 'comes into conflict with the claims of male friendship, producing disequilibrium in the social order' (when Benedick challenges Claudio at Beatrice's behest); however, '[t]he ending of the play "takes care" of this problem. As is the case with many of Shakespeare's comedies, the ending of *Much Ado* has a strongly recuperative function as it attempts to smooth over the contradictions or fissures that have opened in the course of the play'.

I have glossed over a number of interesting points Howard makes about *Much Ado* in my attempt to summarize some of the main ideas of her essay; however, I do want to note one other place in the text where 'history' most palpably intrudes. In her comments on Don Pedro's 'production' of love in Beatrice and Benedick, Howard states that 'by happy sleight of hand, what is their *destiny* within [a gendered social order] is made to seem their *choice*. This maneuver affords another instance of inter-class accommodation as the aristocratic ideology of arranged property marriages is made to appear seamlessly compatible with emergent middle-class ideologies of love and individual choice as preconditions for marital union'. Although Howard has been arguing that the play 'encodes' and 'recuperates' an aristocratic, patriarchal ideology, at this point she suggests that *Much Ado* simultaneously carries out a rather different ideological function in that it incorporates 'emergent middle-class ideologies of love and individual choice'.

This is a shrewd insight, in my view; however, it is also one that depends for its 'truth effect' on a (historical) 'text' (the rise of the middle classes) that is 'prior to and more privileged than' the literary work that has mobilized the emergent ideology in question. Howard, of course, strenuously argued in the beginning of her essay that there can be no such prior and privileged texts, just as she had argued Tony Bennett's postmodern point that 'no discourse . . . lies outside the domain of the ideological'. Neither of these assumptions, it seems to me, is upheld in her discussion of *Much Ado*. Instead, what we ultimately get in this determinately contextualised analysis of Shakespeare's work is the privileged text of (a particular) history via Howard's knowledge of Marxist-feminist ideological critique.

In her essay entitled '(Untimely) Critiques for a Red Feminism', Teresa Ebert argues that '[m]ost postmodern feminists . . . have suppressed "objective reality" in discourse and regimes of signification. Nonetheless, they are feeling (however indirectly) the historical pressures of the return of the suppressed "objective reality"'(Ebert 1995, 113). Such is the case, I would argue, in Howard's work. Despite her efforts to avoid 'the class reductionism and economic determinism of classical Marxism', her practice betrays its reliance on a Marxist-feminist realism that inevitably foregrounds the determining power of the economic base (the 'objective reality' suppressed in Howard's theoretical writings) over the ideological superstructures. Of course, from a classical Marxist position, this 'betrayal' is no bad thing: as Ebert has persuasively argued, '[t]o articulate the relations connecting seemingly disparate events and phenomena is in fact a necessary and unavoidable part of effective knowledge production' (Ebert 1995, 146).

Ebert also notes that, while 'the conflicts over ideology, cultural practices and significations are . . . an important part of the social struggle for emancipation[,] the issue is how do we explain the relation of the discursive to the non-discursive, the relation of cultural practices to the "real existing world"—whose objectivity is the fact of the "working day"—in order to transform it?' (Ebert 1995, 146) The answer, I would claim, lies not in a postmodern renunciation of 'epistemology' and 'truth' but, rather, in a renewed commitment to a classical Marxist concept of determination and a concomitant belief (noted above) that, '[a]lthough we can only talk about, or represent, [the world] within some signifying practice or another, what is said within those practices depends for its validity not on the signifying practice alone . . . but on properties and qualities of the things referred to or represented' (Lovell 1980, 82). In other words, it is not a postmodern Marxist feminism but a Marxist-feminist *realism* by means of which we may labour to make theory adequate to its past and present objects, as well as to 'emergent conditions' (Howard 1994, 21).

Bibliography

Beacon, Thomas. Solon His Follie (1594). Ed. Clare Carroll and Vincent Carey. Binghamton, N.Y.: Medieval and Renaissance Texts and Studies, 1996.

Bhabha, Homi. 'DissemiNation: Time, Narrative and the Margins of the Modern Nation'. The Location of Culture. London: Routledge, 1990.139-70.

Cohen, Stephen. 'Between Form and Culture: New Historicism and the Promise of a Historical Formalism' Renaissance Literature and Its Formal Engagements. Ed. Mark David Rasmussen. London: Palgrave, 2002. 17-33.

Craik, T.W. Introduction. King Henry V. By William Shakespeare. London: Routledge, 1995. 1-111

Denham, John. 'Cooper's Hill' (1642) Expans'd Hieroglyphics: A Study of Sir John Denham's Cooper's Hill, With a Critical Edition of the Poem. By Brendan O Hehir. Berkeley and Los Angeles: U. of California P., 1969. 109-34.

Dollimore, Jonathan and Sinfield, Alan. 'History and Ideology: The Instance of Henry V' Alternative Shakespeares. Ed. John Drakakis. London: Routledge, 1985. 206-27.

Escobedo, Andrew. Nationalism and Historical Loss in Renaissance England. Ithaca and London: Cornell U.P., 2004.

Fineman, Joel. Shakespeare's Perjured Eye: The Invention of Poetic Subjectivity in the Sonnets. Berkeley: U. of California P., 1986.

Greene, Thomas. The Light in Troy: Imitation and Discovery in Renaissance Poetry. New Haven: Yale U.P., 1982.

Griffiths, Huw. 'Letter Writing Lucrece: Shakespeare in

the 1590s' Rhetoric, Women and Politics in Early Modern England. London: Routledge, 2006, 89-110.

Guy, John. (Ed.) The Reign of Elizabeth I: Court and Culture in the Last Decade, Cambridge: Cambridge University Press, 1985.

Hadfield, Andrew. Shakespeare and Republicanism. Cambridge: Cambridge U.P., 2005.

Hammer, Paul. The Polarisation of Elizabethan Politics: The Political Career of Robert Devereux, the 2nd Earl of Essex. Cambridge: Cambridge U.P., 1999.

Hill, Geoffrey. King Log. London: Andre Deutsch, 1968.

Jameson, Fredric. 'Imaginary and Symbolic in Lacan: Marxism, Psychoanalytic Criticism and the Problem of the Subject' Yale French Studies. 55/56 (1977) 338-95.

The Political Unconscious: Narrative as Socially Symbolic Act. London: Methuen, 1981.

Janowitz, Anne. England's Ruins: Poetic Purpose and the National Landscape. Cambridge, Mass.. Blackwell, 1990.

Kerrigan, John. 'Divided Kingdoms and the Local Epic: Mercian Hymns to the King of Britain's Daughter' The Yale Journal of Criticism 13.1 (2000) 1-21

Lewkenor, Lewis. The Common-Wealth and Government of Venice Written By the Cardinall Gasparo Contareno. London, 1599.

Norbrook, David. Writing the English Republic: Poetry, Rhetoric and Politics 1627-1660. Cambridge: Cambridge U.P., 1999.

Parker, Patricia. Shakespeare From the Margins: Language, Culture, Context. Chicago: Chicago U.P., 1996.

Paulin, Tom. 'A Visionary Nationalist: Geoffrey Hill' Minotaur: Poetry and the Nation State. London: Faber and Faber, 1992. 276-84.

Peltonen, Markku. Classical Humanism and Republicanism in English Political Thought 1570-1640. Cambridge: Cambridge U.P., 1995.

Puttenham, George. The Arte of English Poesie. Ed. Gladys Doidge Willcock and Alice Walker. Cambridge: Cambridge U.P., 1936 (reprinted 1970).

Roberts, Andrew. 'Geoffrey Hill and Pastiche: "An Apology for the Revival of Christian Architecture in England" and The Mystery of the Charity of Charles Pegyt'. The Yale Journal of Criticism 13.1 (2000) 153-66.

Shakespeare, William. King Henry V. Ed. T.W. Craik. London: Routledge, 1995.

Complete Sonnets and Poems. Ed. Colin Burrow. Oxford: Oxford U.P., 2002.

Spenser, Edmund. The Faereie Queene. Ed. A.C. Hamilton. London: Longman, 1977.

The Yale Edition of the Shorter Poems of Edmund Spenser. Ed. William A. Oram et al.. New Haven and London: Yale U.P., 1989.